AT HOME
with the WORD
2 0 0 2

Sunday Scriptures and Reflections

Mary Katharine Deeley

Paul Panaretos, SJ
Kathleen Spears Hopkins
Judy Glassco Humowiecki

LTP

LITURGY
TRAINING
PUBLICATIONS

Reprinting from *At Home with the Word 2002*

A parish or an institution may purchase a license to reprint the Reflections (and their discussion questions), the Practices of Faith, Hope and Charity, the Prayer of the Season or the holy day boxes from *At Home with the Word 2002*. Please see page 154 for details.

If a parish or institution wishes to reproduce some or all of the scripture texts, a license must be acquired from the copyright owners (see below). When writing to copyright owners, state clearly which texts you wish to use, the number of copies to be made, and how often you'll be using the copies. There may be a license fee.

Acknowledgments

The Sunday scripture pericopes contained herein are from the New Revised Standard Version of the Bible, © 1989 Division of Christian Education of the National Council of Churches of Christ in the U.S.A. All rights reserved. Used by permission. Text emendations © 1997 Augsburg Fortress. All rights reserved.

Most Roman Catholic parishes in the United States proclaim the Sunday scriptures using the readings from the *Lectionary for Mass, Volume 1: Sundays, Solemnities and Feasts of the Lord,* copyright 1998, 1997, 1970 Confraternity of Christian Doctrine, Washington, D.C. For information on reprint permission, write: Confraternity of Christian Doctrine, 1312 Massachusetts Avenue NW, Washington DC 20005.

The English translation of the *Salve, Regina* from *A Book of Prayers* © 1993 International Committee on English in the Liturgy, Inc. (ICEL); excerpts from the English translation of *The Roman Missal* © 1973 ICEL. Used by permission. All rights reserved. For reprint permission, write: ICEL, 1522 K Street NW, Suite 1000, Washington DC 20005-1202.

The English translation of Psalm 22, 51, 63, 85, 98, 100, 113, 118, 126, 131, 134, 145 and 147 from *Psalms for Praise and Worship: A Complete Liturgical Psalter,* edited by John Holbert, S. T. Kimbrough, Jr., and Carlton R. Young © 1992 Abingdon Press. Used by permission. All rights reserved.

The English translation of the Canticle of Zechariah © 1989 Hope Publishing Co., the Canticle of Mary © 1985 Augsburg Fortress and the Canticle of Simeon © International Consultation on English Texts. Used by permission. All rights reserved.

The art for this year's *At Home with the Word* is the work of Doug Andelin. The seasonal icons were created by Anne Fritzinger.

The Prayers of the Season were written by Gabe Huck. The holy day commentaries were written by Peter Mazar. For December 25 Day, the Practice of Faith was written by Barbara Budde, the Practice of Hope by Kathleen Dewey, and the Practice of Charity by Jennifer Willems.

The design of this book is by Jill Smith. This book was edited by Margaret M. Brennan. Audrey Novak Riley was the production editor. Typesetting was by Anne Fritzinger, in Palatino and Universe. The book was printed and bound by Von Hoffmann Graphics, Inc. of Eldridge, Iowa.

AT HOME WITH THE WORD 2002 © 2001 Archdiocese of Chicago: Liturgy Training Publications, 1800 North Hermitage Avenue, Chicago IL 60622-1101; 1-800-933-1800; orders@ltp.org; fax 1-800-933-7094. All rights reserved.

Visit our website at www.ltp.org.

ISBN 1-56854-374-3

AHW02

How to Use At Home with the Word

SCRIPTURE READINGS These are the heart of *At Home with the Word.* You may want to read the scriptures before going to church, or, better yet, use this book to return to the Sunday scriptures again and again throughout the week.

Because the Sunday readings of many other Christian churches are the same as those proclaimed in Catholic communities, *At Home with the Word* has highlighted the scriptures we share. There are two minor changes that result. First, there may be a few more verses in the reading here than you'll hear proclaimed in the Sunday assembly. Also, when Roman Catholic churches observe a particular feast on a given Sunday that is not celebrated by other Christian communities, there will be two sets of readings.

REFLECTIONS Mary Katharine Deeley is the pastoral associate at Sheil Catholic Center in Evanston, Illinois. She has a PHD degree in Hebrew Bible and early Christian literature from Northwestern University, Evanston, Illinois.

The reflections offer background information on the scriptures and new insights to consider. Households or small groups may share the readings and reflections weekly.

This is Year A, the year of the gospel according to Matthew. Throughout Ordinary Time we will be reading most often from this gospel. See the introduction to the gospel of Matthew, which begins on page 8.

PRACTICE OF FAITH Paul Panaretos is a member of the Society of Jesus and the director of Loyola of the Lake Jesuit Retreat House in Clinton, Ohio.

PRACTICE OF HOPE Kathleen Spears Hopkins holds an MTS degree in spirituality from the Catholic Theological Union at Chicago. She writes regularly for *Markings,* and her work has appeared in *Catechumenate, Emmanuel* and *America.*

PRACTICE OF CHARITY Judy Glassco Humowiecki is a pastoral counselor who practices in Chicago and Oak Park, Illinois. She is active in United Power for Action and Justice and serves as a member of the pastoral team of her parish.

WEEKDAY READINGS Some people may want to read more than the Sunday scriptures. For each week, we've listed the verses of the books of the Bible from which the first readings for daily Mass are taken.

At Home with the Word also includes:

MORNING, EVENING AND NIGHT PRAYERS These simple patterns of prayer for the home take five or ten minutes and are meant to be repeated every day. Don't be afraid of repetition; that's one way to learn to pray.

FRIDAY AND SUNDAY PSALMS AND PRAYERS Sunday is our day of feasting, Friday our day of fasting. Both days need extra prayer and acts of discipleship. Here are psalms, a Lord's Day song and a prayer for Fridays from the U.S. bishops' letter *The Challenge of Peace.*

PRAYERS FROM THE MASS Included here are prayers and other texts from the Mass. Knowing these by heart will help you take full, conscious and active part in Sunday Mass.

SEASONAL PSALMS AND PRAYERS Each season is introduced by a page that includes an acclamation, a psalm and a short prayer. Repeating a single psalm throughout a season is a fine way to learn the psalms by heart.

CALENDAR
TABLE OF CONTENTS

3 How to Use *At Home with the Word*

6 The Lectionary and *At Home with the Word*

8 An Introduction to the Gospel of Matthew

10 Prayers for Various Times and Days

ADVENT PSALM page **21**

22 December 2, 2001
First Sunday of Advent
Immaculate Conception of the Virgin Mary: December 8

24 December 9, 2001
Second Sunday of Advent

26 December 16, 2001
Third Sunday of Advent

28 December 23, 2001
Fourth Sunday of Advent

CHRISTMAS PSALM page **31**
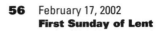

32 December 25, 2001
Christmas, Midnight Mass
34 **Christmas, Mass during the Day**

36 December 30, 2001
Holy Family
First Sunday after Christmas
Mary, Mother of God: January 1

38 January 6, 2002
Epiphany of the Lord

40 January 13, 2002
Baptism of the Lord

WINTER PSALM page **43**

44 January 20, 2002
Second Sunday in Ordinary Time/after Epiphany

46 January 27, 2002
Third Sunday in Ordinary Time/after Epiphany
Presentation of the Lord: February 2

48 February 3, 2002
Fourth Sunday in Ordinary Time/after Epiphany

50 February 10, 2002
Fifth Sunday in Ordinary Time (Roman Catholic)
52 **Transfiguration of the Lord** (RCL)
Ash Wednesday: February 28

LENT PSALM page **55**

56 February 17, 2002
First Sunday of Lent

58 February 24, 2002
Second Sunday of Lent

60 March 3, 2002
Third Sunday of Lent

62 March 10, 2002
Fourth Sunday of Lent

64 March 17, 2002
Fifth Sunday of Lent
Joseph, husband of Mary: March 19

66 March 24, 2002
Palm Sunday of the Lord's Passion

PASCHAL TRIDUUM PSALM page **71**

72 March 28–30, 2002
The Three Days

EASTER PSALM page **75**

76 March 31, 2002
Easter Sunday

78 April 7, 2002
Second Sunday of Easter
Annunciation of the Lord: April 8

80 April 14, 2002
Third Sunday of Easter

82 April 21, 2002
Fourth Sunday of Easter

84 April 28, 2002
Fifth Sunday of Easter

86 May 5, 2002
Sixth Sunday of Easter

88 May 9 or 12, 2002
Ascension of the Lord

90 May 12, 2002
Seventh Sunday of Easter
Pentecost Vigil: May 18–19

92 May 19, 2002
Pentecost

SUMMER PSALM page **95**

96 May 26, 2002
Trinity Sunday
First Sunday after Pentecost

98 June 2, 2002
Roman Catholic: Body and Blood of Christ
Other Churches: See pages 100–101
Sacred Heart of Jesus: June 7

100 June 2, 2002
Second Sunday after Pentecost

102 June 9, 2002
Tenth Sunday in Ordinary Time
Third Sunday after Pentecost

104 June 16, 2002
Eleventh Sunday in Ordinary Time
Fourth Sunday after Pentecost

106 June 23, 2002
Twelfth Sunday in Ordinary Time
Fifth Sunday after Pentecost
Birth of John the Baptist: June 24
Peter and Paul, apostles: June 29

108 June 30, 2002
Thirteenth Sunday in Ordinary Time
Sixth Sunday after Pentecost

110 July 7, 2002
Fourteenth Sunday in Ordinary Time
Seventh Sunday after Pentecost

112 July 14, 2002
Fifteenth Sunday in Ordinary Time
Eighth Sunday after Pentecost

114 July 21, 2002
Sixteenth Sunday in Ordinary Time
Ninth Sunday after Pentecost
Mary Magdalene: July 22

116 July 28, 2002
Seventeenth Sunday in Ordinary Time
Tenth Sunday after Pentecost

118 August 4, 2002
Eighteenth Sunday in Ordinary Time
Eleventh Sunday after Pentecost
Transfiguration of the Lord: August 6

120 August 11, 2002
Nineteenth Sunday in Ordinary Time
Twelfth Sunday after Pentecost
Assumption of Mary into Heaven: August 15

122 August 18, 2002
Twentieth Sunday in Ordinary Time
Thirteenth Sunday after Pentecost

124 August 25, 2002
Twenty-first Sunday in Ordinary Time
Fourteenth Sunday after Pentecost

126 September 1, 2002
Twenty-second Sunday in Ordinary Time
Fifteenth Sunday after Pentecost

128 September 8, 2002
Twenty-third Sunday in Ordinary Time
Sixteenth Sunday after Pentecost
Exaltation of the Holy Cross: September 14

130 September 15, 2002
Twenty-fourth Sunday in Ordinary Time
Seventeenth Sunday after Pentecost

AUTUMN PSALM page **133**

134 September 22, 2002
Twenty-fifth Sunday in Ordinary Time
Eighteenth Sunday after Pentecost

136 September 29, 2002
Twenty-sixth Sunday in Ordinary Time
Nineteenth Sunday after Pentecost

138 October 6, 2002
Twenty-seventh Sunday in Ordinary Time
Twentieth Sunday after Pentecost

140 October 13, 2002
Twenty-eighth Sunday in Ordinary Time
Twenty-first Sunday after Pentecost

142 October 20, 2002
Twenty-ninth Sunday in Ordinary Time
Twenty-second Sunday after Pentecost

144 October 27, 2002
Thirtieth Sunday in Ordinary Time
Twenty-third Sunday after Pentecost
All Saints: November 1; All Souls: November 2

146 November 3, 2002
Thirty-first Sunday in Ordinary Time
Twenty-fourth Sunday after Pentecost
Dedication of the Lateran Basilica in Rome: November 9

148 November 10, 2002
Thirty-second Sunday in Ordinary Time
Twenty-fifth Sunday after Pentecost

150 November 17, 2002
Thirty-third Sunday in Ordinary Time
Twenty-sixth Sunday after Pentecost

152 November 24, 2002
Christ the King
Last Sunday after Pentecost
Thanksgiving Day (U.S.A.): November 28

154 Information on License to Reprint

The Lectionary and At Home with the Word

by Martin F. Connell

WHAT IS A LECTIONARY? A lectionary is an ordered selection of readings, chosen from both testaments of the Bible, for proclamation in the assembly gathered for worship. Lectionaries have been used for Christian worship since the fourth century. At different times and in different places before the invention of the printing press in the fifteenth century, the orders of the readings varied a bit. The variety from church to church often reflected the different issues that were important to the local communities of the time.

For the four centuries from the Council of Trent (1545–1563) to the Second Vatican Council (1963–1965), the readings in most Catholic churches were basically the same from year to year and were proclaimed in Latin, an ancient language that many Catholics did not understand. The use of the language of the people in the liturgy and the revision of the lectionary after the Second Vatican Council have had tremendous effects on the accessibility of the Bible for Catholics. The Bible is again a vibrant source of our faith and tradition.

THE THREE-YEAR LECTIONARY CYCLE The lectionary issued by the church after the Second Vatican Council appeared in 1970. The most exciting feature of the lectionary was its basic plan. This three-year plan incorporates a fuller selection of readings from the books of the Bible. Each of the first three gospels—Matthew, Mark and Luke—corresponds with one year: Matthew for Year A, Mark for Year B and Luke for Year C. The Sunday lectionary cycle, therefore, takes three years to complete. This liturgical year 2002 is Year A, which begins on the First Sunday of Advent, December 2, 2001.

YEAR A: THE GOSPEL OF MATTHEW You will find that most of the gospel readings proclaimed in your Sunday assembly this year and printed in *At Home with the Word 2002* are from the gospel of Matthew. This gospel will be proclaimed on most Sundays from the First Sunday of Advent to the celebration of Christ the King, November 24, 2002. The introduction to the gospel of Matthew on pages 8–9 and the commentaries on the gospel each week will help you recognize and appreciate the contribution of this gospel to our faith.

THE GOSPEL OF JOHN You might ask: What about the Fourth Gospel? The gospel of John is not excluded from proclamation during the three-year cycle. Though it does not have a year during which it is highlighted, the gospel of John punctuates certain seasons and times of the year.

The readings from Year A on the third, fourth and fifth Sundays of Lent are from the gospel of John, and they are proclaimed every year in parishes celebrating the RCIA. These three wonderful stories from the gospel of John—the woman at the well (on the third Sunday), the man born blind (on the fourth Sunday) and the raising of Lazarus (on the fifth Sunday)—are important texts to accompany the celebration of the scrutinies in the process of Christian initiation.

During Years B and C, you will find two sets of readings on these Sundays in *At Home with the Word:* one set for churches celebrating the scrutinies of the RCIA and one set for parishes that are not having the initiation process during that particular liturgical year.

The gospel of John also appears for the Mass of the Lord's Supper on Holy Thursday and for the long passion reading on Good Friday. And on most of the Sundays of Easter—during the fifty days from Easter Sunday until Pentecost—the gospel of John is proclaimed at the liturgy.

THE DIFFERENCE BETWEEN THE BIBLE AND THE LECTIONARY The shape of the lectionary comes from the ancient church practice of *lectio continua*, a Latin term which describes the successive reading through books of the Bible from Sunday to Sunday. You can see such a *lectio continua* in practice if you flip through *At Home with the Word* and, for example, consider the gospel texts assigned to the Sundays from the Thirteenth Sunday in Ordinary Time, June 30, to the Feast of Christ the King, November 24. Though not every verse is included, you will notice that through these Sundays we move from chapter 9 of Matthew to chapter 25.

You will find, moreover, that the first readings often echo some image, character or idea in the gospel, as is the church's intention. The second reading often stands on its own and comes from a letter of Paul or some other letter of the New Testament. You will notice, for example, that the second readings from July through November take us through Romans, Philippians and Thessalonians.

UNITY WITH OTHER CHRISTIAN CHURCHES IN THE WORD OF GOD The basic plan of the lectionary for Catholics is universal. The readings proclaimed in your church on a particular Sunday are the same as those proclaimed in Catholic churches all over the globe. The lectionary is one of the main things that makes our liturgy so "catholic," or universal.

But as time has passed, other Christian churches have adopted the Catholic lectionary also. So not only are the readings the same as those in other Catholic churches, but the revision of the Roman Catholic lectionary has been so well received that other churches have begun to follow its three-year lectionary cycle.

Catholics and their neighbors who attend other Christian churches often hear the same word of God proclaimed and preached in the Sunday gathering. Even though you may not talk about the Sunday readings with you neighbors and therefore haven't realized that your readers read the same lections and your preachers preach on the same scriptural texts, this is really a remarkable change when you consider how very far apart from one another Catholic and Protestant churches were before the Second Vatican Council.

The slight difference between the readings you'll find in *At Home with the Word 2002* and what is proclaimed on Sunday is a result of our efforts to highlight the scriptures shared by many Christian churches. The major parts of the readings will be secure, but there might be a few verses tacked on in *At Home with the Word* at the beginning or end of a reading to match those in the Revised Common Lectionary, which is used in many non–Catholic Christian churches. When the page with the readings is short on space, a shorter version of a reading or two will be printed and the full citation will be provided at the beginning so that you can check out the fuller text in your Bible.

At the bottom of each right-hand column on the odd-numbered pages, you will find citations for the readings of the daily liturgy. When a reading is from the same book of the Bible as the reading from the day before, you will find only the citation of chapter and verse. When the book of the Bible changes from one day to the next, the full citation will be given.

We hope that your celebration of the liturgy in your parish is deepened by the preparation you will find in this book. Have a wonderful liturgical year being "at home with the Word" of God.

An Introduction to the Gospel of Matthew

by Mary Katharine Deeley

The gospel of Matthew sets the stage for the entire New Testament as it narrates the first set of stories we read about the life of Jesus. A long genealogy of Jesus in the first chapter places us firmly in the literary traditions of the Old Testament, particularly in Genesis, where narratives of the patriarchs are often preceded by their genealogies. It is important to Matthew to establish Jesus as an heir to the promise of Abraham and as the messiah king who was to come from the house of David.

Matthew writes primarily to Jewish Christians about 80–85 CE. At that time, Jews and Christians alike were in turmoil. The Romans had destroyed the great Jewish temple in Jerusalem. Christians were under suspicion and attack by Jews, Romans and even other Christians who had set themselves up as prophets. In this turbulent time, Matthew assures his audience that even though the world in which they must preach the good news is a hostile one, with many temptations to turn away from Jesus, those who acknowledge Jesus will inherit the kingdom of God.

The religious, social and political context of Matthew's audience influences the evangelist. Matthew uses the Jewish technique of *midrash* to tell about Jesus' birth and death, adding poetic and creative understandings to the bare bones of the story in order to "seek out" the truth for the community of faith (the word *midrash* comes from a Hebrew root meaning "to seek"). The persecution by the Romans led to a revival of apocalyptic thought, in which God is depicted as the ultimate victor over evil. Matthew's stories of the end-times include the sudden appearance of the divine, a world in turmoil, and God's judgment of the righteous and the wicked. In Matthew's vision, faithfulness to the gospel ethic to love God and neighbor is the crucial determinant of whether a Christian will be invited into heaven or sent to hell. Finally, Matthew's gospel places emphasis on the concept of church. It is in this gospel that Peter is named the rock on which the church is built. Matthew also draws out the understanding of Christian discipleship and community as the fuller and deeper living out of the Jewish Law. Jesus himself says: "I did not come to destroy the Law, but to fulfill it."

Year A is dominated by two themes from Matthew's gospel: urgency and uncompromising choice. Matthew begins the year with warnings to stay awake for the coming of God and ends it with judgment between those who followed a righteous path and those who did not. In between, Matthew exhorts the reader to watch, to listen and to follow Jesus. One either follows Christ or does not; one either lives in the reign of God or dies apart from it. In this, Matthew echoes the great speech of Moses who tells the Jews in Deuteronomy that they have before them life and death, blessing or curse. To read Matthew's gospel is to see this choice laid out before us as well.

The demand to make a choice and the command to keep watch were familiar exhortations for the Jews. Many prophets had spoken of the coming day of the Lord as a day of judgment and justice. Matthew relies on the memory of these prophecies. Quoting the Hebrew scriptures more than the other evangelists, Matthew skillfully reveals Jesus' identity as the Messiah.

To read Matthew is to get a sense of the passion and commitment of early church leaders. They were driven in their mission to preach and to baptize all nations. They accepted no half-hearted commitments. In their time and place, to be a Christian was to risk ostracism, even persecution. The weak-willed and the faint of heart would not survive in such a world. Those who were unsure of the truth that Jesus spoke could not preach the good news of a Messiah who was crucified. Only those who had given themselves wholly to the discipleship of Christ could live in the community of the faithful and bring others to be baptized. The true disciple was one who had eyes to see, ears to hear, and a heart that believed the Lord was coming soon.

ABOUT THE ART
by Gabe Huck

The cover and all the art for the 2002 edition of *At Home with the Word* was created by San Francisco artist Doug Andelin. Working in watercolor and pastels, Andelin takes us through the prayers of the days and the seasons with images that evoke tiny moments of our lives and our communities.

The cover depicts an elderly Matthew, whose gospel we read through the Sundays of 2002. He is at work on a scroll, puzzling out the genealogy with which he will begin his gospel: "An account of the genealogy of Jesus the Messiah, the son of David, the son of Abraham. Abraham was the father of Isaac . . . " Here and there Matthew appears to have caught a mistake: crossed out a name and made a correction. We might see the names of some people whose appearance in Jesus' family is a bit of a surprise. After forty-two generations Matthew is finished: " . . . Jacob the father of Joseph the husband of Mary of whom Jesus was born."

This genealogy is the reason that the symbol of Matthew as an evangelist has been a human or angel figure (alongside Mark's lion, Luke's ox and John's eagle). On the cover we see the angel helping Matthew recall who begot whom as the scroll unwinds and a Spirit-like dove hovers nearby, perhaps helping Matthew tell the tale with some care and imagination. Like many earlier artists, Doug Andelin has Matthew wearing glasses. Where might Matthew be as he writes? Legends are many. Some say he lived and wrote in Syria, others see Matthew in Ethiopia, Iran, Macedonia, even Ireland. In the churches of the West, Matthew's feast day is September 21.

M O R N I N G
p r a y e r

This order of prayer may be said upon waking or before or during breakfast.

Lord, open my lips,
And my mouth will proclaim your praise.

The Sign of the Cross

In the name of the Father
and of the Son
and of the Holy Spirit.

Psalm 63:1–4, 5–8

O God, you are my God, I seek you,
I thirst for you;
my flesh faints for you,
as in a dry and weary land where no water is.
So I have looked upon you in the sanctuary,
beholding your power and glory.

Because your steadfast love is better than life,
my lips will praise you.
So I will bless you as long as I live;
I will lift up my hand and call on your name.

My mouth praises you with joyful lips,
when I think of you upon my bed,
and meditate on you in the watches of the night;
for you have been my help,
and in the shadow of your wings I sing for you.
My soul clings to you;
your right hand upholds me.

*One of the seasonal psalms throughout this book
may be prayed instead of Psalm 63.*

The Canticle of Zechariah

Bless'd be the God of Israel
who comes to set us free
and raises up new hope for us:
a Branch from David's tree.
So have the prophets long declared
that with a mighty arm
God would turn back our enemies
and all who wish us harm.

With promised mercy will God still
the covenant recall,
the oath once sworn to Abraham,
from foes to save us all;
that we might worship without fear
and offer lives of praise,
in holiness and righteousness
to serve God all our days.

My child, as prophet of the Lord
you will prepare the way,
to tell God's people they are saved
from sin's eternal sway.
Then shall God's mercy from on high
shine forth and never cease
to drive away the gloom of death
and lead us into peace.

*This canticle may be sung to the tune FOREST
GREEN or any other CMD tune, such as with the
hymn "I Sing the Almighty Power of God."*

The Lord's Prayer

*You may join hands with others or hold your
hands with palms facing upward while praying
the Lord's Prayer.*

E V E N I N G
p r a y e r

This order of prayer may be said before or after dinner.

God, come to my assistance.
Lord, make haste to help me.

The Lighting of a Candle

*A candle may be lit to welcome the evening
while saying:*

Jesus Christ is the light of the world,
a light no darkness can overcome.

Psalm 113

Praise the Lord!
Praise, O servants of the Lord,
praise the name of the Lord!
Blessed be the name of the Lord
from this time forth and for evermore!

From the rising of the sun to its setting
the name of the Lord is to be praised!
The Lord is high above all nations,
God's glory above the heavens!

Who is like the Lord our God,
who is seated on high,
who looks far down
upon the heavens and the earth?

God raises the poor from the dust,
and lifts the needy from the ash heap,
to make them sit with nobles,
with the nobles of God's people.

God gives the barren woman a home,
making her the joyous mother of children.
Praise the Lord!

amen

The Canticle of Mary

My soul proclaims your greatness, Lord;
I sing my Savior's praise!
You looked upon my lowliness,
and I am full of grace.
Now ev'ry land and ev'ry age
this blessing shall proclaim—
great wonders you have done for me,
and holy is your name.

To all who live in holy fear
your mercy ever flows.
With mighty arm you dash the proud,
their scheming hearts expose.
The ruthless you have cast aside,
the lowly throned instead;
the hungry filled with all good things,
the rich sent off unfed.

To Israel, your servant blest,
your help is ever sure;
the promise to our parents made
their children will secure.
Sing glory to the Holy One,
give honor to the Word,
and praise the Pow'r of the Most High,
one God, by all adored.

*This canticle may be sung to the tune KINGSFOLD
or any other CMD tune, such as with the hymn "I
Heard the Voice of Jesus Say."*

Intercession and Lord's Prayer

*At day's end we offer our petitions in Jesus' name.
We make intercession for our church, our world,
our parish, our neighbors, our family and friends
and ourselves. We seal all our prayers with the
Lord's Prayer. In conclusion, those present may
exchange the sign of peace.*

N I G H T

p r a y e r

This order of prayer may be said before going to sleep.

God, come to my assistance.
Lord, make haste to help me.

Psalm 131

O Lord, my heart is not lifted up,
my eyes are not raised too high;
I do not occupy myself with things
too great and too marvelous for me.

But I have calmed and quieted my life,
like a weaned child with its mother;
I am like a weaned child.

O Israel, hope in the Lord
now and forever.

amen

Or:

Psalm 134

Come, bless the Lord,
all you servants of the Lord,
who stand by night in the house of the Lord!

Lift up your hands in the holy place,
and bless the Lord!
May the Lord who made heaven and earth
bless you from Zion.

The Canticle of Simeon

Lord, now you let your servant go in peace;
your word has been fulfilled:

my own eyes have seen the salvation
which you have prepared in the sight
    of every people:

a light to reveal you to the nations
and the glory of your people Israel.

Invocation to Mary

The final prayer of the day is customarily to Mary.

Hail, holy Queen, Mother of mercy,
our life, our sweetness, and our hope!
To you we cry, the children of Eve;
to you we send up our sighs,
mourning and weeping in this land of exile.
Turn, then, most gracious advocate,
your eyes of mercy toward us;
lead us home at last
and show us the blessed fruit
of your womb, Jesus:
O clement, O loving, O sweet Virgin Mary.

Or:

Hail Mary, full of grace,
The Lord is with you!
Blessed are you among women,
and blessed is the fruit of your womb, Jesus.
Holy Mary, Mother of God,
pray for us sinners,
now and at the hour of our death.

Or during the season of Easter:

Queen of heaven, rejoice, alleluia.
The Son whom you merited to bear, alleluia,
has risen as he said, alleluia.

Rejoice and be glad, O Virgin Mary, alleluia!
For the Lord has truly risen, alleluia.

The Sign of the Cross

We end the day the way we began it,
with the sign of the cross.

May almighty God give us a restful night
    and a peaceful death,
the Father and the Son and the Holy Spirit.
Amen.

FRIDAY

prayer

Friday is our weekly fast day, our day of special prayer, fasting and almsgiving.

Lord, by your cross and resurrection
   you have set us free.
You are the savior of the world.

Psalm 145:13–18, 21

The Lord's words are faithful.
The Lord's deeds are gracious.
The Lord upholds all who are falling,
and raises up all who are bowed down.

The eyes of all look to you,
and you give them their food in due season.
You open your hand,
you satisfy the desire of every living thing.

All the Lord's ways are just,
all the Lord's doings are kind.
The Lord is near to all who call,
to all who call upon the Lord in truth.

My mouth will speak the praise of the Lord;
let all flesh bless God's holy name forever and ever.

Prayer of the Day

All praise be yours, God our Creator,
as we wait in joyful hope
for the flowering of justice
and the fullness of peace.

All praise for this day, this Friday.
By our weekly fasting and prayer,
cast out the spirit of war, of fear and mistrust,
and make us grow hungry for human kindness,
thirsty for solidarity
with all the people of your dear earth.

May all our prayers, our fasting and our deeds
be done in the name of Jesus. Amen.

The wedding feast of the Lamb has begun,
and his bride is prepared to welcome him.

Psalm 100

Make a joyful noise to the Lord, all the lands!
Serve the Lord with gladness!
Come into God's presence with singing!

Know that the Lord, who made us, is God.
We are the Lord's;
we are the people of God,
the sheep of God's pasture.

Enter God's gates with thanksgiving,
and God's courts with praise!
Give thanks and bless God's name!

For the Lord is good;
God's steadfast love endures for ever,
God's faithfulness to all generations.

Song of the Day

O Lord, in whom this day first dawned,
who clothe creation wondrously,
that you should clothe yourself in flesh
is yet more wonderful to see.

Now raised to heights where names all fail,
proclaimed "The Lord," O risen Christ,
in you alone we find our life,
the sun which set that we might rise.

Most Holy God, Word, Spirit: One,
outpoured in love eternally;
you love us unto death that we
might share your own divinity!

Amen

S U N D A Y
p r a y e r

**Sunday is our weekly feast day.
We rejoice in creation and
assemble to hear the word of God
and give thanks and praise.**

Prayers from the Mass

Confiteor

I confess to almighty God,
and to you, my brothers and sisters,
that I have sinned through my own fault
in my thoughts and in my words,
in what I have done,
and in what I have failed to do;
and I ask blessed Mary, ever virgin,
all the angels and saints,
and you, my brothers and sisters,
to pray for me to the Lord our God.

Gloria

Glory to God in the highest,
and peace to his people on earth.
Lord God, heavenly King,
almighty God and Father,
    we worship you, we give you thanks,
    we praise you for your glory.
Lord Jesus Christ, only Son of the Father,
Lord God, Lamb of God,
you take away the sin of the world:
    have mercy on us;
you are seated at the right hand of the Father:
    receive our prayer.

For you alone are the Holy One,
you alone are the Lord,
you alone are the Most High,
    Jesus Christ,
    with the Holy Spirit,
    in the glory of God the Father. Amen.

Nicene Creed

We believe in one God,
   the Father, the Almighty,
   maker of heaven and earth,
   of all that is seen and unseen.

We believe in one Lord, Jesus Christ,
   the only Son of God,
   eternally begotten of the Father,
   God from God, Light from Light,
   true God from true God,
   begotten, not made,
      one in Being with the Father.
Through him all things were made.
For us and for our salvation
      he came down from heaven:
by the power of the Holy Spirit
      he was born of the Virgin Mary,
      and became man.
For our sake he was crucified
      under Pontius Pilate;
   he suffered, died, and was buried.
   On the third day he rose again
      in fulfillment of the scriptures;
   he ascended into heaven and is seated
      at the right hand of the Father.
He will come again in glory
      to judge the living and the dead,
      and his kingdom will have no end.
We believe in the Holy Spirit, the Lord,
   the giver of life,
  who proceeds from the Father and the Son.
  With the Father and the Son
   he is worshiped and glorified.
  He has spoken through the prophets.
We believe in one holy catholic
   and apostolic Church.
We acknowledge one baptism
   for the forgiveness of sins.
We look for the resurrection of the dead,
   and the life of the world to come.
  Amen.

Preface Acclamation

Holy, holy, holy Lord, God of power and might,
heaven and earth are full of your glory.
   Hosanna in the highest.
Blessed is he who comes in the name
     of the Lord.
Hosanna in the highest.

Memorial Acclamation

Christ has died,
Christ is risen,
Christ will come again.
or:
Dying you destroyed our death,
rising you restored our life.
Lord Jesus, come in glory.
or:
When we eat this bread and drink this cup,
we proclaim your death, Lord Jesus,
until you come in glory.
or:
Lord, by your cross and resurrection
you have set us free.
You are the Savior of the world.

Lord's Prayer

Our Father, who art in heaven,
hallowed be thy name;
thy kingdom come;
thy will be done on earth as it is in heaven

Give us this day our daily bread;
and forgive us our tresspasses
as we forgive those who tresspass against us;
and lead us not into temptation,
but deliver us from evil. Amen.

Communion

Lord, I am not worthy to receive you,
but only say the word and I shall be healed.

ADVENT

Maranatha! Come, Lord Jesus!

Let me hear what God the Lord will speak,
for God will speak peace to the people,
to the faithful, to those who turn to God
    in their hearts.

Surely salvation is at hand
    for those who fear the Lord,
that glory may dwell in our land.
Steadfast love and faithfulness
    will meet;
righteousness and peace
    will kiss each other.

Faithfulness will spring up
    from the ground,
and righteousness will look down
    from the sky.
The Lord will give what is good,
and our land will yield its increase.

Righteousness will go before the Lord,
and make a path for God's footsteps.

—Psalm 85:8–13

In the long nights of December,
we listen, Lord, for the words you speak.
How can we hear you
when the markets and machines are so loud,
when the sellers and the entertainers
clamor for our every attention?
Still we would listen for you
and hear of wars so we may long for peace,
and hear of oppression
so we may long for justice,
and hear of hunger so we may long for you.
Then make a path, O God,
so righteousness and peace
shall meet and shall kiss
and with that kiss, with that glory,
shall we and this good creation
praise and bless your coming.

—Prayer of the Season

21

READING I *Isaiah 2:1–5*

The word that Isaiah son of Amoz saw
concerning Judah and Jerusalem.
In days to come
the mountain of the LORD's house
shall be established as the highest of the mountains,
and shall be raised above the hills;
all the nations shall stream to it.

Many peoples shall come and say,
"Come, let us go up to the mountain of the LORD,
to the house of the Jacob's God,
who will teach us the ways of God,
that we may walk in the paths of the LORD."

For out of Zion shall go forth instruction,
and the word of the LORD from Jerusalem.
God shall judge between the nations,
and shall arbitrate for many peoples;
they shall beat their swords into plowshares,
and their spears into pruning hooks;
nation shall not lift up sword against nation,
neither shall they learn war any more.

O house of Jacob,
come, let us walk in the light of the LORD!

The Word of the Lord

READING II *Romans 13:11–14*

Besides this, you know what time it is, how it is now
the moment for you to wake from sleep. For salvation is nearer to us now than when we became
believers; the night is far gone, the day is near. Let
us then lay aside the works of darkness and put on
the armor of light; let us live honorably as in the
day, not in reveling and drunkenness, not in
debauchery and licentiousness, not in quarreling
and jealousy. Instead, put on the Lord Jesus Christ,
and make no provision for the flesh, to gratify its
desires.

The Word of the Lord

GOSPEL *Matthew 24:36–44*

Jesus said, "About that day and hour no one knows,
neither the angels of heaven, nor the Son, but only
the Father.

"For as the days of Noah were, so will be the
coming of the Son-of-Man. For as in those days
before the flood they were eating and drinking, mar-
rying and giving in marriage, until the day Noah
entered the ark, and they knew nothing until the
flood came and swept them all away, so too will be
the coming of the Son-of-Man.

"Then two men will be in the field; one will be
taken and one will be left. Two women will be
grinding meal together; one will be taken and one
will be left. Keep awake therefore, for you do not
know on what day your Lord is coming.

"But understand this: if the owner of the house
had known in what part of the night the thief was
coming, the owner would have stayed awake and
would not have let the house be broken into.

"Therefore you also must be ready, for the Son-
of-Man is coming at an unexpected hour."

The Gospel of the Lord

Saturday, December 8, 2001

IMMACULATE CONCEPTION OF THE VIRGIN MARY

Genesis 3:9–15, 20 *Eve is "the mother of the living."*

Ephesians 1:3–6, 11–12 *God chose us before the world began.*

Luke 1:26–38 *I am the servant of the Lord.*

Sin means separation from God. We believe Mary was
never separated from God from the moment of her conception in her mother's womb. On this Advent feast of
Mary, her "yes" undoes Eve's "no." Mary is our new
Eve, the mother of the living God.

REFLECTION

Matthew's vision of the day of the Lord shows it coming in the midst of day-to-day living—eating and drinking, plowing and grinding meal. The life of a farm family provides Matthew with many of the images for Advent this year. Matthew understands that God will appear in the most ordinary times, when men and women are working and playing and getting on with the business of their lives.

Matthew also presents the disturbing notion of God coming as a thief in the night, a time when most people are asleep. Night is when dishonorable activities are more likely to happen. The letter to the Romans mentions drunkenness, quarreling and jealousy. Is this what is meant by night? Is it a spiritual night, a time when we abandon or are ignorant of our identities as children of God? Is it the time when we engage as individuals and as communities in injustice, war, greed or oppression?

The irony, of course, is that we do not know when God is coming, and we are often unaware of just how benighted are some of the activities, attitudes and identities we treasure. Matthew's surprising identity of God as a thief wakes us up to the understanding that God willingly enters our night to remove these things from us so that we can realize what we truly need. God, the thief, comes to rob us of everything that keeps us from living as children of light. God's coming heralds a new era of light in which our most ordinary activities will be filled with the presence of God.

At the beginning of Advent, the call to trust in God's timing and live awake and in the light is the work of the whole church.

■ **What are the "works of darkness" that the church can name and begin to lay aside this Advent? What would you yourself name?**

■ **How do you envision the "justice of God" among nations and people? How can you participate in and act according to that vision now?**

PRACTICE OF FAITH

ENDINGS AND BEGINNINGS. As the calendar year ends, the church year begins. Isaiah's prophecies make a friend think of the genesis of everything: the beginning of creation when beasts and humans lived in peace. Advent can be a time to make New Year's resolutions. How can you put on Jesus afresh so that the light of the Lord shines more brightly in our world?

PRACTICE OF HOPE

THE DAY IS NEAR. The night is almost gone. Stay awake! Watch and pray! You do not know the day or the hour! These are words filled with expectation and hope. It is time to abandon worldly cares and wait for the Lord. In this time of Christmas shopping and preparation, these words seem to clash with the spirit of the secular season, and they do. Lucky for us, Advent violet and rose clash with red and green! If you keep your eyes open for the coming of the Holy One, you will know what is important and what is not.

PRACTICE OF CHARITY

THE PROMISE OF ADVENT. Isaiah tells us that when the Lord comes again, nations will be at peace and there will be no need for swords or spears. The prophecy was clearly waiting to come true in 1980 when civil war tore the nation of El Salvador. The four American women martyred on December 2 were there to preach the gospel promise of justice for the poor and oppressed. But the ruling class of that tiny Central American country saw the work of Maura Clarke, Ita Ford, Dorothy Kazel and Jean Donovan as a threat to their privileged way of life. In many countries of our world, the poor continue to wait for God's reign of justice. As one effort to bring about the promise of the Messiah, consider a gift to The Heifer Project, which provides farm animals to Third World families. Your children can choose to purchase a chicken, lamb or pig, and a picture of your animal will be mailed in time to put it in the child's stocking. Write to The Heifer Project International at PO Box 998175, Washington DC 20077-7137.

WEEKDAY READINGS (Mo)Isaiah 4:2–6; (Tu)11:1–10; (We)25:6–10; (Th)26:1–6; (Fr)29:17–24; (Sa)Immaculate Conception (see box)

READING I *Isaiah 11:1–10*

A shoot shall come out from the stump of Jesse,
and a branch shall grow out of its roots.
The spirit of the LORD shall rest on him,
the spirit of wisdom and understanding,
the spirit of counsel and might,
the spirit of knowledge and the fear of the LORD.
His delight shall be in the fear of the LORD.

He shall not judge by what his eyes see,
or decide by what his ears hear;
but with righteousness shall judge the poor,
and decide with equity for the meek of the earth;
he shall strike the earth with the rod of his mouth,
and with the breath of his lips shall kill the wicked.
Righteousness shall be the belt around his waist,
and faithfulness the belt around his loins.

The wolf shall live with the lamb,
the leopard shall lie down with the kid,
the calf and the lion and the fatling together,
and a little child shall lead them.
The cow and the bear shall graze,
their young shall lie down together;
and the lion shall eat straw like the ox.
The nursing child shall play over the hole of the asp,
and the weaned child shall put its hand
   on the adder's den.
They will not hurt or destroy on all
   my holy mountain;
for the earth will be full of the knowledge of the
Lord as the waters cover the sea.

On that day there will stand as a signal to the peoples
   the root of Jesse,
of whom the nations shall inquire,
and whose dwelling shall be glorious.

The word of the Lord

READING II *Romans 15:4–9*

Revised Common Lectionary: Romans 15:4–13

Whatever was written in former days was written for
our instruction, so that by steadfastness and by the
encouragement of the scriptures we might have hope.
May the God of steadfastness and encouragement
grant you to live in harmony with one another, in
accordance with Christ Jesus, so that together you
may with one voice glorify the God and Father of
our Lord Jesus Christ.

Welcome one another, therefore, just as Christ
has welcomed you, for the glory of God. For I tell
you that Christ has become a servant of the Jewish
people on behalf of the truth of God in order to confirm the promises given to the ancestors, and in
order that the Gentiles might glorify our merciful
God. As it is written, "Therefore I will confess you
among the Gentiles, and sing praises to your name."

GOSPEL *Matthew 3:1–12*

The word of the Lord

In those days John the Baptist appeared in the
wilderness of Judea, proclaiming, "Repent, for the
dominion of heaven has come near." This is the one
of whom the prophet Isaiah spoke when he said,

   "The voice of one crying out in the wilderness:
   'Prepare the way of the Lord,
   make straight the paths of the Lord.'"

Now John wore clothing of camel's hair with a
leather belt around his waist, and his food was
locusts and wild honey. Then the people of Jerusalem
and all Judea were going out to him, and all the
region along the Jordan, and they were baptized by
him in the river Jordan, confessing their sins.

But when John saw many Pharisees and
Sadducees coming for baptism, he said to them,
"You brood of vipers! Who warned you to flee from
the wrath to come? Bear fruit worthy of repentance.
Do not presume to say to yourselves, 'We have
Abraham as our ancestor'; for I tell you, God is able
from these stones to raise up children to Abraham.
Even now the ax is lying at the root of the trees;
every tree therefore that does not bear good fruit is
cut down and thrown into the fire.

"I baptize you with water for repentance, but
one who is more powerful than I is coming after me;
I am not worthy to carry his sandals. He will baptize you with the Holy Spirit and fire. With a win-
nowing fork in hand, he will clear his threshing floor
and will gather his wheat into the granary; but the
chaff he will burn with unquenchable fire."

The Gospel of the Lord

REFLECTION

Isaiah's description of the peaceable kingdom and John the Baptist's metaphor of the wheat and the chaff present contrasting images of the same reality. How can such radically different pictures teach us about the coming of Jesus? In the Hebrew scriptures, the day of the Lord is described alternately as a feast and delight for the righteous and as a day of wrath and judgment for those who had not turned to God or were hypocritical in their actions. The prophets challenged, cajoled and warned the people that God's coming would be unlike anything they had known. The shoot from Jesse's branch in Isaiah meant both the renewal of life for the line of David and the reversal of the natural order of things. Even mortal enemies would lie down together.

Like the prophets of old, John the Baptist knew that the reign of God was a time for repentance. He called on people to change their lives as completely as God would change the world. John is described as like Elijah who, according to the prophet Malachi, would come before the day of the Lord.

John the Baptist, however, does not think of God's coming as peaceful. He uses the metaphor of the threshing floor to explain it. This image called to mind the place where wheat is beaten to separate the good grain from the waste, the chaff. John challenges his listeners to see themselves on the threshing floor: Will they be gathered in as good grain or burned as chaff?

The Pharisees and Sadducees believe that their claim to be Abraham's descendents guarantees them a place among the righteous. They have come for baptism because they think it looks good, not because they desire to repent. John warns them that everything they think they know is about to be changed. If they do not bear good fruit, they will be destroyed; only the truly repentant will be gathered into the granary.

Depending on the disposition of one's heart, the contrasting images of the kingdom and the threshing floor can be comfort or challenge.

■ **Newborn children change their parents' lives radically. How might the presence of the newborn child, Jesus, change your life? How might the church as a whole show the world the change this newborn brings?**

■ **Reflect on the command, "prepare the way of the Lord." How are you preparing for the coming of Jesus at Christmas?**

PRACTICE OF FAITH

BEAR FRUIT. Today's gospel is clear that deeds, not just words, are needed to usher in the reign of God. John wants evidence of a change of heart. The Pharisees and Sadducees cannot assume that because they are children of Abraham they are living according to God's law. Likewise, simply calling ourselves Christian is not enough. How do we live our faith? What life changes must we make if we are to live the Christian life?

PRACTICE OF HOPE

STEADFASTNESS AND ENCOURAGEMENT. As the pace of Christmas preparations becomes faster, take time this week to have coffee or breakfast with a friend. Encourage each other in slowing down, and enjoy your time together as a gift from God.

Begin by slowing down and letting go of the frantic pace; let the wonder of the season fill your heart. Remember that the coming of Christ is the focus of our hope and our joy. The Holy Spirit brings all good gifts, and peace is the most wondrous of gifts. Imagine a world without war, where children can play in safety and none will go hungry.

PRACTICE OF CHARITY

LIVE IN HARMONY. Isaiah tells us again of the coming of the Messiah. The idyllic description of the animals living together in peace contrasts sharply with John's rebuke of the Pharisees and Sadducees. They cannot rely on their identity as children of Abraham but must repent and change their ways. In our own time, with religious wars all over the world, we are reminded that all of us have looked to our religion at one time or another to feel assured that we are in the right. The Fellowship of Reconciliation recognizes the inherent contradiction when people of faith war against one another. Since 1915, they have gone to many parts of the world where religious groups are at war to urge the combatants to find a way to peace. Learn more about the work of the Fellowship of Reconciliation, Box 271, Nyack NY 10960; www.forusa.org.

WEEKDAY READINGS (Mo)Isaiah 35:1–10; (Tu)40:1–11; (We)Zechariah 2:14–17; (Th)Isaiah 41:13–20; (Fr)48:17–19; (Sa)Sirach 48:1–4; 9–11

READING I *Isaiah 35:1–10*

Roman Catholic: Isaiah 35:1–6a, 10

The wilderness and the dry land shall be glad,
the desert shall rejoice and blossom;
like the crocus it shall blossom abundantly,
and rejoice with joy and singing.
The glory of Lebanon shall be given to it,
the majesty of Carmel and Sharon.
They shall see the glory of the LORD,
the majesty of our God.

Strengthen the weak hands,
and make firm the feeble knees.
Say to those who are of a fearful heart,
"Be strong, do not fear!
Behold, your God will come with vengeance,
with terrible recompense.
God will come and save you."

Then the eyes of the blind shall be opened,
and the ears of the deaf unstopped;
then the lame shall leap like a deer,
and the tongue of the speechless sing for joy.
For waters shall break forth in the wilderness,
and streams in the desert;
the burning sand shall become a pool,
and the thirsty ground springs of water;
the haunt of the jackals shall become a swamp,
the grass shall become reeds and rushes.

A highway shall be there,
and it shall be called the Holy Way;
the unclean shall not travel on it,
but it shall be for God's people;
no traveler, not even fools, shall go astray.
No lion shall be there,
nor shall any ravenous beast come up upon it;
they shall not be found there,
but the redeemed shall walk there.
And the ransomed of the LORD shall return,
and come to Zion with singing;
everlasting joy shall be upon their heads;
they shall obtain joy and gladness,
and sorrow and sighing shall flee away.

READING II *James 5:7–10*

Be patient, therefore, beloved, until the coming of the Lord. The farmer waits for the precious crop from the earth, being patient with it until it receives the early and the late rains. You also must be patient. Strengthen your hearts, for the coming of the Lord is near. Beloved, do not grumble against one another, so that you may not be judged. See, the Judge is standing at the doors! As an example of suffering and patience, beloved, take the prophets who spoke in the name of the Lord.

GOSPEL *Matthew 11:2–11*

When John heard in prison what the Messiah was doing, he sent word by his disciples and said to him, "Are you the one who is to come, or are we to wait for another?" Jesus answered them, "Go and tell John what you hear and see: those who are blind receive their sight, those who are lame walk, those with leprosy are cleansed, those who are deaf hear, the dead are raised, and the poor have good news brought to them. And blessed is anyone who takes no offense at me."

As they went away, Jesus began to speak to the crowds about John: "What did you go out into the wilderness to look at? A reed shaken by the wind? What then did you go out to see? Someone dressed in soft robes? Look, those who wear soft robes are in royal palaces. What then did you go out to see? A prophet? Yes, I tell you, and more than a prophet. This is the one about whom it is written,

'See, I am sending my messenger ahead of you,
who will prepare your way before you.'

Truly I tell you, among those born of women no one has arisen greater than John the Baptist; yet the least in the dominion of heaven is greater than he."

26

REFLECTION

"Go and tell John what you and hear and see," Jesus tells John's disciples when they ask if he is the one for whom they are waiting. In that simple request, Jesus asks them to witness to what is happening in the world. If they know the promise of Isaiah and the other prophets, the people and John will recognize who Jesus is. In the poetry of the prophets, the coming of God will restore the people of God to wholeness, beautifully symbolized by the opening of eyes, ears and lips. Jesus goes even further by talking about the dead being raised and the good news preached to the poor. Jesus' command forces John's disciples to see the transformation of the world that is taking place around them a little at a time.

Last week, the farmer's threshing floor gave us an image of upheaval that the coming of God would bring. This week, James points to the farmer's patience in waiting for a crop to ripen. Change and growth can seem painfully slow, whether we are waiting for a crop of wheat or the dominion of God. But the farmer can see the signs of the harvest coming closer. Jesus challenges the crowd to see the signs of the reign of God already begun in their midst. He challenges them to be wakeful and repentant, even as they come to know him for who he is.

We can look in our world for signs that signal the presence of God: a mother embracing her child's killer in forgiveness and compassion; the coming together of children from opposite sides of war-torn areas like Northern Ireland or the Middle East; neighbors and friends rallying to help a family burned out of its home five days before Christmas. These moments and many like them show where God has changed the world a little at a time. "Tell the world what you see," Jesus might say to us. If we have remained awake and patient, we might be able to do that.

■ **Reflect on the signs of God's presence around you. If Jesus asked you to tell what you have seen, what would you say? How can the church proclaim God's transformation of the world?**

■ **For children, waiting for Christmas can be difficult. What are difficult waiting times for adults? What helps to get through these periods?**

PRACTICE OF FAITH

FEAR NOT! Many times God's messengers announce themselves with the words: Do not be afraid. Recall the angel Gabriel at the Annunciation or the angels appearing to the shepherds in the fields. In fact, this greeting appears in scripture at least 44 times! These are heartening words. Fear prevents our ability to recognize God's presence and respond to God's call. Of what are you afraid? Let the light of God's promise shine on your fears.

PRACTICE OF HOPE

BE PATIENT, BELOVED. We are all on the road. And what a road it is—not even a fool can go astray on it! Take a walk this week, through the snow or the slush or the dryness; for no matter what the weather, the road goes on. Pause to look at the people around you. Say a quiet prayer for their wellbeing, and pray for a blessing for yourself as well! Wait in joyful, hopeful expectation for the coming of the Lord.

PRACTICE OF CHARITY

DO NOT JUDGE ANOTHER. The letter of James cautions the early Christians not to grumble against one another lest they themselves be judged. All too often people speak of understanding those who suffer—the homeless, the mentally ill, the addicted—but in the depths of their hearts suspect that these people brought their situation on themselves because of moral weakness or failure.

In the United States there is a movement to build more prisons rather than to commit our resources to help these people become productive citizens. Contact a local prison ministry to find out how to help those who are in trouble with the law instead of merely condemning them.

WEEKDAY READINGS (Mo)Genesis 49:2, 8–10; (Tu)Jeremiah 23:5–8; (We)Judges 13:2–7, 24–25a; (Th)Isaiah 7:10–14; (Fr)Zephaniah 3:14–18a; (Sa)1 Samuel 1:24–28

READING I *Isaiah 7:10–16*

The LORD spoke to Ahaz, saying,
Ask a sign of the LORD your God;
let it be deep as Sheol or high as heaven.
But Ahaz said,
I will not ask, and I will not put the LORD to the test.

Then Isaiah said:
Hear then, O house of David!
Is it too little for you to weary mortals,
that you weary my God also?
Therefore this very LORD will give you a sign.
Look, the young woman is with child
    and shall bear a son,
and shall name him Immanuel.
He shall eat curds and honey
by the time he knows how to refuse the evil
    and choose the good.
For before the child knows how to refuse the evil
    and choose the good,
the land before whose two kings you are in dread
will be deserted."

The Word of the Lord

READING II *Romans 1:1–7*

Paul, a servant of Jesus Christ, called to be an apostle, set apart for the gospel of God, which God promised beforehand through the prophets in the holy scriptures, the gospel concerning God's Son, who was descended from David according to the flesh and was declared to be Son of God with power according to the spirit of holiness by resurrection from the dead, Jesus Christ our Lord, through whom we have received grace and apostleship to bring about the obedience of faith among all the Gentiles for the sake of his name, including yourselves who are called to belong to Jesus Christ,

To all God's beloved in Rome,
who are called to be saints:
Grace to you and peace
from God, our Father,
and the Lord Jesus Christ.

The Word of the Lord

GOSPEL *Matthew 1:18–25*

Now the birth of Jesus the Messiah took place in this way. When his mother Mary had been engaged to Joseph, but before they lived together, she was found to be with child from the Holy Spirit.

Her husband Joseph, being a righteous man and unwilling to expose her to public disgrace, planned to dismiss her quietly. But just when he had resolved to do this, an angel of the Lord appeared to him in a dream and said, "Joseph, son of David, do not be afraid to take Mary home as your wife, for the child conceived in her is from the Holy Spirit. She will bear a son, and you are to name him Jesus, for he will save his people from their sins." All this took place to fulfill what had been spoken by the Lord through the prophet: "Look, the virgin shall conceive and bear a son, and they shall name him Emmanuel," which means, "God is with us."

When Joseph awoke from sleep, he did as the angel of the Lord commanded him; he took her home as his wife, but had no marital relations with her until she had borne a son; and he named him Jesus.

The Gospel of the Lord

28

REFLECTION

Paul writes that through Jesus he is called to be an apostle, his hearers are called to belong to Jesus Christ, and those to whom he is writing are called to be saints. In the trying times of the first century, none of these were easy. Paul was misunderstood and persecuted by the Jews for his mission to the Gentiles. Christians, still part of the Jewish synagogue, constituted an increasingly vocal religious minority. Rome viewed both the Christians and the Jews as a threat to political power and the prevailing religion of the emperor. What gave the early Christians the courage to name themselves followers of Christ and beloved of God?

The answer is deceptively simple: It was because in Jesus, God became human. When Paul reflected on the experience of Jesus, he saw in him the fulfillment of Isaiah's prophecy about Emmanuel, the child who was "God with us." In Jewish belief, all things were possible with God. God could conquer the most stubborn of enemies. Just remembering what God had done, as related in the Hebrew scriptures, gave courage to the faintest of hearts.

For the Christians, Jesus was the living sign that once again God had broken into human existence. The belief that Jesus was God, the Lord of all, gave Paul and the early Christians a boldness to preach about the reign of God.

What does it mean for us that God became human? It means that God found goodness in a world that sometimes makes us despair. It means that God did not despise a body that we sometimes find weak. It means that we have an example of how to live our lives as children of God. Can we be less bold, then, in our proclamation of the good news? Can we fail to model the peace and justice of Christ in our dealings with the world? At the end of our season of anticipation, the reality of "God with us" strengthens feeble knees and gives us courage, for we know that we are not and have never been alone.

■ In what ways can the church preach the good news that "God is with us" to those on the margins of our society?

■ God's presence and transforming power often go unnoticed. Review what has happened in the world in the last ten years and name where God may have been active. Do the same thing for your own lives.

PRACTICE OF FAITH

TRUE FAITH. Pope Pius XII said, "True religion and profound humaneness are not rivals. They are sisters." Joseph seemed to know that. In his time and culture, betrothal bonded a couple as solidly as marriage itself. Perplexed as he was, he refused to be anything but humane toward Mary. He accepted the word of God's messenger and courageously stood by Mary, his betrothed.

True religion and profound humaneness show us what is most real, even if this sometimes flies in the face of convention. Can you recall a time when you were faced with a choice that called you to act with compassion, even if it meant going against the norm?

PRACTICE OF HOPE

HIS NAME IS "GOD WITH US." Attentiveness can be especially hard to come by this week, but Joseph is a good role model for us. He is attentive and obedient to God. The Latin root of the word *obedience* means "to listen." To listen attentively is to obey. Listen to a recording of Handel's *Messiah* this week as you bake cookies or wrap gifts, and be attentive to the presence of God in your dreams and in your waking.

PRACTICE OF CHARITY

GOD WITH US. The child Mary will bear is to be named Jesus because he will save the people from their sins. This last week of Advent is a good time to repent a chief sin of our American culture: commercialism run wild. This holiday requires Christians to realize that we belong to a minority group that lives differently from those who view Christmas as a civil holiday. As you wrap your gifts and place them under the tree, also give to those who lack material comforts. Local soup kitchens are busy preparing baskets of food for the Christmas dinners of those without the means to feed their families. They are usually looking for volunteers to help with packing and delivery.

WEEKDAY READINGS (Mo)2 Samuel 7:1–5, 8–12, 14a, 16; (Tu)Christmas; (We)Acts 6:8–10; 7:54–59; (Th)1 John 1:1–4; (Fri)1 John 1:5—2:2; (Sat)1 John 2:3–11

CHRISTMAS

All creatures a choir!

O sing to the Lord a new song,
for the Lord has done marvelous things!
God's right hand and holy arm
have gotten the victory.

The Lord has remembered
     steadfast love and faithfulness
to the house of Israel.
All the ends of the earth have seen
the victory of our God.

Make a joyful noise to the Lord,
     all the earth;
break forth into joyous song
     and sing praises!
Sing praises to the Lord with the lyre,
with the lyre and the sound of melody!
With trumpets and the sound
     of the horn
make a joyful noise before the Ruler,
     the Lord!

Let the sea roar, and all that fills it;
the world and those who dwell in it!
Let the floods clap their hands;
let the hills sing for joy together
     before the Lord.

—Psalm 98:1, 3–8

When people witness deeds like these—
mercy winning victories
and justice welcomed
     in the public places—
then the earth itself will be an orchestra
and all creatures a choir,
and we shall sing together a song
that announces you,
God of poor shepherds and stargazers.
Rehearse us now in that Christmas song:
Like those shepherds may we know where
     to look,
like the magi may we know
     when to listen to the powerful
and when to mere dreams.
Come, Lord, and lift us up in song.

—Prayer of the Season

READING I *Isaiah 9:2–7*

The people who walked in darkness
  have seen a great light;
those who lived in a land of deep darkness—
on them light has shined.
You have multiplied the nation,
you have increased its joy;
they rejoice before you as with joy at the harvest,
as people exult when dividing plunder.
For the yoke of their burden,
and the bar across their shoulders,
the rod of their oppressor,
you have broken as on the day of Midian.
For all the boots of the tramping warriors
and all the garments rolled in blood
shall be burned as fuel for the fire.

For a child has been born for us,
a son given to us;
authority rests upon his shoulders;
and he is named
Wonderful Counselor, Mighty God,
Everlasting Father, Prince of Peace.
His authority shall grow continually,
and there shall be endless peace
for the throne and dominion of David,
to establish and uphold it
with justice and with righteousness
from this time onward and forevermore.

The zeal of the LORD of hosts will do this.

READING II *Titus 2:11–14*

The grace of God has appeared, bringing salvation to all, training us to renounce impiety and worldly passions, and in the present age to live lives that are self-controlled, upright, and godly, while we wait for the blessed hope and the manifestation of the glory of our great God and Savior, Jesus Christ. It is Jesus Christ who gave himself for us to redeem us from all iniquity and purify for himself a people of his own who are zealous for good deeds.

GOSPEL *Luke 2:1–14*

In those days a decree went out from Emperor Augustus that all the world should be registered. This was the first registration and was taken while Quirinius was governor of Syria. All went to their own towns to be registered. Joseph also went from the town of Nazareth in Galilee to Judea, to the city of David called Bethlehem, because he was descended from the house and family of David. He went to be registered with Mary, to whom he was engaged and who was expecting a child. While they were there, the time came for her to deliver her child. And she gave birth to her firstborn son and wrapped him in bands of cloth, and laid him in a manger, because there was no place for them in the inn.

In that region there were shepherds living in the fields, keeping watch over their flock by night. Then an angel of the Lord stood before them, and the glory of the Lord shone around them, and they were terrified. But the angel said to them, "Do not be afraid; for see—I am bringing you good news of great joy for all the people: to you is born this day in the city of David a Savior, who is the Messiah, the Lord. This will be a sign for you: you will find a child wrapped in bands of cloth and lying in a manger." And suddenly there was with the angel a multitude of the heavenly host, praising God and saying,

"Glory to God in the highest heaven,
  and on earth peace among those
    whom God favors!"

REFLECTION

Why does this story never wear out? Could it be because the story witnesses to faith that says God breaks into human existence in surprising and unexpected ways? Could it be that in the coming of Jesus, God makes holy the human body and human birth? Why does this matter? What does it change?

During and after the Babylonian exile, the Jews struggled with the question of God's seeming absence in their lives. The prophets challenged the people to see that they had turned away from God. They also made known God's promise to renew the divine relationship with Israel. The child of Isaiah's prophecy was the herald of the new age of justice and peace.

The Hebrew scriptures outline a pattern of sin and redemption that shows us that even though we are blessed, we are also tempted and we fall. The promise of God to send a messiah appealed not only to the political aspirations of an oppressed people, but also to the spiritual desolation of those who were lost.

Why does the Christmas story never wear out? It is because in this birth the pattern of sin is broken. In Jesus' birth, God becomes one of us and shows us how to live. In Jesus, the divine becomes human so that we can know that the reign of God is at hand.

Luke records that shepherds heard the announcement first. Shepherds were in a unique position to understand the message of the angels. The messiah, born in the city of the shepherd king, was the one who would shepherd them.

If the birth of Jesus means anything it means that we no longer have to fear sin; we have already been freed from it. We no longer have to fear being lost, we have already been found. Jesus becomes human and takes on the role of shepherd so that we can be led to God. In God, all that we are has been blessed.

■ **In the nativity story of Luke, which character are you most like this year? What is your reaction to the birth of Jesus and the events surrounding it?**

■ **Shepherds figure prominently in the story of Jesus' birth. Why does Luke emphasize their participation and their proclamation of the birth?**

PRACTICE OF FAITH

A GREAT LIGHT. "I hate TV news," a friend said as the local broadcast began. "It always emphasizes the darker side, warning you of everything that can go wrong." I could not disagree. Yet we know that the darkness is not the whole story. The truth we celebrate this Christmas night is that a light shone in the darkness, the grace of God has appeared, bringing salvation to all.

The light of Christmas is not a brief flash or a rare event like a comet's appearance. Jesus illuminates the darkness and "his authority shall grow continually." He does not mock our darkness, but desires us to see him in spite of it.

PRACTICE OF HOPE

WE WAIT FOR THE BLESSED HOPE. After all the anticipation of Advent, why do the readings for Christmas Eve still mention waiting? Why are we still awaiting "our blessed hope . . . Jesus Christ"? Hasn't he already come? Didn't he come two thousand years ago at his birth in Bethlehem? Hasn't he come this night, when we celebrate his birth?

Of course he came in the past; of course we celebrate his incarnation on this holy night, but there is more: we still look for "the manifestation of the glory of our great God . . . ."

Titus urges us to wait in hope for this second coming. With Mary, "ponder all things in [your] heart." Remember the great and saving acts of a mighty God, and then see the miracle of a tiny child. Ponder and wait, celebrate and hope. Wait for the fullness of time when God's work and ours will be complete.

PRACTICE OF CHARITY

HOSPITALITY. This feast is a time for families to spend together. The story of the birth of Jesus reminds us that our God became human in order to be fully immersed in our day to day history including the daily life of our families. As Christians we believe that we continue the work of Jesus—to bring God into our world and into the lives of all those we meet. Take this opportunity to include someone who is far away from family, or even estranged from them, in your celebrations. Let them experience first-hand the love of this Christian feast. Henri Nouwen, the twentieth-century spiritual guide to so many, said that our ability to offer hospitality, a space in our lives and homes to others, was the sign of our Christianity.

READING I *Isaiah 52:7–10*

How beautiful upon the mountains
are the feet of the messenger
who announces peace,
who brings good news,
who announces salvation,
who says to Zion, "Your God reigns."

Listen! Your sentinels lift up their voices,
together they sing for joy;
for in plain sight
they see the return of the LORD to Zion.

Break forth together into singing,
   you ruins of Jerusalem;
for the LORD has comforted the chosen people,
and has redeemed Jerusalem.
The holy arm of the LORD is bared
before the eyes of all the nations;
and all the ends of the earth
shall see the salvation of our God.

READING II *Hebrews 1:1–6*

Long ago God spoke to our ancestors in many and various ways by the prophets, but in these last days God has spoken to us by a Son, whom God appointed heir of all things, through whom God also created the worlds. He is the reflection of God's glory and the exact imprint of God's very being, and sustains all things by his powerful word. When the Son had made purification for sins, he sat down at the right hand of the Majesty on high, having become as much superior to angels as the name he has inherited is more excellent than theirs.

For to which of the angels did God ever say, "You are my Son; today I have begotten you"? Or again, "I will be a Father to him, and he will be a Son to me"? And again, when bringing the firstborn into the world, God says, "Let all God's angels worship him."

GOSPEL *John 1:1–18*

In the beginning was the Word, and the Word was with God, and the Word was God. The Word was in the beginning with God. All things came into being through the Word, without whom not one thing came into being. What has come into being in the Word was life, and the life was the light of all people. The light shines in the darkness, and the darkness did not overcome it.

There was a man sent from God, whose name was John. He came as a witness to testify to the light, so that all might believe through him. He himself was not the light, but he came to testify to the light. The true light, which enlightens everyone, was coming into the world.

The light was in the world, and the world came into being through him; yet the world did not know him. He came to what was his own, and his own people did not accept him. But to all who received him, who believed in his name, he gave power to become children of God, who were born, not of blood or of the will of the flesh or of the will of a man, but of God.

And the Word became flesh and lived among us, and we have seen his glory, the glory as of a father's only son, full of grace and truth; we have beheld his glory, glory as of the only Son from the Father. (John bore witness to the Word, and cried, "This is the one of whom I said, 'The one who comes after me ranks before me, for he was before me.'") And from his fullness have we all received, grace upon grace. For the law was given through Moses; grace and truth came through Jesus Christ. No one has ever seen God; the only Son, who is in the bosom of the Father, has made God known.

REFLECTION

"In the beginning . . . " calls up images of the chaotic universe into which God speaks words like "let there be light," and thus makes an entire world. Deliberately modeling his opening on the beginning of Genesis, John surprises his audience not with creation but with an existence. This prologue of John's gospel offers us the understanding that Jesus is God's Word of love to the world, coexisting with God from before the creation and finally coming to dwell among us.

What John does is unique among the gospels. The synoptic writers begin with prophecy or genealogy or annunciation, but they begin in the world of human beings and their traditions. They begin with what we expected and show how Jesus fulfills that expectation. John, however, begins in God's world and shows how Jesus fulfills God's plan to love the world into redemption. Immediately the major themes of John come into focus. The Word is light and life; the world that opposes it is darkness and death. John has no middle ground. To John, those who follow Jesus are born of the Spirit. They do not follow the ways of the world, but have eternal life.

Why is this important for us to hear on Christmas day? In a busy season, we often lose our focus, even ourselves in the preparation for the holiday. Stores clamor for our attention. Advertisers tout more and more items we cannot afford to be without. Family pressures seem to heighten, and depression actually increases. It is hard to find time to reflect on the meaning of Christmas when the world demands every minute.

John reminds us that our life is not tied up with the world of parties and presents and last-minute shopping. He remembers for us that God's Word was spoken before the beginning of the world and became the creative force by which the world, and we, were made. John stands as a witness to the new creation in Jesus, the Word made flesh who comes to dwell among us.

John is the poet of the evangelists. His words, like poetry, need to be repeated over and over because they evoke different images and levels of meaning. There is no better time to do this than on Christmas morning, when the church remembers and celebrates the one who brings the fullness of God to us.

■ The Greek word *logos* is translated as "word" but literally means "reason." How would it change or deepen your understanding to think that John's gospel might start: "In the beginning was the Reason . . ."?

PRACTICE OF FAITH

SING PRAISE TO GOD. Sing out during the liturgy today. Celebrate the assurance that the kingdom will come, that all will be brought to perfection. Take your cues from today's first reading from Isaiah: Sing, break forth in singing, lift up your voice! What better way to proclaim the joy of Christmas! Notice how satisfying it is to participate in the music of the liturgy.

After Christmas dinner tonight, plan on some quiet time. Reflect on the peace of Christmas. God's love is real—Christ came, died, and rose again, just as promised. Christ is alive and present in our lives today and every day. Rest in that assurance tonight.

PRACTICE OF HOPE

THE WORD BECAME FLESH. Mary had a habit of doing inconvenient things. She seemed to attract all the "broken" people of the world, and this didn't fit into her teenage daughter's agenda at all.

Why did Mary have to spend so much time away from her own home to prepare a home for a refugee family? And then there was the homeless man who joined them while they were out shopping. Instead of giving him a few dollars and moving on, Mary stopped to chat with him. He ended up riding to the local shelter in their car.

Mary knew her daughter was uncomfortable, but she didn't apologize. She knew the face of Jesus when she saw it. And in the years to come, the daughter was able to see what her mother saw—especially when she looked at her mother.

PRACTICE OF CHARITY

THE MESSENGER WHO PUBLISHES PEACE. As we celebrate this holy feast, we are invited again to recognize that Christ was born to bring God's message of peace to all people. We still need to learn the ways of peace; peacemaking requires both prayer and study. Begin this Christmas season by reading or re-reading the U.S. Catholic bishops' pastoral letter, The "Challenge of Peace." Make note of one area you may want to work on this year. Pray about how you might be a messenger who publishes peace in the months to come. Copies of the pastoral are available from the United States Catholic Conference, 3211 Fourth Street NE, Washington DC 20017-1194; 800-235-8722.

READING I *Sirach 3:2–6, 12–14*

Revised Common Lectionary: Isaiah 63:7–9

For the Lord honors a father above his children
and confirms a mother's right over her children.
Those who honor their father atone for sins,
and those who respect their mother
   are like those who lay up treasure.
Those who honor their father
   will have joy in their own children,
and when they pray they will be heard.
Those who respect their father will have long life,
and those who honor their mother obey the Lord.
My child, help your father in his old age
and do not grieve him as long as he lives;
even if his mind fails, be patient with him;
because you have all your faculties
   do not despise him.
For kindness to a father will not be forgotten,
and will be credited to you against your sins.

READING II *Colossians 3:12–17*

Complete reading: Colossians 3:12–21
Revised Common Lectionary: Hebrews 2:10–18

As God's chosen ones, holy and beloved, clothe yourselves with compassion, kindness, humility, meekness, and patience. Bear with one another and, if anyone has a complaint against another, forgive each other; just as the Lord has forgiven you, so you also must forgive. Above all, clothe yourselves with love, which binds everything together in perfect harmony. And let the peace of Christ rule in your hearts, to which indeed you were called in the one body. And be thankful. Let the word of Christ dwell in you richly; teach and admonish one another in all wisdom; and with gratitude in your hearts sing psalms, hymns, and spiritual songs to God. And whatever you do, in word or deed, do everything in the name of the Lord Jesus, giving thanks to God, the Father, through him.

GOSPEL *Matthew 2:13–22*

Now after the magi had left, an angel of the Lord appeared to Joseph in a dream and said, "Get up, take the child and his mother, and flee to Egypt, and remain there until I tell you; for Herod is about to search for the child, to destroy him."

Then Joseph got up, took the child and his mother by night, and went to Egypt, and remained there until the death of Herod. This was to fulfill what had been spoken by the Lord through the prophet, "Out of Egypt I have called my son."

When Herod saw that he had been tricked by the magi, he was infuriated, and he sent and killed all the children in and around Bethlehem who were two years old or under, according to the time that he had learned from the magi. Then was fulfilled what had been spoken through the prophet Jeremiah: "A voice was heard in Ramah, wailing and loud lamentation, Rachel weeping for her children; she refused to be consoled, because they are no more."

When Herod died, an angel of the Lord suddenly appeared in a dream to Joseph in Egypt and said, "Get up, take the child and his mother, and go to the land of Israel, for those who were seeking the child's life are dead." Then Joseph got up, took the child and his mother, and went to the land of Israel. But when he heard that Archelaus was ruling over Judea in place of his father Herod, he was afraid to go there. And after being warned in a dream, he went away to the district of Galilee.

Tuesday, January 1, 2002

MARY, MOTHER OF GOD

Numbers 6:22–27 *The Lord let his face shine on you!*

Galatians 4:4–7 *You are no longer slaves but children of God.*

Luke 2:16–21 *Mary pondered these things in her heart.*

Our merry Christmastime unfolds with the blessing of a new year, with the astonishing good news of peace on earth and with the treasures pondered within the heart of Mary.

R E F L E C T I O N

We speak of Jesus as our redeemer. The root meaning of the word redeemer, *go'el* in the Hebrew, is "next of kin." In the Hebrew scriptures, the next of kin is the one who can redeem a family's debts. Jesus' sacrificial atonement is the act of a brother to redeem our debt of sin.

Family bonds both comfort and challenge us. Our family is where we can experiment with our gifts and strengths, and where our weaknesses are well-known. Families can be a place of redemption. But they can also be a place of profound loneliness, if trust is betrayed and compassion is absent. Human families can be far from holy families and yet God chose to be revealed as redeemer by being born into a family.

In the family of the church, we live as brothers and sisters, children of God, knowing one another's strengths and weaknesses. The Letter to the Colossians celebrates Jesus as the abiding presence of God, the brother who saves us, and it also points to him as the model who invites us to transform our lives and live according to God's command. Jesus became like us in every respect; we need to become like him in every way we can. This means living in obedience to God and becoming signs of God's presence in the world.

Our choice to live in freedom as children of God shows itself first in our relationships with our families and then with the church itself. The proverb "charity begins at home" carries something of this idea in it. If we cannot redeem the bad situations for those closest to us, how can we possibly do so for the wider community?

The power of God's love allows us to reach out, forgive one another and work for the justice of God. This is what brothers and sisters do in the holy family of God.

■ **Many things today threaten the integrity of families of all kinds, from poverty to substance abuse to emotional or physical abuse. What holds families together? What are the ties that bind? What is your experience of strength in families? How does this understanding illuminate your relationship with God, with the faith community, and with the world?**

■ **What is the first step you would take in becoming more like Christ, your brother? How does the church become the sign of Christ in the world? Read and reflect on the things Jesus does in the gospel stories.**

PRACTICE OF FAITH

COMING HOME. Holy Family Sunday celebrates God with us now, present in our households and family relationships. We speak of "coming home," yet home is often strained by more goings than comings. Taking the children to doctors, dentists and school events; the demands of work; grocery shopping and volunteer meetings — all these can make us strangers to our home and to one another. Take time to be mindful of each person in your home. Schedule meals together and talk to one another. These practices help to ease our harried pace and keep us aware of God's presence in those closest to us.

PRACTICE OF HOPE

ALL IN GOOD TIME. Sirach reminds us that all things unfold in their time. Joseph once again responds to the commands of God. He takes Mary and Jesus to a place of safety, and when the word of God comes to him again, brings them back to their land. In his trusting and faithful actions, God's word is fulfilled.

Joseph knew the scriptures and loved God, but it must have been difficult for him to trust that all of these disruptions in his family life were part of God's saving action in the world. How often we assume that our little actions are of no consequence in the "big picture." To live in hope means to listen to God, and to do God's will as we understand it, trusting that God is bringing about the fulfillment of salvation.

PRACTICE OF CHARITY

FAMILY. The United States sees itself as a society that respects and cherishes families and especially children. Yet our spending patterns belie this. Caregivers for the elderly and for children are among the lowest-paid workers in the country. In the year 2000, their average hourly pay was $6.50. A full-time daycare worker could earn an annual wage of approximately $13,000, almost $5,000 under the poverty level for a family of four. Few of these jobs carry such benefits as sick leave, vacation time and health insurance. Recently there have been efforts to organize and find union support so these caregivers can bargain for better working conditions. This is the kind of action that Pope Leo XIII urged in 1891 in his encyclical *Rerum Novarum*.

WEEKDAY READINGS (Mo)1 John 2:18–21; (Tu)Solemnity of Mary, the Mother of God, see box; (We)2:22–28; (Th)2:29—3:6; (Fr)3:7–10; (Sa)3:11–21

READING I *Isaiah 60:1–6*

Arise, shine; for your light has come,
and the glory of the LORD has risen upon you.
For darkness shall cover the earth,
and thick darkness the peoples;
but the LORD will arise upon you,
and the glory of the LORD will appear over you.
Nations shall come to your light,
and rulers to the brightness of your dawn.

Lift up your eyes and look around;
they all gather together, they come to you;
your sons shall come from far away,
and your daughters shall be carried
   on their nurses' arms.

Then you shall see and be radiant;
your heart shall thrill and rejoice,
because the abundance of the sea
   shall be brought to you,
the wealth of the nations shall come to you.
A multitude of camels shall cover you,
the young camels of Midian and Ephah;
all those from Sheba shall come.
They shall bring gold and frankincense,
and shall proclaim the praise of the LORD.

READING II *Ephesians 3:1–10a*

Roman Catholic: Ephesians 3:2–3a, 5–6

This is the reason that I Paul am a prisoner for Christ Jesus for the sake of you Gentiles—for surely you have already heard of the commission of God's grace that was given me for you, and how the mystery was made known to me by revelation.

In former generations this mystery was not made known to humankind, as it has now been revealed to his holy apostles and prophets by the Spirit: that is, the Gentiles have become heirs with us, members of the same body, and sharers in the promise in Christ Jesus through the gospel.

Of this gospel I have become a servant according to the gift of God's grace that was given me by the working of God's power. Although I am the very least of all the saints, this grace was given to me to bring to the Gentiles the news of the boundless riches of Christ, and to make everyone see what is the plan of the mystery hidden for ages in God who created all things; so that through the church the wisdom of God in its rich variety might now be made known to the rulers and authorities.

GOSPEL *Matthew 2:1–12*

In the time of King Herod, after Jesus was born in Bethlehem of Judea, magi from the East came to Jerusalem, asking, "Where is the child who has been born king of the Jews? For we observed his star at its rising, and have come to pay him homage."

When King Herod heard this, he was frightened, and all Jerusalem with him; and calling together all the chief priests and scribes of the people, he inquired of them where the Messiah was to be born. They told him, "In Bethlehem of Judea; for so it has been written by the prophet:

"'And you, Bethlehem, in the land of Judah,
are by no means least among the rulers
   of Judah;
for from you shall come a ruler
who is to shepherd my people Israel.' "

Then Herod secretly called for the magi and learned from them the exact time when the star had appeared. Then he sent them to Bethlehem, saying, "Go and search diligently for the child; and when you have found him, bring me word so that I may also go and pay him homage."

When they had heard the king, they set out; and there, ahead of them, went the star that they had seen at its rising, until it stopped over the place where the child was. When they saw that the star had stopped, they were overwhelmed with joy.

On entering the house, they saw the child with Mary his mother; and they knelt down and paid him homage. Then, opening their treasure chests, they offered him gifts of gold, frankincense, and myrrh.

And having been warned in a dream not to return to Herod, they left for their own country by another road.

REFLECTION

In the church year, the feast of Epiphany, which means *manifestation,* is the climax of the twelve days of Christmas, with readings focused on God's gift of light to the entire world. When we listen to Matthew's story, what strikes us is that the light appeared, but it was up to the astrologers to interpret the sign and move toward it. Signs of the presence of God appear in many disguises. Some people dream; some have visions. Some are able to look at the wonders of creation and know that God is with them. The astrologers (they have also been called wise men, kings and magicians) consulted the sky, the thing they knew best, to learn of wondrous events. They did not have to find some esoteric object, nor did they have to learn an entirely new craft. The birth of Jesus was made manifest in what they already knew.

The second thing that strikes us is that their journey did not end at the manger, but at the place where they began. The encounter with God does not end with the travelers laying gifts before the newborn king. Rather, it manifests itself in the change that comes afterward. The astrologers returned home by a different way. They had been warned not to go back to Herod, but these different roads also stand for the change that occurs when we encounter the divine. We cannot go back the way we came because we are now different people. We do not see the world in the same way; we do not see ourselves the same way. Like the astrologers, when we lay our gifts at the feet of God, we come away infinitely richer. We change direction.

■ **The church has the responsibility of preaching the good news of God's light, justice and peace. It must live out of the belief that God has enlightened the world. What are the principal areas of injustice and strife in the world now? What can the church do to witness to God's light in those areas?**

■ **What changes have happened in your life because of your encounter with God? How has the world come to know God through you?**

PRACTICE OF FAITH

COMING TOGETHER. Arise, shine, your light has come. The Magi traveled together, seeking a new king. Did each one feel an inner stirring and so decide to join the others on the search? The light of Christ draws together many from far and near to be members of the same body. Look around the assembly today and notice this facet of the mystery of God-with-us. Some variations are visible, while other differences of personality, desires, needs and talents are less obvious.

As the year 2000 waned, Pope John Paul II called on us to let go of past conflicts and to move forward in unity. Perhaps this unity is reflected not so much in expecting others to think and be like us, but in recognition that Jesus came for all.

PRACTICE OF HOPE

OVERWHELMED WITH JOY. This feast of the church year should give those of us who are not of Jewish descent great joy, for the word of the Lord is fulfilled in a special way today for us. The people who walked in darkness, the Gentiles, have seen a great light! The salvation of the Jews is extended to all nations and all peoples. This manifestation of God's Word, Jesus the Christ, to the Magi symbolizes the great generosity of God in extending the reign of God to all.

From God's promise to Abraham, to the epiphany of the Magi, to the realization of Paul that all are called to be one in the reign of God, the mystery is unfolding day by day. Our hope is that we, like the Magi, will be "overwhelmed by joy" at the fulfillment of God's promise. Despite our many differences, our God is the God of all peoples and all nations.

PRACTICE OF CHARITY

ACCEPTING ALL. Not long ago, a civic group that includes churches, synagogues and mosques was invited to the Islamic Center for a prayer service and dinner to mark the end of Ramadan, the annual period of fasting and penance for Muslims. I found it moving to pray with the women upstairs while the men prayed downstairs.

Our host later told us that he was very grateful for our participation. He and other Muslims who have immigrated to the United States have experienced discrimination because Islam is so little understood in this country. With tears in his eyes, he told us that our civic group was the first to honor his religion and treat him with respect for it. Tears came to my eyes when I realized that this gentle, kind, educated man had been treated as a second-class citizen because of his faith.

WEEKDAY READINGS (Mo)1 John 3:22 — 4:6; (Tu)4:7–10; (We)4:11–18; (Th)4:19 — 5:4; (Fr)5:5–13; (Sa)5:14–21

READING I *Isaiah 42:1–9*

Here is my servant, whom I uphold,
my chosen, in whom my soul delights,
upon whom I have put my spirit,
to bring forth justice to the nations.
Not crying out, not lifting up his voice,
not making it heard in the street,
a bruised reed my servant will not break,
nor quench a dimly burning wick,
but will faithfully bring forth justice.
My chosen one will not grow faint or be crushed
until he has established justice in the earth;
and the coastlands wait for his teaching.

Thus says God, the LORD,
who created the heavens and stretched them out,
who spread out the earth and what comes from it,
who gives breath to the people upon it
and spirit to those who walk in it:
I am the LORD,
I have called you in righteousness,
I have taken you by the hand and kept you;
I have given you as a covenant to the people,
a light to the nations,
to open the eyes that are blind,
to bring out the prisoners from the dungeon,
from the prison those who sit in darkness.

I am the LORD, that is my name;
my glory I give to no other,
nor my praise to idols.
See, the former things have come to pass,
and new things I now declare;
before they spring forth, I tell you of them.

READING II *Acts 10:34–43*

Roman Catholic: Acts 10:34–38

Peter began to speak to Cornelius and his household: "I truly understand that God shows no partiality, but in every nation anyone who is God-fearing and does what is right is acceptable to God.

"You know the message God sent to the people of Israel, preaching peace by Jesus Christ, who is Lord of all. That message spread throughout Judea, beginning in Galilee after the baptism that John announced: how God anointed Jesus of Nazareth with the Holy Spirit and with power; how Jesus went about doing good and healing all who were oppressed by the devil, for God was with him. We are witnesses to all that Jesus did both in Judea and in Jerusalem. They put him to death by hanging him on a tree; but God raised Jesus on the third day and allowed him to appear, not to all the people but to us who were chosen by God as witnesses, and who ate and drank with him after he rose from the dead.

"Jesus commanded us to preach to the people and to testify that he is the one ordained by God as judge of the living and the dead. All the prophets testify about him that everyone who believes in him receives forgiveness of sins through his name."

GOSPEL *Matthew 3:13–17*

Jesus came from Galilee to John at the Jordan, to be baptized by him. John would have prevented him, saying, "I need to be baptized by you, and do you come to me?" But Jesus answered him, "Let it be so now; for it is proper for us in this way to fulfill all righteousness." Then John consented.

And when Jesus had been baptized, just as he came up from the water, suddenly the heavens were opened to him and he saw the Spirit of God descending like a dove and alighting on him. And a voice from heaven said, "This is my Son, the Beloved, with whom I am well pleased."

REFLECTION

We begin our Christian lives with a symbolic death. The baptismal waters cleanse us, bury us and become the waters of our rebirth as a new creation. Jesus enters into the waters of baptism as a sign of his unity with us and his willingness to be transparent to the will of God.

Isaiah's servant song provides a clearer picture of what this means. Isaiah did not necessarily have Jesus in mind when he wrote these words, but for the early church and for us, his poetry provides a way of talking about our experience of Jesus. As God's chosen servant who establishes justice, Jesus is the one for whom the world waits. But Isaiah uses a more intriguing word to describe the servant. This servant is God's *covenant* to the people. Covenant means agreement. Unlike the agreements and contracts of our time which are written on paper, Christians believe that the covenant between God and the world is embodied in a person, Jesus. When we look at what the servant does as God's covenant— enlightens the nations, opens the eyes of the blind, brings out prisoners from the dungeon—we realize that God's covenant with us is a commitment to helping us live wholly and freely as children of God.

When the heavens open after his baptism, Jesus is revealed as God's beloved son. Our baptism is the moment of challenge for us. Like Jesus, we put to death anything that keeps us from God; we take on the role of servant and child of God. We enlighten nations by living as though our baptism made a difference. We open blind eyes by publicly proclaiming our faith. We free others from the prison of their fear and doubt by taking on the responsibility to foster God's justice and peace in the world. To be baptized is to transform our lives and follow the example that Jesus set.

■ **Christians think of baptism as the welcome into the community of faith. The early church saw it as the beginning of a new life and demanded that those undergoing baptism transform themselves into new people. How can we recapture some of that early zeal in our celebration of baptism and beyond?**

■ **In what way is the church the embodiment of God's covenant to the world today? How do we participate in that covenant?**

PRACTICE OF FAITH

LET IT BE SO NOW. Today's feast closes the Christmas season. The mystery of God-with-us is too expansive for a one-day celebration, or three days, or even a whole week. As we begin 2002, God's word suggests a sense of the new. Isaiah evokes the creative power of God and God's constant desire: "New things I now declare."

This is what Jesus' life and ministry announce: He shows us a new way to live that will bring forth justice and healing. What needs to be made new in your life?

PRACTICE OF HOPE

GOD SHOWS NO PARTIALITY. What a paradox we see in the baptism of Jesus! God proclaims Jesus as the Chosen One, the Son, and yet, "anyone who is God-fearing and does what is right is acceptable to God." To be "partial," to prefer one or some over others, is to be incomplete. In showing no partiality, God is manifesting the great generosity of the love of Christ that extends to all. No part of humanity is excluded from God's love, but all are included with Christ.

The gift of our baptism in Christ makes us beloved children of God. We nurture hope when we live as though we believed this. The outpouring of the Spirit at Jesus' baptism is still present and active in the world, and in our lives. As we, like the coastlands, "wait for his teaching," we wait in hope of our own "fulfillment." No "partiality" but fullness and generosity are God's promise to those who wait in hope.

PRACTICE OF CHARITY

BRING FORTH JUSTICE. "Here is my servant, whom I uphold, my chosen, in whom my soul delights, upon whom I have put my spirit, to bring forth justice to the nations." Isaiah points to the Messiah as God's chosen who will "not grow faint or be crushed until he has established justice in the earth...." As followers of Jesus, we too have been baptized and called by God to work for justice. In our country, justice is sometimes seen as an individual being rewarded richly for his or her hard work, and the slacker being rewarded accordingly. We forget that the earth and all it contains belongs to the Lord and all the children of God. Our good fortune is probably more a matter of chance, of being born in the right place at the right time, than the result of our efforts. If we truly understand that we are all God's beloved, perhaps the notion of the "common good" can resume its place of honor in our society.

WEEKDAY READINGS (Mo)1 Samuel 1:1–8; (Tu)1:9–20; (We)3:1–10, 19–20; (Th)4:1–11; (Fr)8:4–7, 10–22a; (Sa)9:1–4, 17–19; 10:1a

WINTER ORDINARY TIME

Blessed are you in the sleep of winter!

Praise the Lord, O Jerusalem!
Praise your God, O Zion!
The Lord strengthens the bars
    of your gates,
blesses your children among you,
makes peace in your borders,
fills you with the finest wheat.

The Lord sends out commands
    to the earth;
the word of God runs swiftly.
The Lord sends snow like wool,
scatters hoarfrost like ashes,
throws out ice like crumbs;
who can withstand its cold?

The Lord sends forth the word
    and melts them;
makes the wind blow,
    and the waters flow.
The Lord declares the divine word to Jacob,
divine statutes and ordinances to Israel.
Praise the Lord!

—Psalm 147:12–19

Shall we praise you, hail-hurling God,
in winter's splendor,
in the grace of snow
that covers with brightness
and reshapes both your creation and ours?
Or shall we curse the fierce cold
that punishes homeless people
and shortens tempers?
Blessed are you
in the earth's tilt and course.
Blessed are you in the sleep of winter
and in the oncoming lenten spring.
Now and then and always,
fill these lands with peace.

—Prayer of the Season

READING I *Isaiah 49:1–7*

Listen to me, O coastlands,
pay attention, you peoples from far away!
The LORD called me before I was born,
and while I was in my mother's womb
  God named me.
The LORD made my mouth like a sharp sword;
I was hid in the shadow of God's hand.
The LORD made me a polished arrow;
I was hid away in God's quiver.

And the LORD said to me, "You are my servant,
Israel, in whom I will be glorified."
But I said, "I have labored in vain,
I have spent my strength for nothing and vanity;
yet surely my cause is with the LORD,
and my reward with my God."

And now the LORD says,
who formed me as a servant from the womb,
to bring Jacob back to God,
and that Israel might be gathered to the LORD,
for I am honored in the sight of the LORD,
and my God has become my strength—
the LORD says,
"It is too light a thing that you should be my servant
to raise up the tribes of Jacob
and to restore the survivors of Israel;
I will give you as a light to the nations,
that my salvation may reach to the end of the earth."

Thus says the LORD,
the Redeemer of Israel, the Holy One of Israel,
to one deeply despised, abhorred by the nations,
the slave of rulers,
"Monarchs shall see and stand up,
chieftains, and they shall prostrate themselves,
because of the LORD, who is faithful,
the Holy One of Israel, who has chosen you."

READING II *1 Corinthians 1:1–3*

Paul, called to be an apostle of Christ Jesus by the will of God, and our brother Sosthenes, To the church of God that is in Corinth, to those who are sanctified in Christ Jesus, called to be saints, together with all those who in every place call on the name of our Lord Jesus Christ, both their Lord and ours: Grace to you and peace from God, our Father, and the Lord Jesus Christ.

GOSPEL *John 1:29–42*

Roman Catholic: John 1:29–34

John the Baptist saw Jesus coming toward him and declared, "Here is the Lamb of God who takes away the sin of the world! This is the one of whom I said, 'After me comes a man who ranks ahead of me because he was before me.' I myself did not know him; but I came baptizing with water for this reason, that he might be revealed to Israel."

And John testified, "I saw the Spirit descending from heaven like a dove, and it remained on him. I myself did not know him, but the one who sent me to baptize with water said to me, 'The one on whom you see the Spirit descend and remain is the one who baptizes with the Holy Spirit.' And I myself have seen and have testified that this is the Son of God."

The next day John again was standing with two of his disciples, and as he watched Jesus walk by, he exclaimed, "Look, here is the Lamb of God!" The two disciples heard him say this, and they followed Jesus. When Jesus turned and saw them following, he said to them, "What are you looking for?" They said to him, "Rabbi" (which translated means Teacher), "where are you staying?" He said to them, "Come and see." They came and saw where Jesus was staying, and they remained with him that day. It was about four o'clock in the afternoon.

One of the two who heard John speak and followed him was Andrew, Simon Peter's brother. Andrew first found his brother Simon and said to him, "We have found the Messiah" (which is translated Anointed). He brought Simon to Jesus, who looked at him and said, "You are Simon son of John. You are to be called Cephas" (which is translated Peter).

REFLECTION

All the evangelists identify John the Baptist as the one who prepares the way for Jesus. But the Gospel of John shows us that the Baptist began his ministry without any clear picture of the one for whom he was waiting. John baptized people in the Jordan because something had told him that the anointed one would come to him. In his attentiveness to the signs around him, John lived very much as an "Advent prophet," expecting to see the Messiah at any time.

John the Baptist was not interested in reaping glory for himself or in getting people to follow him. John's task was simply to point to Jesus. Thus, when two disciples saw Jesus walk by and did not know him, John told them Jesus was the Lamb of God. The two disciples would later accept Jesus' invitation to "come and see" where he was staying. They did not question John, but went on to witness for themselves. Thus John's legacy was passed on to the world.

To prepare the way for the unknown Christ, John was willing to see the signs of God in every person who came, in every crowd that gathered. The description of the servant of God in Isaiah's prophecy told of a person who was God's polished arrow ready to strike at the heart of the world. The servant was also a light to all the nations and not to Israel alone. In Jesus, John saw all of this and more.

■ **To see the extraordinary in the ordinary is one of the marks of a saint. When have you noticed the divine shining in the routine, ordinary events of your life?**

■ **Jesus continues to invite us to "come and see." When have you responded, and what did you see?**

PRACTICE OF FAITH

CALLED TO BE SAINTS. When I went camping for the first time I discovered how natural it was to go to sleep at dusk and to awaken at dawn. Usually, we try to control the darkness with artificial light. Yet, how often, as we burn the midnight oil, do we echo Isaiah, "I have labored in vain"? God, however, does nothing in vain.

Can we believe that God gives us what we need to be saints? Through our participation in Christ's life we will not lack any spiritual gift. Whenever we help one another to discover and express our gifts, we cooperate with grace.

PRACTICE OF HOPE

COME AND SEE. John the Baptist was Jesus' kinsman, and they must have known each other well. Yet John says to his disciples, "I myself did not know him." Obviously, there is a deeper level of knowing intended here. John recognizes Jesus as the Lamb of God when he sees the Holy Spirit descend on Jesus. "I myself have seen and testified that this is the Son of God."

Like those who waited for the Anointed of God, the Messiah, we hope for better things, but we do not know how to see. We will recognize Christ in the familiar and the unfamiliar if we listen, look and pay attention to the Holy Spirit's movements in our own lives and in the lives of those around us.

PRACTICE OF CHARITY

"I HAVE LABORED IN VAIN, I HAVE SPENT MY STRENGTH FOR NOTHING. . . ." Each generation laments the cynicism and selfishness of the next, the seeming indifference that prompts them to ignore the problems that afflict our world because they see no possibility of effecting a change. Yet, the evidence shows us that there are plenty of young people whose optimism and faith in God lead them to join a volunteer program for a year or two. Approximately 10% of the University of Notre Dame graduates do so each year. Such programs have a profound effect on their participants. Whether in the hills of Appalachia or the streets of Harlem, these young people meet the problems that accompany poverty. They see first-hand illness, lack of education, addiction rooted in hopelessness. They finally know first-hand what it means when one must rely on God for one's strength.

WEEKDAY READINGS (Mo)1 Samuel 15:16–23; (Tu)16:1–13; (We)17:32–33, 37, 40–51; (Th)18:6–9, 19:1–7; (Fr)Acts 22:3–16; (Sa)2 Timothy 1:1–8

READING I *Isaiah 9:1–4*

Roman Catholic: Isaiah 8:23—9:3

There will be no gloom for those who were in anguish. In the former time the LORD brought into contempt the land of Zebulun and the land of Naphtali, but in the latter time the LORD will make glorious the way of the sea, the land beyond the Jordan, Galilee of the nations.

The people who walked in darkness
have seen a great light;
those who lived in a land of deep darkness—
on them light has shined.
You have multiplied the nation,
you have increased its joy;
they rejoice before you as with joy at the harvest,
as people exult when dividing plunder.
For the yoke of their burden,
and the bar across their shoulders,
the rod of their oppressor,
you have broken as on the day of Midian.

READING II *1 Corinthians 1:10–18*

Now I appeal to you, brothers and sisters, by the name of our Lord Jesus Christ, that all of you be in agreement and that there be no divisions among you, but that you be united in the same mind and the same purpose. For it has been reported to me by Chloe's people that there are quarrels among you, my brothers and sisters. What I mean is that each of you says, "I belong to Paul," or "I belong to Apollos," or "I belong to Cephas," or "I belong to Christ." Has Christ been divided? Was Paul crucified for you? Or were you baptized in the name of Paul?

I thank God that I baptized none of you except Crispus and Gaius, so that no one can say that you were baptized in my name. (I did baptize also the household of Stephanas; beyond that, I do not know whether I baptized anyone else.) For Christ did not send me to baptize but to proclaim the gospel, and not with eloquent wisdom, so that the cross of Christ might not be emptied of its power.

For the message about the cross is foolishness to those who are perishing, but to us who are being saved it is the power of God.

GOSPEL *Matthew 4:12–22*

Now when Jesus heard that John had been arrested, he withdrew to Galilee. He left Nazareth and made his home in Capernaum by the sea, in the territory of Zebulun and Naphtali, so that what had been spoken through the prophet Isaiah might be fulfilled:

"Land of Zebulun, land of Naphtali, on the road by the sea, across the Jordan, Galilee of the Gentiles— the people who sat in darkness have seen a great light, and for those who sat in the region and shadow of death light has dawned."

From that time Jesus began to proclaim, "Repent, for the dominion of heaven has come near."

As Jesus walked by the Sea of Galilee, he saw two brothers, Simon, who is called Peter, and Andrew his brother, casting a net into the sea—for they were fishermen. And Jesus said to them, "Follow me, and I will make you fish for human beings." Immediately they left their nets and followed Jesus.

Going on from there, Jesus saw two other brothers, James son of Zebedee and his brother John, in the boat with their father Zebedee, mending their nets, and he called them. Immediately they left the boat and their father, and followed him.

Saturday, February 2, 2002

THE PRESENTATION OF THE LORD

Malachi 3:1–4 *But who can endure the day of his coming?*

Hebrews 2:14–18 *He became like us in every way.*

Luke 2:22–40 *Simeon took the child in his arms.*

The light of Christmas shone feebly at first, rising to shine brightly from a star at Epiphany. Today this light is placed in our very arms. Like old Simeon, we are hand in hand with God.

REFLECTION

The prophet Isaiah figures prominently in the first reading and the gospel reading this week. Isaiah speaks of the great light that will come to those who have lived in darkness. He couples that with the glory that God will bring to the land beyond the Jordan. Matthew sees the fulfillment of this prophecy in Jesus' choice of a home, since Capernaum was in the territory of Zebulon and Naphtali, two lands that Isaiah specifically names.

The light that comes, however, requires a response. Jesus' first words are a command to repent. To repent is to change one's way of thinking and acting, to move in a different direction. We associate repentance with turning away from sin, but Matthew gives a graphic illustration of what people might turn from and what they turn toward when they repent. In the call of Peter and Andrew, Jesus does not ask them to stop being the fishermen that they are. Instead, he commands them to follow and be fishermen in the service of God.

Peter and Andrew leave their nets, the sign of their livelihood, and follow Jesus. James and John are called as well, and leave their boat, a symbol of their possessions, and their father, who represents their family and home ties. They, too, turn away from what they know and turn toward Jesus and toward their new lives in the service of God while Jesus proclaims the gospel throughout Galilee.

God's incarnation and revelation to the world is made known in the response of people. It is not enough to turn away from sin; we must turn toward God with all our hearts and souls. God asks us to be who we are fully and authentically, serving and witnessing to God in the world.

■ **The culture identifies us in many ways—by who we are in our families, by what we own, by what we do. What would you find hard to leave behind in following Jesus? How would you identify yourself when you do follow Jesus?**

■ **Can you recall an instance when you have truly repented, that is, changed your mind about someone or something? Where was God in that movement?**

PRACTICE OF FAITH

THIS IS IT! For us, the dominion of God is as near at hand as it was when Jesus was on earth. The light that came into the world in Jesus has never gone out. On Saturday we will celebrate the Feast of the Presentation and Candlemas.

Light the candles in your home and say the Nunc Dimittis, the prayer of Simeon when he saw the child Jesus presented in the temple.

PRACTICE OF HOPE

DARKNESS AND LIGHT. What hope is there for a people who live in the darkness of scorn? Zebulun and Naphtali were the butt of jokes and scorned as lands of the Gentiles. Many people come from places that are considered second-class. Having grown up in Buffalo, New York, I know the sting of jokes and scorn for my native place.

And yet, it is to just such places and people that Jesus is sent to bring the good news. It is to the scorned and the marginalized that Jesus brings the greatest hope. If you have nothing to lose, then you have everything to hope for. If we are in darkness now, we know that upon us the Light of Christ will dawn. Be patient in the darkness and look for the Light.

PRACTICE OF CHARITY

POLITICAL PEOPLE. Many people object to mixing religion and politics. After all, politics leads to division and dissension, while religion should lead to unity and harmony. In November 1999, the American bishops wrote a letter, *Faithful Citizenship: Civic Responsibility for a New Millennium.* They directed the faithful to participate fully in the political process because in a democracy, the political arena is where our commitment to justice for all is carried out. We can practice individual acts of charity by ourselves, but there is power in joining with others to vote for people and programs that work for peace and justice. We may disagree about how best to achieve adequate housing, education, food and health care for all, but we agree on what we seek because we all belong to Christ.

WEEKDAY READINGS (Mo)2 Samuel 5:1–7,10; (Tu)6:12b–15, 17–9; (We)7:4–17; (Th)7:18–19, 24–29; (Fr)11:1–4a,5–10a, 13–17; (Sa)Presentation, see box.

READING I *Zephaniah 2:3; 3:12–13*

Revised Common Lectionary: Micah 6:1–8

Seek the LORD, all you humble of the land,
who do his commands;
seek righteousness, seek humility;
perhaps you may be hidden
on the day of the LORD's wrath.
For I will leave in the midst of you
a people humble and lowly.
They shall seek refuge
in the name of the Lord
the remnant of Israel;
they shall do no wrong and utter no lies,
nor shall a deceitful tongue
be found in their mouths.
Then they will pasture and lie down,
and no one shall make them afraid.

READING II *1 Corinthians 1:18–31*

Roman Catholic: 1 Corinthians 1:26–31

The message about the cross is foolishness to those who are perishing, but to us who are being saved it is the power of God.

For it is written, "I will destroy the wisdom of the wise, and the discernment of the discerning I will thwart."

Where is the one who is wise? Where is the scribe? Where is the debater of this age? Has not God made foolish the wisdom of the world?

For since, in the wisdom of God, the world did not know God through wisdom, God decided, through the foolishness of our proclamation, to save those who believe. For Jews demand signs and Greeks desire wisdom, but we proclaim Christ crucified, a stumbling block to Jews and foolishness to Gentiles, but to those who are called, both Jews and Greeks, Christ the power of God and the wisdom of God. For God's foolishness is wiser than human wisdom, and God's weakness is stronger than human strength.

Consider your own call, brothers and sisters: not many of you were wise by human standards, not many were powerful, not many were of noble birth. But God chose what is weak in the world to shame the strong; God chose what is low and despised in the world, things that are not, to reduce to nothing things that are, so that no one might boast in the presence of God.

God is the source of your life in Christ Jesus, who became for us wisdom from God, and righteousness and sanctification and redemption, in order that, as it is written, "Let the one who boasts, boast in the Lord."

GOSPEL *Matthew 5:1–12*

When Jesus saw the crowds, he went up the mountain and sat down; and his disciples came to him. Then Jesus began to speak, and taught them, saying:

"Blessed are the poor in spirit,
    for theirs is the dominion of heaven.
Blessed are those who mourn,
    for they will be comforted.
Blessed are the meek,
    for they will inherit the earth.
Blessed are those who hunger and thirst
    for righteousness,
for they will be filled.
Blessed are the merciful,
    for they will receive mercy.
Blessed are the pure in heart,
    for they will see God.
Blessed are the peacemakers,
    for they will be called children of God.
"Blessed are those who are persecuted
    for righteousness' sake,
for theirs is the dominion of heaven.
Blessed are you when people revile you
    and persecute you
and utter all kinds of evil
    against you falsely on my account.
Rejoice and be glad,
    for your reward is great in heaven,
for in the same way they persecuted
    the prophets who were before you."

R E F L E C T I O N

Paul's message to the Corinthians is good news for all who have felt they were not good enough, talented enough, even lucky enough to be of use to God in the world. Paul boldly proclaims that the foolishness of the cross is, in part, that God chose what is weak, low and despised, to redeem the world. Today the sign of the cross is as countercultural as it was in first-century Corinth.

The early Christians looked for security in economic and social status; we also find comfortable bank accounts and the right friends suitable shields against the world's woes. Christianity in Corinth drew many of its converts from the poor and outcast and from Gentile God-fearers who embraced Jewish theology but were not circumcised. Learning to live with charity and love for every member of the new religion was difficult, and Paul had to remind the Corinthians of their responsibilities to their neighbors. Are we so different?

The beatitudes from the Sermon on the Mount echo the theology of Paul. Jesus' teaching blesses those who are poor in spirit, those who mourn and those who hunger for righteousness. To people expecting a glorious victory over their Roman oppressors, Jesus must have seemed very weak. For those who believed that God rewarded good behavior with wealth, success and possessions, Jesus must have seemed very foolish. Jesus preaches about the possibility of a worthy and full life that is far different than what the world expects or understands.

■ In what ways have you gone against what the world or society expects? How has the church supported that effort? How might the church provide guidance and support in the future to envision a world with a different set of values?

■ Many think that belief in a God who would sacrifice his own son is absurd. How do you answer those objections? What does the cross say to you about God?

PRACTICE OF FAITH

THE OUTLINE. A book's table of contents gives quick and ready access to the whole book. It is its plan, an outline of the book. In similar fashion, Jesus' Beatitudes function as a table of contents for how to live. However countercultural they sound to our ears, we realize they speak the truth.

Who do you know whose life reflects the Beatitudes, or even just one of them? In what way are they blessed? What blessing do you seek?

PRACTICE OF HOPE

LET NO ONE BOAST. Are you credentialed? Did you go to the best schools? Are your parents rich and famous? Maybe and maybe not. It doesn't matter! The good news is: We are God's own!

Have you ever felt poor, regardless of your financial status? Have you ever mourned a loss? Have you ever been hungry? Reviled and persecuted? Ridiculed for doing the right thing? Re-read the Beatitudes this week (Matthew 5:1–12) and pick just one to carry with you in your heart. Be comforted by God's promise of hope for you, and then offer some of that loving kindness to another. You are blessed.

PRACTICE OF CHARITY

DO JUSTICE. The scriptures this week are especially rich. Zephaniah summarizes what the Lord asks of us: to seek righteousness and humility. In the Sermon on the Mount, Jesus tells us very concretely what these mean. It is all there—to mourn with those who mourn for the loss of a loved one or their own illness, to act with mercy toward all we meet no matter how much they annoy us, to work for peace wherever we encounter the lack of it. One organization whose work is based on the Sermon on the Mount is Pax Christi. Their statement of purpose reads: "Pax Christi advocates primacy of conscience, economic and social justice, and respect for creation." Get in touch with them at Pax Christi, 532 W. 8th St., Erie PA 16502-1343; 814-453-4955; info@paxchristiusa.org.

WEEKDAY READINGS (Mo)2 Samuel 15:13–14, 30; 16:5–13a; (Tu)18:9–10, 14b, 24—25a, 30—19:3; (We)24:2, 9–17; (Th)1 Kings 2:1–4, 10–12; (Fr)Sirach 47:2–11; (Sa)1 Kings 3:4–13

READING I *Isaiah 58:6–10*

Is not this the fast that I choose:
to loose the bonds of injustice,
to undo the thongs of the yoke,
to let the oppressed go free,
and to break every yoke?
Is it not to share your bread with the hungry,
and bring the homeless poor into your house;
when you see the naked, to cover them,
and not to hide yourself from your own kin?

Then your light shall break forth like the dawn,
and your healing shall spring up quickly;
your vindicator shall go before you,
the glory of the LORD shall be your rear guard.
Then you shall call, and the LORD will answer;
you shall cry for help, and God will say,
    Here I am.

If you remove the yoke from among you,
the pointing of the finger, the speaking of evil,
if you offer your food to the hungry
and satisfy the needs of the afflicted,
then your light shall rise in the darkness
and your gloom like the noonday.

READING II *1 Corinthians 2:1–5*

When I came to you, brothers and sisters, I did not come proclaiming the mystery of God to you in lofty words or wisdom. For I decided to know nothing among you except Jesus Christ, and him crucified. And I came to you in weakness and in fear and in much trembling. My speech and my proclamation were not with plausible words of wisdom, but with a demonstration of the Spirit and of power, so that your faith might rest not on human wisdom but on the power of God.

GOSPEL *Matthew 5:13–16*

Jesus said: "You are the salt of the earth; but if salt has lost its taste, how can its saltiness be restored? It is no longer good for anything, but is thrown out and trampled under foot.

"You are the light of the world. A city built on a hill cannot be hid. No one after lighting a lamp puts it under the bushel basket, but on the lampstand, and it gives light to all in the house. In the same way, let your light shine before others, so that they may see your good works and give glory to your Father in heaven."

Wednesday, February 13, 2002

ASH WEDNESDAY

Joel 2:12–18 *Proclaim a fast. Rend your hearts.*

2 Corinthians 5:20—6:2 *Now is the time to be reconciled.*

Matthew 6:1–6, 16–18 *Pray, fast and give alms.*

The Spirit urges us into the desert discipline of the Lenten spring. For forty days we will strip away everything that separates us from God, beginning today, as we are marked with a cross of ashes. Death and life in a single sign!

REFLECTION

Isaiah does not waste words telling Israel what God requires of a holy people. The condemnation of fasting and worship without a true transformation of heart and soul is frequent in the writings of the Old Testament prophets. Here it is at the heart of Isaiah's message. Here, too, we see that the beatitudes have their source in the ancient prophetic tradition of Israel. God's care for the poor was part of the covenant between God and Israel from its very beginning.

After the exile, the Israelites quarreled about the rituals and practices that identified the true Israelite. Among these were the right way to fast and the correct way to pray. In their zeal to re-establish a group identity, many Israelites forgot that fasting and prayer by themselves mean nothing to God. Sincere prayer results in obedience to the law and in particular to concern for the poor, the disenfranchised, and the stranger in Israel. Those who draw near to God are those who feed the hungry, clothe the naked and work for justice in the world.

There is true wisdom in this understanding that God's spirit reveals itself in the relationship between believers and the world. Respect for creation, love for one another, and true prayer and worship are hallmarks of the faithful. They are also the legacy of Jesus, who was crucified for everyone. In him Christians find the example and the challenge to live a life of righteousness. Matthew reminds us that the grace of God dwelling in us makes us salt and light for the world. As salt, we add flavor, we scrub clean, we preserve what is good. As light, we illuminate the path for ourselves and others who are in darkness. Jesus did not come to make an easier path or to gather an elite group around him. Our discipleship is realized precisely in our loving relationship with the world, modeling for others what Jesus has modeled for us. This is the Law of Moses; this is the prophetic vision; this is the teaching of Jesus.

■ **Think of the many ways salt is used. In what ways does the analogy with salt speak to our mission as Christian disciples?**

■ **The church has a responsibility to witness to God in the world. How does your community work for justice in its day-to-day life?**

PRACTICE OF FAITH

SALT. About two years ago the newspapers reported an emerging culinary twist: coarse salt lavished on chocolate and fruity desserts to sharpen the flavors by contrast. My taste buds shivered at the thought: a new savor, a new purpose for salt.

In the Torah, salt was prescribed for every sacrifice in order to remind God's people that God had joined them in perpetual covenant, "a covenant of salt forever" (Numbers 18:19). "You are the salt of the earth" reminds us of our role in this covenant: to free the oppressed, to feed the hungry, to shelter the homeless, to clothe the naked, to serve one another. As we approach the season of Lent, what needs salt in your life? How will you add salt to it to give it vitality?

PRACTICE OF HOPE

"YOU CALL THIS A FAST?" Sometimes we get stuck in a rut. We think we are doing God's will when we fast and do penitential works, but when these are done without mindfulness, Isaiah reminds us of their worthlessness. It is in freeing others from oppression that we truly do the work of God. When we are lying around in the gloom and ashes of our own discouragement and hopelessness, that is when we need to feed the hungry, shelter the homeless and comfort those who are, like us, oppressed.

We are never alone; we are always linked to others in community. When we do the work of God, when we feed, comfort and set people free, then our light shines and we are like salt that gives flavor and zest to life.

PRACTICE OF CHARITY

LIGHT FOR THE WORLD. There is a parish in Chicago that buried a 58-year-old wife, nurse and mother of six after a long struggle with cancer. She was truly someone whose light "broke forth like the dawn"; it shone in her eyes, even in the last days of her illness. In accompanying this woman during her final days, however, the community also became a light for the world. Neighbors were amazed at the steadfast care given by so many people. Several women took turns spending half-days with her so that her family did not bear the entire burden of her care. Communion ministers brought her the eucharist daily. It is possible for parishes to offer this kind of informal hospice care, especially if there is a parish nurse. Consider starting such a program in your church. Or contact a local hospice agency and offer to volunteer there.

WEEKDAY READINGS (Mo)1 Kings 8:1–7, 9–13; (Tu)8:22–23, 27–30; (We)Ash Wednesday, see box; (Th)Deuteronomy 30:15–20; (Fr)Isaiah 58:1–9a; (Sa)Isaiah 58:9b–14

READING I *Exodus 24:12–18*

The LORD said to Moses, "Come up to me on the mountain, and wait there; and I will give you the tablets of stone, with the law and the commandment which I have written for their instruction." So Moses set out with his assistant Joshua, and Moses went up into the mountain of God. To the elders Moses had said, "Wait here for us, until we come to you again; for Aaron and Hur are with you; whoever has a dispute may go to them."

Then Moses went up on the mountain, and the cloud covered the mountain. The glory of the LORD settled on Mount Sinai, and the cloud covered it for six days; on the seventh day God called to Moses out of the cloud. Now the appearance of the glory of the LORD was like a devouring fire on the top of the mountain in the sight of the people of Israel. Moses entered the cloud, and went up on the mountain. Moses was on the mountain for forty days and forty nights.

READING II *2 Peter 1:26–21*

We did not follow cleverly devised myths when we made known to you the power and coming of our Lord Jesus Christ, but we had been eyewitnesses of his majesty. For Jesus received honor and glory from God, the Father, when that voice was conveyed to him by the Majestic Glory, saying, "This is my Son, my Beloved, with whom I am well pleased." We ourselves heard this voice come from heaven, while we were with Jesus on the holy mountain.

So we have the prophetic message more fully confirmed. You will do well to be attentive to this as to a lamp shining in a dark place, until the day dawns and the morning star rises in your hearts. First of all you must understand this, that no prophecy of scripture is a matter of one's own interpretation, because no prophecy ever came by human will, but men and women moved by the Holy Spirit spoke from God.

GOSPEL *Matthew 17:1–9*

Six days later, Jesus took with him Peter and James and his brother John and led them up a high mountain, by themselves. And Jesus was transfigured before them, and his face shone like the sun, and his clothes became dazzling white.

Suddenly there appeared to them Moses and Elijah, talking with him. Then Peter said to Jesus, "Lord, it is good for us to be here; if you wish, I will make three dwellings here, one for you, one for Moses, and one for Elijah."

While Peter was still speaking, suddenly a bright cloud overshadowed them, and from the cloud a voice said, "This is my Son, the Beloved, with whom I am well pleased; listen to him!" When the disciples heard this, they fell to the ground and were overcome by fear. But Jesus came and touched them, saying, "Get up and do not be afraid." And when they looked up they saw no one except Jesus alone.

As they were coming down the mountain, Jesus ordered them, "Tell no one about the vision until after the Son-of-Man has been raised from the dead."

REFLECTION

In the ancient world, clouds were a sign of mystery and majesty. Clouds inhibit our vision and disorient us. Hikers on mountains take extra care when they walk through clouds because a step in the wrong direction can be fatal. In this situation, clouds sharpen our senses, for they put us on alert. In the book of Exodus, God speaks from the midst of clouds. In Psalm 68 God is given the title "Cloud Rider."

The disciples are overshadowed by a cloud as they see Jesus converse with Moses and Elijah, symbols of the Law and the Prophets. What visions were inhibited? What did they find disorienting about their cloud experience? Where were they made more aware? This vision of Jesus occurs in the midst of the prophecies about Jesus' passion and death (Matthew 16:21–33 and 17:22–23). The disciples did not understand Jesus when he talked of this. The Messiah was supposed to be a conquering hero, a miracle worker, the one who freed them from tyranny. The Messiah was not supposed to be put to death. The disciples came to the top of the mountain unsure, a little disoriented already. The cloud made them lose their bearings and frightened them. But that was the only way they could see the true nature of Jesus, whose glory shone more brightly than anything they had ever known.

Jesus' glory is understood only in the light of his suffering and death. The cloud allows us to lay aside our expectations of what we think the Savior is and begin to see the paradox of faith that stands before us. Jesus' power and majesty are shown ultimately in his surrender. In telling the disciples to keep quiet about the vision until after the Son of Man rises from the dead, Jesus wanted them to understand that his suffering, death and resurrection were necessary for the working out of God's plan of salvation.

■ **Peter's desire to capture the experience by building three tents or dwellings is understandable. We often want to hold onto special moments or revelations. Why is this not possible or even desirable?**

■ **In its evangelization, the church must witness both to Jesus' suffering and death and to his glorious resurrection and ascension. How are these realities manifested in the world today?**

PRACTICE OF FAITH

FEAR AND AWE. Confronted with the presence of God, humans first tend to cower in fear. Why? We hear the story of Moses encountering God's glory, which was like a devouring fire, on the top of the mountain, and the people were afraid. When Jesus radiated glory, his disciples were also overcome by fear. Does fear have a place in our response to the divine? How is awe different from fear? Recall a time you were fearful or in awe of God. What was revealed to you?

PRACTICE OF HOPE

VISION AND HOPE. Most people of faith can tell of an experience of God. For some, it was a moment of recognition or clarity. For others, it might have been a deeply peaceful experience of nature's beauty. Or it have been in witnessing a death, sensing the closeness of the Holy in the process of dying. Maybe it happened on retreat, or maybe it happened in the kitchen. These peak experiences are a gift to be treasured. We do not and cannot make them happen. They are transformations, reminding us of the life to come and encouraging us to have faith and hope in God's promises. Receive them as a gift and a reminder of God's love.

PRACTICE OF CHARITY

LISTEN TO HIM. As Lent begins, we are instructed to listen to him, God's beloved Son. What has Jesus been saying up to this point in his ministry? One message he has repeated over and over is that we are to care for those on the margins and without influence— widows, orphans, lepers, even tax collectors. Witness for Peace continues to speak Jesus' message. It is important that we listen to *them*. The work of Witness for Peace is summarized in a bumper sticker they created: "Stop the War against the Poor." They have produced many educational materials and programs about the causes of poverty in our world. Witness for Peace deserves our support. Contact them at 1229 15th Street N.W., Washington DC 20078-2223; 202-588-1471; email witness@witnessforpeace.org.

WEEKDAY READINGS (Mo)1 Kings 8:1–7, 9–13; (Tu)8:22–23, 27–30; (We)Ash Wednesday, see box on page 51; (Th)Deuteronomy 30:15–20; (Fr)Isaiah 58:1–9a; (Sa)Isaiah 58:9b–14

LENT

Have mercy on me, O God!

Have mercy on me, O God,
according to your steadfast love;
according to your abundant mercy
blot out my transgressions.

Wash me thoroughly from my iniquity,
and cleanse me from my sin!
For I know my transgressions,
and my sin is ever before me.
Against you, you only, I have sinned,
and done that which is evil in your sight.

Let me hear with joy and gladness;
let the bones which you have broken rejoice.
Hide your face from my sins,
and blot out all my iniquities.

Create in me a clean heart, O God,
and put a new and right spirit within me.
Cast me not away from your presence,
and take not your holy spirit from me.

Deliver me from bloodshed,
    O God, God of my salvation,
and my tongue shall sing aloud
    of your deliverance.
O Lord, open my lips,
and my mouth shall show forth your praise.

—Psalm 51:1–4a, 8–11, 14–15

Like a gift we only want to want,
these forty days surround us once more
and you set about washing us, God.
Scrub and scour these stubborn ashes.
Separate what we are
from what we are not
and so bring on the lenten ordeal:
the prayer by day and night,
the fast that clears our sight,
the alms that set things right.
At the end, when we have lost again,
you alone make dry bones come together
and bruised bones dance
round the cross where sinners live
now and for ever.

—Prayer of the Season

READING I *Genesis 2:7–9, 15–18, 25; 3:1–7*

Revised Common Lectionary: Genesis 2:15–17; 3:1–7

Then the LORD God formed man from the dust of the ground, and breathed into his nostrils the breath of life; and the man became a living being. And the LORD God planted a garden in Eden, in the east; and there he put the man whom he had formed. Out of the ground the LORD God made to grow every tree that is pleasant to the sight and good for food, the tree of life also in the midst of the garden, and the tree of the knowledge of good and evil.

The Lord God took the man and put him in the garden of Eden to till it and keep it. And the LORD God commanded the man, "You may freely eat of every tree of the garden; but of the tree of the knowledge of good and evil you shall not eat, for in the day that you eat of it you shall die."

Then the Lord God said, "It is not good that the man should be alone; I will make him a helper as his partner."

And the man and his wife were both naked, and were not ashamed.

Now the serpent was more crafty than any other wild animal that the LORD God had made. The serpent said to the woman, "Did God say, 'You shall not eat from any tree in the garden'?" The woman said to the serpent, "We may eat of the fruit of the trees in the garden; but God said, "'You shall not eat of the fruit of the tree that is in the middle of the garden, nor shall you touch it, or you shall die.'" But the serpent said to the woman, "You will not die; for God knows that when you eat of it your eyes will be opened, and you will be like God, knowing good and evil."

So when the woman saw that the tree was good for food, and that it was a delight to the eyes, and that the tree was to be desired to make one wise, she took of its fruit and ate; and she also gave some to her husband, who was with her, and he ate.

Then the eyes of both were opened, and they knew that they were naked; and they sewed fig leaves together and made loincloths for themselves.

READING II *Romans 5:12, 17–19*

Just as sin came into the world through one human being, and death came through sin, so death spread to all because all have sinned. If, because of the trespass of one, death exercised dominion through that one, much more surely will those who receive the abundance of grace and the free gift of righteousness exercise dominion in life through the one, Jesus Christ.

Therefore just as the trespass of one person led to condemnation for all, so the act of righteousness of one person leads to justification and life for all. For just as by the disobedience of one the many were made sinners, so by the obedience of one the many will be made righteous.

GOSPEL *Matthew 4:1–11*

Jesus was led up by the Spirit into the wilderness to be tempted by the devil. He fasted forty days and forty nights, and afterwards was famished.

The tempter came and said to him, "If you are the Son of God, command these stones to become loaves of bread." But Jesus answered, "It is written, 'One does not live by bread alone, but by every word that comes from the mouth of God.'"

Then the devil took Jesus to the holy city and placed him on the pinnacle of the temple, saying to him, "If you are the Son of God, throw yourself down; for it is written, 'God will give you into the angels' charge,' and 'On their hands they will bear you up, so that you will not dash your foot against a stone.'" Jesus said to the devil, "Again it is written,' 'Do not put the Lord your God to the test.'"

Again, the devil took Jesus to a very high mountain and showed him all the realms of the world and their splendor; and said to him, "All these I will give you, if you will fall down and worship me." Jesus said to the devil, "Away with you, Satan! for it is written, 'Worship the Lord your God; serve God alone.'"

Then the devil left him, and suddenly angels came and waited on him.

REFLECTION

It is hard to believe that the desire for wisdom could be a bad thing, yet that seems to be the message of the Genesis reading. Adam and Eve take the fruit because "it is to be desired to make one wise." They take it because the serpent tells them they will be like God. They take it because for one minute they believe that they can live apart from their Creator. Adam and Eve sin because they believe they themselves can supply all they need, and so they are willing to put God aside. It is not their desire for wisdom, but their lack of faith in God's love and care that is the source of their sin.

Jesus is also tempted to take matters into his own hands. The tempter's opening remark: "If you are the Son of God..." is designed to play on every doubt that Jesus might have, either of his identity or of God's power. The tempter entices Jesus with the three things human beings need to feel independent, even of God: self-sufficiency, pride and power. To provide one's own food, to test God's love and to wield control over people and places—these make us think we know and can do all things.

A closer look at each temptation reveals that the outcome is transient and ultimately unsatisfying. Bread will make a meal, but hunger will return. Being held up by angels may prove God's love, but pride will demand more and more extreme tests. The world and all its splendor is not enough to fill the thirst for power. Jesus fights these temptations by remembering the scriptures: "Worship the Lord your God; serve God alone." Faced with temptation, Jesus calls to mind who God is. In the face of such confidence, the tempter has to leave.

■ **Where do we get the idea that we do not need God to live? In what ways does that idea become temptation? What do you do to resist it?**

■ **Using scripture was one way Jesus reminded himself of who God was in his life. What are favorite scripture passages or stories that help you remember who God is?**

PRACTICE OF FAITH

JOYFUL DISCIPLINE. Lent, the springtime of the church, is a joyful season. That phrase, a joyful season, is from the beginning of the lenten eucharistic prayer. The Jesuit priest and paleontologist Teilhard de Chardin said that joy is the surest sign of the presence of God. In what ways does the discipline of Lent make us joyful? Why would joy be a sign of God's presence?

PRACTICE OF HOPE

FREE GIFTS! No purchase necessary! We are all used to "gift with purchase" enticements of every kind: frequent flyer miles, cash back for using charge cards, rebates. In the economy of salvation, the offer has a twist: God's grace is free, no strings attached! Hard to believe? We are so accustomed to "this for that" and "no free lunch" that we think we owe God something in exchange for God's great love.

But there is nothing we could do or give that would earn us "bonus points" to the Reign of God. It has been paid in full with the blood of Christ. It may be that we are more comfortable with guilt than with gratitude. We'd rather wallow in self-loathing than accept that God loves us even when we are unworthy of that love. This first week of Lent, be grateful for the gift and just accept it.

PRACTICE OF CHARITY

KNOWLEDGE. Eve and Adam succumbed to the temptation to eat of the forbidden fruit so that they would have all knowledge and be equal with God. Their desire does not imply that the search for knowledge is evil; the evil is in the pride that makes us believe we should or could be equal to God.

Among the troubles of the Native American people is the poor education provided by the Bureau of Indian Affairs in years past. In recent years, however, the schools have been turned over to the local Indian communities. Increasingly, young Native Americans want a college education. The American Indian College Fund raises at least $100,000 in scholarship money each year. Contact them at 8333 Greenwood Blvd., Denver CO 80221; www.collegefund.org.

WEEKDAY READINGS (Mo)Leviticus 19:1–2, 11–18; (Tu)Isaiah 55:10–11; (We)Jonah 3:1–10; (Th)Esther C:12, 14–16, 23–25; (Fr)1 Peter 5:1–4; (Sa)Deuteronomy 26:16–19

READING I *Genesis 12:1–4*

The LORD said to Abram, "Go from your country and your kindred and your father's house to the land that I will show you. I will make of you a great nation, and I will bless you, and make your name great, so that you will be a blessing. I will bless those who bless you, and the one who curses you I will curse; and in you all the families of the earth shall be blessed."

So Abram went, as the LORD had told him; and Lot went with him.

READING II *2 Timothy 1:8–10*

Revised Common Lectionary: Romans 4:1–5, 13–17

Join with me in suffering for the gospel, relying on the power of God, who saved us and called us with a holy calling, not according to our works but according to God's own purpose and grace. This grace was given to us in Christ Jesus before the ages began, but it has now been revealed through the appearing of our Savior Christ Jesus, who abolished death and brought life and immortality to light through the gospel.

GOSPEL *Matthew 17:1–9*

Revised Common Lectionary: John 3:1–7

Jesus took with him Peter and James and his brother John and led them up a high mountain, by themselves. And Jesus was transfigured before them, and his face shone like the sun, and his clothes became dazzling white.

Suddenly there appeared to them Moses and Elijah, talking with him. Then Peter said to Jesus, "Lord, it is good for us to be here; if you wish, I will make three dwellings here, one for you, one for Moses, and one for Elijah."

While Peter was still speaking, suddenly a bright cloud overshadowed them, and from the cloud a voice said, "This is my Son, the Beloved, with whom I am well pleased; listen to him!" When the disciples heard this, they fell to the ground and were overcome by fear. But Jesus came and touched them, saying, "Get up and do not be afraid." And when they looked up, they saw no one except Jesus alone.

As they were coming down the mountain, Jesus ordered them, "Tell no one about the vision until after the Son-of-Man has been raised from the dead."

REFLECTION

Paul's letter to Timothy supports the argument that we did nothing to merit God's attention; it is only through God's design that Jesus came bearing grace to a sinful world. In other letters Paul uses the story of Abraham to illustrate this point. Abraham did nothing to merit God's blessing; his faith was sufficient. But note that Abraham also believed in God when God had done nothing more than promise a blessing of land and descendents. Faith in God's promise led Abraham to leave his birthplace.

For Peter, James and John, the transfigured Jesus who appeared with Moses and Elijah on the top of a mountain was far removed from the compassionate healer and wise teacher with whom they had traveled. Some scholars believe that the story is an appearance of the glorified Jesus after the resurrection, but Matthew places it in the midst of Jesus' prophecies of his suffering and death.

First, faith alone will allow the disciples to see through the suffering and death of the one they called friend and teacher and realize that glory can come in weakness and the hand of God can turn even the most horrible events into a saving act. Second, the disciples had no control over either the suffering or the glory. It was no human act that brought God to earth; God chose to become human because God so loved the world. God chose the path of crucifixion, the sacrifice to end all sacrifice, in order to free us.

For us who read this story year after year, it is a reminder that Jesus is the Messiah, whether on a cross or on a mountain in glory.

■ Do you find witness and testimony about Jesus and the Spirit in the church? In what way?

■ What does the story of the transfiguration tell you about Jesus' relationship with God and with the Hebrew scriptures? Is this important to your understanding of Jesus?

PRACTICE OF FAITH

TRANSFIGURED. Few have seen Jesus as the disciples Peter, James and John did at the Transfiguration or heard the voice of God as clearly as Abraham did. Yet, many of us have "heard" something we recognize as God. Sometimes these moments of revelation are mountaintop experiences; other times they are quiet moments of awareness or understanding. Reflect on those times in your life that you have heard God's voice. How has your life changed because you listened?

PRACTICE OF HOPE

FAITH OR GOOD WORKS? Sometimes we Christians sound as if these two are opposed. The law or grace? Abraham was a man of faith and believed what God promised, and it was credited to him as good works. What does this mean? Do we only have to believe and do nothing? Well, yes and no. God loved us while we were sinners; in fact, before we even existed! But to live in God's love draws us to loving acts for God and neighbor.

What looks like a contradiction between faith and charity might be clearer if we consider hope. We believe, and out of that belief comes love. Because we love and are loved, we trust and we hope. Hope is the fruit of faith and love working together. Hope is forward-looking. It looks to the future when all contradiction will be resolved and God's peace will reign.

PRACTICE OF CHARITY

LISTEN TO HIM. As Jesus is transfigured before his disciples, God the Father calls out that this is his Son, the Beloved. And we are to listen to him. What has Jesus been saying up to this point in his ministry? One message he has repeated is that we are to care for the marginalized, those without influence—widows, orphans, lepers, even tax collectors. Witness for Peace continues to speak Jesus's message. The work of Witness for Peace is summarized in its bumper sticker, "Stop the War against the Poor." They have produced educational materials about the causes of poverty. Witness for Peace deserves our support. Contact them at 1229 15th St. NW, Washington DC 20078-2223; 202-588-1471; email witness@witnessforpeace.org

WEEKDAY READINGS (Mo)Daniel 9:4b–10; (Tu)Isaiah 1:10, 16–20; (We)Jeremiah 18:18–20; (Th)17:5–10; (Fr)Genesis 37: 3–4, 12–13a, 17b–28; (Sa)Micah 7:14–15, 18–20

READING I *Exodus 17:2–7*

The people quarreled with Moses, and said, "Give us water to drink." Moses said to them, "Why do you quarrel with me? Why do you test the LORD?" But the people thirsted there for water; and the people complained against Moses and said, "Why did you bring us out of Egypt, to kill us and our children and livestock with thirst?"

So Moses cried out to the LORD, "What shall I do with this people? They are almost ready to stone me." The LORD said to Moses, "Go on ahead of the people, and take some of the elders of Israel with you; take in your hand the staff with which you struck the Nile, and go. I will be standing there in front of you on the rock at Horeb. Strike the rock, and water will come out of it, so that the people may drink."

Moses did so, in the sight of the elders of Israel. He called the place Massah and Meribah, because the Israelites quarreled and tested the LORD, saying, "Is the LORD among us or not?"

READING II *Romans 5:1–2, 6–8*

Revised Common Lectionary: Romans 5:1–11

Since we are justified by faith, we have peace with God through our Lord Jesus Christ, through whom we have obtained access to this grace in which we stand.

For while we were still weak, at the right time Christ died for the ungodly. Indeed, rarely will anyone die for a righteous person—though perhaps for a good person someone might actually dare to die. But it is proof of God's own love for us in that while we still were sinners Christ died for us.

GOSPEL *John 4:5–10, 14–26, 39, 40–42*

Complete reading: John 4:5–42

Jesus came to a Samaritan city called Sychar, near the plot of ground that Jacob had given to his son Joseph. Jacob's well was there, and Jesus, tired out by his journey, was sitting by the well. It was about noon. A Samaritan woman came to draw water, and Jesus said to her, "Give me a drink." (His disciples had gone to the city to buy food.) The Samaritan woman said to him, "How is it that you, a Jewish man, ask a drink of me, a woman of Samaria?" (Jewish people do not share things in common with Samaritans.) Jesus answered her, "If you knew the gift of God, and who it is that is saying to you, 'Give me a drink,' you would have asked him, and he would have given you living water. Everyone who drinks of this water will be thirsty again, but those who drink of the water I will give them will never be thirsty. The water that I will give will become in them a spring of water gushing up to eternal life." The woman said to Jesus, "Sir, give me this water, so that I may never be thirsty or have to keep coming here to draw water."

Jesus said to her, "Go, call your husband, and come back." The woman answered him, "I have no husband." Jesus said to her, "You are right in saying, 'I have no husband'; for you have had five husbands, and the one you have now is not your husband. What you have said is true!" The woman said to Jesus, "Sir, I see that you are a prophet. Our ancestors worshiped on this mountain, but you say that the place where people must worship is in Jerusalem."

Jesus said to her, "Woman, believe me, the hour is coming when you will worship the Father neither on this mountain nor in Jerusalem. You worship what you do not know; we worship what we know, for salvation is from the Jewish people. But the hour is coming, and is now here, when the true worshipers will worship the Father in spirit and truth, for such worshipers the Father seeks. God is spirit, and those who worship God must worship in spirit and truth." The woman said to him, "I know that Messiah is coming" (who is called Christ). "When he comes, he will proclaim all things to us." Jesus said to her, "Here I am, the one who is speaking to you."

Many Samaritans from that city believed in Jesus because of the woman's testimony. They asked him to stay with them; and Jesus stayed there two days. And many more believed because of his word. They said to the woman, "It is no longer because of what you said that we believe, for we have heard for ourselves, and we know that this is truly the Savior of the world."

REFLECTION

The exchange between the Samaritan woman and Jesus is all the more powerful for the honesty and respect between them. The woman has no illusions about her identity, and she has refused to let others determine what she is to think and how she is to behave. She lives her life apart from the rest of her village, drawing water in the heat of midday, rather than in the cooler hours, when others would be at the well. She draws her water as everyone does, to wash, to drink, to live.

Jesus has no illusions about his identity either. Just as she is honest about who she is with him, he reveals himself as the source of living water that leads to eternal life. Imagine never having to draw water again! To someone who has to draw water every day, this must be an incredible claim. And yet this woman who does not quite understand what Jesus means responds by proclaiming her faith: "I know that the Messiah is coming." When he hears this, Jesus opens the next level of understanding to her: "I am he."

The story of the Samaritan woman is the story of two people who are open to one another. One finds acceptance; the other finds faith. The living water that is Jesus cleanses and purifies the woman's heart and soul. The result for her is instantaneous. She leaves her water jar to witness to the village about him. She spills the good news like water and it fills the town.

For the elect, the third, fourth and fifth Sundays in Lent mark the time of the scrutinies, a series of exorcisms and prayers. In special intercessions, the community of faith asks God to cast out sin and temptation and to fill the elect with grace. We also remind ourselves that at baptism we were washed in the living water that leads to eternal life, and now we are to witness to the one who led us there.

■ **Jesus pushes aside the artificial boundaries of gender and nationality when he converses with the Samaritan woman. What are the boundaries in your social group that marginalize people? How do you and your church work to eliminate those boundaries?**

■ **The gospel does not talk about sin, but about a woman who does not hide her true identity from Jesus. What is your true identity before God?**

PRACTICE OF FAITH

THIRST. Jesus asked someone for a drink: a woman, a foreigner. He stunned her and his apostles because he ignored the rules that said Jewish men were not to talk to Gentile women. A simple question began an autobiographical exchange that transformed everything for the woman.

For what do we thirst? What prevents us asking for what we need to quench our thirst? Sometimes we are called to step out in faith. We need to trust that in asking for what we need, we will receive living water. Pray for the elect and catechumens whose thirst has brought them to ask for the sacraments.

PRACTICE OF HOPE

HOPE DOES NOT DISAPPOINT. Suffering can make us or break us. The people of God, thirsting for water, complained bitterly in the desert, not trusting God's promises. The woman at the well had suffered scorn and rejection. She too thirsted. But she heard the message Jesus proclaimed, and her suffering and endurance flowered into hope. She became the first to proclaim the Messiah to the Samaritan people, a people scorned and given up for spiritually dead by the Jewish people.

In the deserts of our life, we can have hope if we believe and endure, "because God's love has been poured into our hearts" like "living water."

PRACTICE OF CHARITY

CHRIST DIED FOR SINNERS. Paul tells us that Christ died for us while we were sinners. Jesus promised the Samaritan woman life forever if she believed in him. This Messiah turns rules upside down. It is not the righteous for whom he came, but for sinners. Are we Christians to do any less? How can we believe we have the right to judge people and put them to death? The United States still sentences criminals to death while the rest of the civilized world has rejected the death penalty. There are many groups working to end this, including the American Friends Service Committee (AFSC), whose motto is "seeing what love can do." To learn more, contact AFSC, 1501 Cherry Street, Philadelphia PA 19102-1479; 888-588-2372; www.afsc.org.

WEEKDAY READINGS (Mo)2 Kings 5:1–15a; (Tu)Daniel 3:25, 34–43; (We)Deuteronomy 4:1, 5–9; (Th)Jeremiah 7:23–28; (Fr)Hosea 14:2–10; (Sa)6:1–6

READING I *1 Samuel 16:1, 5–7, 10–13*

The LORD said to Samuel, "I will send you to Jesse the Bethlehemite, for I have provided for myself a king among his sons." And Samuel sanctified Jesse and his sons and invited them to the sacrifice.

When they came, Samuel looked on Eliab and thought, "Surely the LORD's anointed is now before the LORD." But the LORD said to Samuel, "Do not look on his appearance or on the height of his stature, because I have rejected him; for the LORD does not see as mortals see; they look on the outward appearance, but the LORD looks on the heart." Jesse made seven of his sons pass before Samuel, and Samuel said to Jesse, "The LORD has not chosen any of these."

Samuel said to Jesse, "Are all your sons here?" And he said, "There remains yet the youngest, but he is keeping the sheep." And Samuel said to Jesse, "Send and bring him; for we will not sit down until he comes here." Jesse sent and brought him in. Now he was ruddy, and had beautiful eyes, and was handsome. The LORD said, "Rise and anoint him; for this is the one." Then Samuel took the horn of oil, and anointed him in the presence of his brothers; and the spirit of the LORD came mightily upon David from that day forward. Samuel then set out and went to Ramah.

READING II *Ephesians 5:8–14*

Once you were darkness, but now in the Lord you are light. Live as children of light—for the fruit of the light is found in all that is good and right and true. Try to find out what is pleasing to the Lord. Take no part in the unfruitful works of darkness, but instead expose them. For it is shameful even to mention what such people do secretly; but everything exposed by the light becomes visible, for everything that becomes visible is light.

Therefore it says, "Sleeper, awake! Rise from the dead, and Christ will shine on you."

GOSPEL *John 9:1, 6–17, 34–38*
Complete reading: John 9:1–41

As Jesus walked along, he saw a man blind from birth. Jesus spat on the ground and made mud with the saliva and spread the mud on the man's eyes, saying to him, "Go, wash in the pool of Siloam" (which means Sent). Then he went and washed and came back able to see.

The neighbors and those who had seen him before as a beggar began to ask, "Is this not the man who used to sit and beg?" Some were saying, "It is he." Others were saying, "No, but it is someone like him." He kept saying, "I am the man." But they kept asking him, "Then how were your eyes opened?" He answered, "The man called Jesus made mud, spread it on my eyes, and said to me, 'Go to Siloam and wash.' Then I went and washed and received my sight." They said to him, "Where is he?" He said, "I do not know."

They brought to the Pharisees the man who had formerly been blind. Now it was a sabbath day when Jesus made the mud and opened his eyes. Then the Pharisees also began to ask him how he had received his sight. He said to them, "He put mud on my eyes. Then I washed, and now I see." Some of the Pharisees said, "This man is not from God, for he does not observe the sabbath." But others said, "How can a man who is a sinner perform such signs?" And they were divided. So they said again to the blind man, "What do you say about him? It was your eyes he opened." He said, "He is a prophet."

They answered him, "You were born entirely in sins, and are you trying to teach us?" And they drove him out.

Jesus heard that they had driven him out, and when he found him, he said, "Do you believe in the Son-of-Man?" He answered, "And who is he, sir? Tell me, so that I may believe in him." Jesus said to him, "You have seen him, and he is the one speaking with you." He said, "Lord, I believe." And he worshiped Jesus.

REFLECTION

In the story of the man born blind, Jesus exposes the hypocrisy of those who refuse to see evidence in front of them and continue to live as though they alone have the truth. The lesson begins with the disciples' assumption that sin is the cause of illness. Jesus dispels that notion by pointing out that God works out the divine plan in all people regardless of their physical imperfections. The disciples watch Jesus put mud on the man and then send him to wash in the pool of Siloam, which means "sent," and is a veiled reference to Jesus himself. Washing in the pool is interpreted as a sign of baptism.

The man born blind tells the leaders the truth about what has happened to him—"I do not know whether he is a sinner. One thing I do know, that though I was blind, now I see." As he repeats his story, he comes to realize that Jesus is from God, perhaps a prophet. When the leaders cannot force him to change his story, they return to the disciples' original position and calling the man a sinner, cast him out of the temple.

The Pharisees are caught in their own knowledge of the law. They believe that God does not listen to sinners. They hold to the belief that they alone are the righteous to whom God listens. In the face of Jesus' miracle, they must either find another explanation or admit that God listens to Jesus and a poor blind beggar as well. When Jesus finds the man after he is cast out of the temple, Jesus reveals himself as the light of the world.

Light can penetrate the smallest crack. The glow of a single candle can brighten the darkest room. Jesus can take advantage of the smallest opening to shine light into our world. Let us pray for eyes to see.

■ **Many things blind us to the truth. What are sources of blindness in your life?**

■ **Paul writes that the disciples should expose the unfruitful works of darkness and let the light shine forth in all that is good, right and true. What in our culture are the "works of darkness"? How might you bring the light of Christ to shine on them?**

PRACTICE OF FAITH

CAN YOU SEE IN THAT LIGHT? My dad often asked me that question when he found me reading in dim light. Turning on a lamp always made reading easier. Are you trying to live without the benefit of the Light who has come into the world? During these last weeks of Lent, ponder how your faith in Jesus as the Christ sheds light on what you think and do.

PRACTICE OF HOPE

WALK AS CHILDREN OF THE LIGHT. These words from Ephesians appear in the rite of baptism. We are encouraged to walk in the light of God. In today's readings, the metaphors of light and darkness, of sight and blindness are used to dispel our misconceptions about sin. Still, even today some people consider certain illnesses to be punishment for sin. Pray for the light of Christ to reveal our prejudices so that in seeing the truth, we may live God's love more fully.

PRACTICE OF CHARITY

SIN DOES NOT CAUSE BLINDNESS. We know people in the ancient world believed that any deformity or illness was the result of sin. That belief is not absent in our modern world. Isn't thinking God will punish us if we do the wrong thing a definition of superstition?

Amnesty International has devoted itself to the plight of political prisoners for many years. These men and women are seen as threats by their governments and imprisoned on some pretext. They suffer not because of their own sins but because we still live in a world where people are spiritually blind. Amnesty International, 322 Eighth Ave., New York NY 10001; 212-807-8400.

WEEKDAY READINGS (Mo)Isaiah 65:17–21; (Tu)Ezekiel 47:1–9, 12; (We)Isaiah 49:8–15; (Th)Exodus 32:7–14; (Fr)Wisdom 2:1a, 12–22; (Sa)Jeremiah 11:18–20

READING I *Ezekiel 37:12–14*

Revised Common Lectionary: Ezekiel 37:1–14

Thus says the Lord GOD: I am going to open your graves, and bring you up from your graves, O my people; and I will bring you back to the land of Israel. And you shall know that I am the LORD, when I open your graves, and bring you up from your graves, O my people. I will put my spirit within you, and you shall live, and I will place you on your own soil; then you shall know that I, the LORD, have spoken and will act, says the LORD.

READING II *Romans 8:8–11*

Those who are in the flesh cannot please God. But you are not in the flesh; you are in the Spirit, since the Spirit of God dwells in you. Anyone who does not have the Spirit of Christ does not belong to Christ. But if Christ is in you, though the body is dead because of sin, the Spirit is life because of righteousness. If the Spirit of the one who raised Jesus from the dead dwells in you, the one who raised Christ from the dead will give life to your mortal bodies also through this Spirit dwelling in you.

GOSPEL *John 11:17, 20–27, 33–45*

Complete Reading: John 11:1–45

When Jesus arrived, he found that Lazarus had already been in the tomb four days.

When Martha heard that Jesus was coming, she went and met him, while Mary stayed at home. Martha said to Jesus, "Lord, if you had been here, my brother would not have died. But even now I know that whatever you ask from God, God will give you." Jesus said to her, "Your brother will rise again." Martha said to him, "I know that he will rise again in the resurrection on the last day." Jesus said to her, "I am the resurrection and the life. Those who believe in me, even though they die, will live, and everyone who lives and believes in me will never die. Do you believe this?" She said to him, "Yes, Lord, I believe that you are the Messiah, the Son of God, the one coming into the world."

Jesus was greatly disturbed in spirit and deeply moved. He said, "Where have you laid him?" They said to him, "Lord, come and see." Jesus began to weep. So the Judeans said, "See how he loved him!" But some of them said, "Could not the one who opened the eyes of the blind man have kept this man from dying?"

Then Jesus, again greatly disturbed, came to the tomb. It was a cave, and a stone was lying against it. Jesus said, "Take away the stone." Martha, the sister of the dead man, said to him, "Lord, already there is a stench because he has been dead four days." Jesus said to her, "Did I not tell you that if you believed, you would see the glory of God?"

So they took away the stone. And Jesus looked upward and said, "Father, I thank you for having heard me. I knew that you always hear me, but I have said this for the sake of the crowd standing here, so that they may believe that you sent me." When Jesus had said this, he cried with a loud voice, "Lazarus, come out!" The dead man came out, his hands and feet bound with strips of cloth, and his face wrapped in a cloth. Jesus said to them, "Unbind him, and let him go."

Many of the Judeans therefore, who had come with Mary and had seen what Jesus did, believed in him.

Monday, March 19, 2001

JOSEPH, HUSBAND OF MARY

2 Samuel 7:4–5, 12–14, 16 *I will make David's throne endure.*

Romans 4:13, 16–18, 22 *He is father of us all.*

Matthew 1:16, 18–21, 24 *Joseph, Son of David, fear not!*

Near the beginning of spring, as the earth is about to awaken from its sleep, we tell the story of Joseph. In the Book of Genesis, Joseph is the "dreamer of dreams." In the Gospel of Matthew, Joseph dreams of the coming kingdom. Then he awakens to find himself the father of the king.

REFLECTION

We have two very different stories before us. We recognize Ezekiel's vision as a promise of restoration that shows Israel who God is. John's story is more disturbing. Lazarus is a person, not a vision. He is known and loved by many, including Jesus. His death, like the bones Ezekiel saw, will reveal God's power.

Even the details of the story before Jesus raises Lazarus reveal how fully Jesus enters into human life and suffering. John shows us Jesus' human emotion three times: first, Jesus loved Lazarus, Mary and Martha; second, Jesus was greatly disturbed; third, Jesus wept. In these observations John shows Jesus grieving over the death of a friend as all people do. Martha, aware of Jesus' love for her and for Lazarus, does not need to see a miracle to believe that Jesus is the resurrection and the life. But her trust makes it possible for Jesus to call Lazarus forth.

When Lazarus comes out of the tomb, he is bound in burial cloths. Jesus commands the crowd to unbind Lazarus, and they see that death has no power over them. The word used here for unbinding is the same as the word used for releasing someone from sin. Jesus has power over sin and death.

■ **How does the death and resurrection of Lazarus prefigure Jesus' death and resurrection? Who are the people around each? What are the circumstances of the burials of each?**

■ **What does it mean for us to "unbind" another person? Why is it necessary for our faith life?**

PRACTICE OF FAITH

"UNBIND HIM." Often activities and obligations, habits and compulsions bind us up. As Lent continues, we are invited to welcome Jesus as the one who unbinds us and sets us free. Very often when we hear these words we do not ponder their meaning.

Do we know that the same spirit of God that raised Lazarus from the dead seeks to free us? Can we turn to God and honestly name those things that bind us: our addictions, grudges, resentments, compulsions? As Martha pleaded on behalf of her brother, let us plead for release and freedom. Then we too will have a foretaste of resurrection.

PRACTICE OF HOPE

CAN THESE BONES LIVE? Sometimes our hopes clash with reality. Ezekiel's vision of the dry bones and the raising of Lazarus both fly in the face of common sense. But God asks us, as Jesus asked Martha, "Do you believe...?" Martha's love for the Lord nourished her faith and her hope in the resurrection. But she received more than she hoped for. The promise of the resurrection defies human logic, and yet, our love for God and God's great love for us makes our hope possible. Like those who came to comfort Mary and Martha and became witnesses to a miracle, we comfort each other, carry each other's burdens and encourage each other in faith. This week, unbind someone and let them go free.

PRACTICE OF CHARITY

HELPING REFUGEES. In cities like New York, Chicago and Philadelphia, there are Saint Patrick's Day parades this week. They say that on this day everyone is Irish, regardless of their actual ethnic background. Look around at the people watching the parade: You'll see people who are Irish, Italian, Polish, Korean, Indian, Cuban, Iranian, Russian, Mexican and more. As always, people come to the United States to make a better life. In some cases, they have left political persecution but in others they are fleeing economic hardships. The International Relief Committee helps more than 8,500 refugees to resettle in the United States each year. In fact, the IRC is there wherever refugees need their help. They use more than $.92 of every dollar raised for direct services to people in need. Send contributions to IRC, P.O. Box 98152, Washington DC 20090-8152.

WEEKDAY READINGS (Mo)Daniel 13:41–62; (Tu)Joseph, husband of Mary, see box; (We)Daniel 3:14–20; (Th)Genesis 17:3–9; (Fr)Jeremiah 20:10–13; (Sa)Ezekiel 37:21–28.

READING I *Isaiah 50:4–9*

The Lord GOD has given me the tongue of a teacher,
that I may know how to sustain the weary
  with a word.
Morning by morning the Lord GOD wakens—
wakens my ear to listen as those who are taught.
The Lord GOD has opened my ear,
and I was not rebellious,
I did not turn backward.
I gave my back to those who struck me,
and my cheeks to those who pulled out the beard;
I did not hide my face from insult and spitting.

The Lord GOD helps me;
therefore I have not been disgraced;
therefore I have set my face like flint,
and I know that I shall not be put to shame;
the one who vindicates me is near.
Who will contend with me?
Let us stand up together.
Who are my adversaries?
Let them confront me.
It is the Lord GOD who helps me;
who will declare me guilty?

READING II *Philippians 2:5–11*

Let the same mind be in you that was in Christ
Jesus, who, although being in the form of God, did
not regard equality with God as something to be
exploited, but relinquished it all, taking the form of a
slave, being born in human likeness. And being
found in human form, he humbled himself and
became obedient to the point of death—even death
on a cross.

Therefore God also highly exalted him and gave
him the name that is above every name, so that at
the name of Jesus every knee should bend, in
heaven and on earth and under the earth, and every
tongue should confess that Jesus Christ is Lord, to
the glory of God, the Father.

GOSPEL *Matthew 26:14—27:54*

One of the twelve, who was called Judas Iscariot,
went to the chief priests and said, "What will you
give me if I betray him to you?" They paid him
thirty pieces of silver. And from that moment Judas
began to look for an opportunity to betray him.

On the first day of Unleavened Bread the disciples came to Jesus, saying, "Where do you want us
to make the preparations for you to eat the
Passover?" Jesus said, "Go into the city to a certain
man, and say to him, 'The Teacher says, My time is
near; I will keep the Passover at your house with my
disciples.'" So the disciples did as Jesus had directed
them, and they prepared the Passover meal.

When it was evening, Jesus took his place with
the twelve; and while they were eating, he said,
"Truly I tell you, one of you will betray me." And
they became greatly distressed and began to say to
him one after another, "Surely not I, Lord?" Jesus
answered, "The one who has dipped his hand into
the bowl with me will betray me. The Son-of-Man
goes as it is written of him, but woe to that one by
whom the Son-of-Man is betrayed! It would have
been better for that one not to have been born."
Judas, who betrayed him, said, "Surely not I, Rabbi?"
He replied, "You have said so."

While they were eating, Jesus took a loaf of
bread, and after blessing it he broke it, gave it to the
disciples, and said, "Take, eat; this is my body."
Then he took a cup, and after giving thanks he gave
it to them, saying, "Drink from it, all of you; for this
is my blood of the covenant, which is poured out for
many for the forgiveness of sins. I tell you, I will
never again drink of this fruit of the vine until that
day when I drink it new with you in my Father's
dominion."

When they had sung the hymn, they went out to
the Mount of Olives.

Then Jesus said to them, "You will all become
deserters because of me this night; for it is written, 'I
will strike the shepherd, and the sheep of the flock
will be scattered.' But after I am raised up, I will go
ahead of you to Galilee." Peter said to him, "Though
all become deserters because of you, I will never

desert you." Jesus said to him, "Truly I tell you, this very night, before the cock crows, you will deny me three times." Peter said to him, "Even though I must die with you, I will not deny you." And so said all the disciples.

Then Jesus went with them to a place called Gethsemane; and he said to his disciples, "Sit here while I go over there and pray." He took with him Peter and the two sons of Zebedee, and began to be grieved and agitated. Then he said to them, "I am deeply grieved, even to death; remain here, and stay awake with me." And going a little farther, he threw himself on the ground and prayed, "My Father, if it is possible, let this cup pass from me; yet not what I want but what you want." Then he came to the disciples and found them sleeping; and he said to Peter, "So, could you not stay awake with me one hour? Stay awake and pray that you may not come into the time of trial; the spirit indeed is willing, but the flesh is weak." Again Jesus went away for the second time and prayed, "My Father, if this cannot pass unless I drink it, your will be done." Again Jesus came and found them sleeping, for their eyes were heavy. So leaving them again, he went away and prayed for the third time, saying the same words. Then he came to the disciples and said to them, "Are you still sleeping and taking your rest? See, the hour is at hand, and the Son-of-Man is betrayed into the hands of sinners. Get up, let us be going. See, my betrayer is at hand."

While he was still speaking, Judas, one of the twelve, arrived; with him was a large crowd with swords and clubs, from the chief priests and the elders of the people. Now the betrayer had given them a sign, saying, "The one I will kiss is the man; arrest him." At once he came up to Jesus and said, "Greetings, Rabbi!" and kissed him. Jesus said to him, "Friend, do what you are here to do." Then they came and laid hands on Jesus and arrested him. Suddenly, one of those with Jesus put his hand on his sword, drew it, and struck the slave of the high priest, cutting off his ear. Then Jesus said to him, "Put your sword back into its place; for all who take the sword will perish by the sword. Do you think

that I cannot appeal to my Father, who will at once send me more than twelve legions of angels? But how then would the scriptures be fulfilled, which say it must happen in this way?" At that hour Jesus said to the crowds, "Have you come out with swords and clubs to arrest me as though I were a bandit? Day after day I sat in the temple teaching, and you did not arrest me. But all this has taken place, so that the scriptures of the prophets may be fulfilled." Then all the disciples deserted him and fled.

Those who had arrested Jesus took him to Caiaphas the high priest, in whose house the scribes and the elders had gathered. But Peter was following him at a distance, as far as the courtyard of the high priest; and going inside, he sat with the guards in order to see how this would end.

Now the chief priests and the whole council were looking for false testimony against Jesus so that they might put him to death, but they found none, though many false witnesses came forward. At last two came forward and said, "This fellow said, 'I am able to destroy the temple of God and to build it in three days.'" The high priest stood up and said, "Have you no answer? What is it that they testify against you?" But Jesus was silent. Then the high priest said to him, "I put you under oath before the living God, tell us if you are the Messiah, the Son of God." Jesus said to him, "You have said so. But I tell you, from now on you will see the Son-of-Man seated at the right hand of Power and coming on the clouds of heaven." Then the high priest tore his clothes and said, "He has blasphemed! Why do we still need witnesses? You have now heard his blasphemy. What is your verdict?" They answered, "He deserves death." Then they spat in his face and struck him; and some slapped him, saying, "Prophesy to us, you Messiah! Who is it that struck you?"

Now Peter was sitting outside in the courtyard. A servant-girl came to him and said, "You also were with Jesus the Galilean." But he denied it before all of them, saying, "I do not know what you are talking about." When he went out to the porch, another servant-girl saw him, and she said to the bystanders, "This man was with Jesus of Nazareth." Again he denied it with an oath, "I do not know the man." After a little while the bystanders came up and said to Peter, "Certainly you are also one of them, for your accent betrays you." Then he began to curse, and he swore an oath, "I do not know the man!" At that moment the cock crowed. Then Peter remembered what Jesus had said: "Before the cock crows, you will deny me three times." And he went out and wept bitterly.

When morning came, all the chief priests and the elders of the people conferred together against Jesus in order to bring about his death. They bound him, led him away, and handed him over to Pilate the governor.

When Judas, his betrayer, saw that Jesus was condemned, he repented and brought back the thirty pieces of silver to the chief priests and the elders. He said, "I have sinned by betraying innocent blood." But they said, "What is that to us? See to it yourself." Throwing down the pieces of silver in the temple, he departed; and he went and hanged himself. But the chief priests, taking the pieces of silver, said, "It is not lawful to put them into the treasury, since they are blood money." After conferring together, they used the silver to buy the potter's field as a place to bury foreigners. For this reason that field has been called the Field of Blood to this day. Then was fulfilled what had been spoken through the prophet Jeremiah, "And they took the thirty pieces of silver, the price of the one on whom a price had been set, on whom some of the people of Israel had set a price, and they gave the silver for the potter's field, as the Lord commanded me."

Now Jesus stood before the governor; and the governor asked him, "Are you the King of the Jews?" Jesus said, "You say so." But when he was accused by the chief priests and elders, he did not answer. Then Pilate said to him, "Do you not hear how many accusations they make against you?" But Jesus gave Pilate no answer, not even to a single charge, so that the governor was greatly amazed.

Now at the festival the governor was accustomed to release a prisoner for the crowd, anyone whom they wanted. At that time they had a notori-ous prisoner, called Jesus Barabbas. So after they had gathered, Pilate said to them, "Whom do you want me to release for you, Jesus Barabbas or Jesus who is called the Messiah?" For he realized that it was out of jealousy that they had handed him over. While he was sitting on the judgment seat, his wife sent word to him, "Have nothing to do with that innocent man, for today I have suffered a great deal because of a dream about him." Now the chief priests and the elders persuaded the crowds to ask for Barabbas and to have Jesus killed. The governor again said to them, "Which of the two do you want me to release for you?" And they said, "Barabbas." Pilate said to them, "Then what should I do with Jesus who is called the Messiah?" All of them said, "Let him be crucified!" Then Pilate asked, "Why, what evil has he done?" But they shouted all the more, "Let him be crucified!"

So when Pilate saw that he could do nothing, but rather that a riot was beginning, he took some water and washed his hands before the crowd, saying, "I am innocent of this man's blood; see to it your-selves." Then all the people answered, "His blood be on us and on our children!" So Pilate released Barabbas for them; and after flogging Jesus, he handed him over to be crucified.

Then the soldiers of the governor took Jesus into the governor's headquarters, and they gathered the whole cohort around him. They stripped him and put a scarlet robe on him, and after twisting some thorns into a crown, they put it on his head. They put a reed in his right hand and knelt before him and mocked him, saying, "Hail, King of the Jews!" They spat on him, and took the reed and struck him on the head. After mocking him, they stripped him of the robe and put his own clothes on him. Then they led him away to crucify him.

As they went out, they came upon a man from Cyrene named Simon; they compelled this man to carry his cross. And when they came to a place called Golgotha (which means Place of a Skull), they offered Jesus wine to drink, mixed with gall; but when he tasted it, he would not drink it. And when they had crucified him, they divided his clothes among themselves by casting lots; then they sat down there and kept watch over him. Over his head they put the charge against him, which read, "This is Jesus, the King of the Jews."

Then two bandits were crucified with him, one on his right and one on his left. Those who passed by derided him, shaking their heads and saying, "You who would destroy the temple and build it in three days, save yourself! If you are the Son of God, come down from the cross." In the same way the chief priests also, along with the scribes and elders, were mocking him, saying, "He saved others; he cannot save himself. He is the King of Israel; let him come down from the cross now, and we will believe in him. He trusts in God; let God deliver him now, if God wants to; for he said, 'I am God's Son.'" The bandits who were crucified with him also taunted him in the same way.

From noon on, darkness came over the whole land until three in the afternoon. And about three o'clock Jesus cried with a loud voice, "Eli, Eli, lema sabachthani?" that is, "My God, my God, why have you forsaken me?" When some of the bystanders heard it, they said, "This man is calling for Elijah." At once one of them ran and got a sponge, filled it with sour wine, put it on a stick, and gave it to him to drink. But the others said, "Wait, let us see whether Elijah will come to save him." Then Jesus cried again with a loud voice and breathed his last.

At that moment the curtain of the temple was torn in two, from top to bottom. The earth shook, and the rocks were split. The tombs also were opened, and many bodies of the saints who had fallen asleep were raised. After his resurrection they came out of the tombs and entered the holy city and appeared to many.

Now when the centurion and those with him, who were keeping watch over Jesus, saw the earthquake and what took place, they were terrified and said, "Truly this man was God's Son!"

REFLECTION

For Jesus, who began his public ministry with a temptation in the desert, this is a new time of temptation both in the garden and on the cross. Jesus is tempted not to take the cup his Father gives him, tempted to come down from the cross, tempted with the same words the devil used in the desert—"if you are the Son of God . . . ." The passion begins with a betrayal, yet Jesus sits down at table with Judas and shares bread and wine. Jesus loves Judas to the end, even knowing what he is about. In the garden, Jesus' impassioned prayers are lost on the sleeping disciples. He could have left them: He had prophesied they would all desert him. In the high priest's house, his prophethood is mocked, even as his prophecy comes true in the courtyard when Peter denies him. On the cross, in agony, he is mocked again. The urge to show the mockers who he really is must have been great. The passion ends in death and Jesus is laid in a tomb secured by a rock, but not before the earth shakes and the centurion speaks: "Truly this man was God's Son." Jesus is known for who he really is in his death for the world.

The disciples are also tempted—to turn their backs on one another, to fall asleep, to fight, to deny in fear. It would seem that the tempter wins. But there are ways in which temptation does not win: The Roman centurion could not turn a blind eye to what was happening; the women stayed with Jesus and refused to lose faith in the one they loved.

The passion is a story of Jesus who has entered the very heart of human existence with its choices, sorrows, betrayals and great loves. Through it all he walks a steady path, focused on the one who calls him, loving those who follow him, forgiving those who persecute him.

■ **Paul tells us that Jesus did not regard equality with God as something to be exploited. The gospel tells us that Jesus did not regard the human condition as something to be despised. What does that teach us?**

PASCHAL TRIDUUM

Holy is God! Holy and Strong!
Holy immortal One, have mercy on us!

I am poured out like water,
and all my bones are out of joint;
my heart is like wax,
melted within my breast.

My tongue sticks to my jaws;
you lay me in the dust of death.
I can count all my bones.
They stare and gloat over me;
they divide my garments among them,
and cast lots for my clothing.

But you, O Lord, be not far away!
O my help, hasten to my aid!
Deliver my soul from the sword,
my life from the power of the dog!

I will tell of your name to my kindred;
in the midst of the congregation
    I will praise you.
All who fear the Lord, shout praise!
For God did not despise or abhor
the affliction of the afflicted,
nor hide from me,
but heard when I cried out.

The poor shall eat and be satisfied;
those who seek the Lord shall praise the Lord!
May your hearts live forever!
All the ends of the earth shall remember
and turn to the Lord.

—Psalm 22:14, 15bc, 17–20, 22–23a, 24, 26–27b

Holy God,
praise be yours for this tree of Paradise,
this tree that made Noah's saving Ark,
this tree whose branches embraced Jesus
and so shade and shelter us all.
Here may all the weary rest
these holy days,
hungry and thirsty for your word,
eating and drinking only your word
until, in the darkness between
Saturday and Sunday,
heaven and earth shall here be wed.
Then drowning waters shall be
waters of life
and the Savior's blood a banquet.
Holy God, praise be yours.

—Prayer of the Triduum

THE THREE DAYS

Holy Thursday brings the end to the Forty Days of Lent, which make up the season of anticipation of the great Three Days. Composed of prayer, almsgiving, fasting and the preparation of the catechumens for baptism, the season of Lent is now brought to a close and the Three Days begin as we approach the liturgy of Holy Thursday evening. As those to be initiated into the church have prepared themselves for their entrance into the fullness of life, so have we been awakening in our hearts, minds and bodies our own entrances into the life of Christ, experienced in the life of the church.

The Three Days, this Easter *Triduum* (Latin for "three days"), is the center, the core, of the entire year for Christians. These days mark the mystery around which our entire lives are played out. Adults in the community are invited to plan ahead so that the whole time from Thursday night until Easter Sunday is free of social engagements, free of entertainment and free of meals except for the simplest nourishment. We measure these days—indeed, our very salvation in the life of God—in step with the catechumens themselves; our own rebirths are revitalized as we participate in their initiation rites and as we have supported them along the way.

We are asked to fast on Good Friday and to continue fasting, if possible, all through Holy Saturday as strictly as we can so that we come to the Easter Vigil hungry and full of excitement, parched and longing to feel the sacred water of the font on our skin. Good Friday and Holy Saturday are days of paring down distractions so that we may be free for prayer and anticipation, for reflection, preparation and silence. The church is getting ready for the Great Night of the Easter Vigil.

As one who has been initiated into the church, as one whose life has been wedded to this community gathered at the table, you should anticipate the Triduum with concentration and vigor. With you, the whole church knows that our presence for the liturgies of the Triduum is not just an invitation.

Everyone is needed. We "pull out all the stops" for these days. As human persons, wedded to humanity by the joys and travails of life and grafted onto the body of the church by the sanctifying waters of baptism, we lead the new members into new life in this community of faith.

To this end, the Three Days are seen not as three liturgies distinct from one another but as one movement. These days have been connected intimately and liturgically from the early days of the Christian church. As a member of this community, you should be personally committed to preparing for and anticipating the Triduum and its culmination in the Vigil of the Great Night, Holy Saturday.

The church proclaims the direction of the Triduum by the opening antiphon of Holy Thursday, which comes from Paul's Letter to the Galatians (6:14). With this verse the church sets a spiritual environment into which we as committed Christians enter the Triduum:

We should glory in the cross of our Lord Jesus Christ, for he is our salvation, our life and resurrection; through him we are saved and made free.

HOLY THURSDAY

On Thursday evening we enter into this Triduum together. Whether presider, baker, lector, preacher, wine maker, greeter, altar server, minister of the eucharist, decorator or person in the remote corner in the last pew of the church, we begin, as always, by hearkening to the word of God. These are the scriptures for the liturgy of Holy Thursday:

Exodus 12:1–8, 11–14
Ancient instructions for the meal of the Passover

1 Corinthians 11:23–26
Eat the bread and drink the cup until the return of the Lord

John 13:1–15
Jesus washes the feet of the disciples

Then we, like Jesus, do something strange: We wash feet. Jesus gave us this image of what the church is supposed to look like, feel like, act like. Our position—whether as washer or washed, servant or served—is a difficult one for us to take. Yet we learn from the discomfort, from the awkwardness.

Then we celebrate the eucharist. Because it is connected to the other liturgies of the Triduum on Good Friday and Holy Saturday night, the evening liturgy of Holy Thursday has no ending. Whether we stay to pray awhile or leave, we are now in the quiet, peace and glory of the Triduum.

GOOD FRIDAY

We gather quietly in community on Friday and again listen to the Word of God:

Isaiah 52:13—53:12
The servant of the Lord was crushed for our sins

Hebrews 4:14–16; 5:7–9
The Son of God learned obedience through his suffering

John 18:1—19:42
The passion of Jesus Christ

After the sermon, we pray at length for all the world's needs: for the church; for the pope, the clergy and all the baptized; for those preparing for initiation; for the unity of Christians; for Jews; for non–Christians; for atheists; for all in public office; and for those in special need.

Then there is another once-a-year event: The holy cross is held up in our midst and we come forward one by one to do reverence with a kiss, bow or genu-flection. This communal reverence of an instrument of torture recalls the painful price, in the past and today, of salvation, the way in which our redemp-tion is wrought, the stripes and humiliation of Jesus Christ that bring direction and life back to a human-ity that is lost and dead. During the veneration of the cross, we sing not only of the sorrow but of the glory of the cross by which we have been saved.

Again, we bring to mind the words of Paul: "The cross of Jesus Christ...our salvation, our life and resurrection; through him we are saved and made free."

We continue in fasting and prayer and vigil, in rest and quiet, through Saturday. This Saturday for us is God's rest at the end of creation. It is Christ's repose in the tomb. It is Christ's visit with the dead.

EASTER VIGIL

Hungry now, pared down to basics, lightheaded from vigilance and full of excitement, we committed members of the church, the already baptized, gather in darkness and light a new fire. From this blaze we light a great candle that will make this night bright for us and will burn throughout the Easter season. We hearken again to the Word of God with some of the most powerful narratives and proclamations of our tradition:

Genesis 1:1—2:2
Creation of the world

Genesis 22:1–18
The sacrifice of Isaac

Exodus 14:15—15:1
The Red Sea

Isaiah 54:5–14
You will not be afraid

Isaiah 55:1–11
Come, come to the water

Baruch 3:9–15, 32—4:4
The shining light

Ezekiel 36:16–28
The Lord says: I will sprinkle water

Romans 6:3–11
United with him in death

Mark 16:1–8
Jesus has been raised up

After the readings, we pray to all our saints to stand with us as we go to the font and bless the waters. The chosen of all times and all places attend to what is about to take place. The catechumens renounce evil, profess the faith of the church and are baptized and anointed.

All of us renew our baptism. For us these are the moments when death and life meet, when we reject evil and give our promises to God. All of this is in the communion of the church. So together we go to the table and celebrate the Easter eucharist.

EASTER

Christ is risen! Christ is truly risen!

O give thanks to the Lord, who is good;
whose steadfast love endures forever!
Let Israel say,
"God's steadfast love endures forever."

I was pushed hard, so that I was falling,
but the Lord helped me.
The Lord is my strength and my power;
the Lord has become my salvation.

I shall not die, but I shall live,
and recount the deeds of the Lord.
The Lord disciplined me severely,
but did not give me over to death.

Open to me the gates of righteousness,
that I may enter through them
and give thanks to the Lord.
The stone which the builders rejected
has become the cornerstone.
This is the Lord's doing;
it is marvelous in our eyes.

This is the day which the Lord has made;
let us rejoice and be glad in it.

—Psalm 118:1–2, 13–14, 17–19, 22–24

The heavens rumble alleluias,
earth dances to the tune
and the wail of the graves
itself becomes song.
All are singing with you, savior God,
at this wedding feast
for you have turned the world around,
inside out and upside down.
Now the homeless are at home
and the martyred embrace their assassins
and the rulers and bosses wonder
whose world this is after all.
After all, let us stand and sing
with the heavens and earth and the graves
and so proclaim that we live now only
in Christ who is Lord for ever and ever.

—Prayer of the Season

READING I *Acts 10:34–43*

Peter began to speak to the people: "I truly understand that God shows no partiality, but in every nation anyone who is God-fearing and does what is right is acceptable to God.

"You know the message God sent to the people of Israel, preaching peace by Jesus Christ—who is Lord of all. That message spread throughout Judea, beginning in Galilee after the baptism that John announced: how God anointed Jesus of Nazareth with the Holy Spirit and with power; how Jesus went about doing good and healing all who were oppressed by the devil, for God was with him. We are witnesses to all that he did both in Judea and in Jerusalem. They put him to death by hanging him on a tree; but God raised him on the third day and allowed him to appear, not to all the people but to us who were chosen by God as witnesses, and who ate and drank with him after he rose from the dead.

"Jesus commanded us to preach to the people and to testify that he is the one ordained by God as judge of the living and the dead. All the prophets testify about him that everyone who believes in him receives forgiveness of sins through his name."

READING II *Colossians 3:1–4*

If you have been raised with Christ, seek the things that are above, where Christ is, seated at the right hand of God. Set your minds on things that are above, not on things that are on earth, for you have died, and your life is hidden with Christ in God. When Christ who is your life is revealed, then you also will be revealed with him in glory.

GOSPEL *John 20:1–18*

Or: Matthew 28:1–10

Early on the first day of the week, while it was still dark, Mary Magdalene came to the tomb and saw that the stone had been removed from the tomb. So she ran and went to Simon Peter and the other disciple, the one whom Jesus loved, and said to them, "They have taken the Lord out of the Lord the tomb, and we do not know where they have laid him."

Then Peter and the other disciple set out and went toward the tomb. The two were running together, but the other disciple outran Peter and reached the tomb first. He bent down to look in and saw the linen wrappings lying there, but he did not go in. Then Simon Peter came, following him and went into the tomb. He saw the linen wrappings lying there and the cloth that had been on Jesus' head, not lying with the linen wrappings but rolled up in a place by itself. Then the other disciple, who reached the tomb first, also went in, and he saw and believed; for as yet they did not understand the scripture, that Jesus must rise from the dead. Then the disciples returned to their homes.

But Mary stood weeping outside the tomb. As she wept, she bent over to look into the tomb; and she saw two angels in white, sitting where the body of Jesus had been lying, one at the head and the other at the feet. They said to her, "Woman, why are you weeping?" She said to them, "Thy have taken away my Lord, and I do not know where they have laid him." When she had said this, she turned around and saw Jesus standing there, but she did not know that it was Jesus. Jesus said to her, "Woman, why are you weeping? Whom are you looking for?" Supposing him to be the gardener, she said to him, tell me where you have laid him, and I will take him away." Jesus said to her, "Mary!" She turned and said to him in Hebrew, "Rabbouni!" (which means Teacher). Jesus said to her, "Do not hold on to me, because I have not yet ascended to the Father. But go to my brothers and say to them, 'I am ascending to my Father and your Father, to my God and your God.'"

Mary Magdalene went and announced to the disciples, "I have seen the Lord"; and she told them that Jesus had said these things to her.

REFLECTION

The first thing that Peter tells us at Easter is that Jesus is seated at God's right hand and will judge the living and the dead. But Mary Magdalene does not see this picture of Christ in glory and victory. The first thing she sees is an empty tomb. Her first thought, which she announces to the astounded disciples, is that the Lord has been taken away. Mary's statement is more profound than it first appears. With the death of Jesus, the disciples have had to "take away" their expectation that the Messiah would be a great king. They had to put aside the notion that the Lord would free Israel from Roman oppression. They had to start over at the beginning with no expectations and read the scriptures with fresh eyes.

When the unnamed disciple reaches the tomb, he too sees that it is empty but notices the shroud lying on the ground. Bold Peter enters the dark tomb and sees both the wrappings and carefully rolled head cloth. This was not the sign of a cataclysmic event or the hasty work of thieves. The importance of these wrappings is borne out in the transformation of the first disciple: "He went in. He saw and believed."

Our understanding of Jesus starts by confronting the empty tomb, and our own emptiness. It is not enough to peer in, but like Peter, we must boldly enter. We will be surprised by what we find!

■ **What are some Easter experiences in your life?**

■ **What does it mean to believe "in the resurrection of the dead"? Why is this important to the Christian life?**

PRACTICE OF FAITH

ONLY CLOTH. When Peter, John and Mary looked in the tomb, all they saw was the cloth in which Jesus had been wrapped. Peter and John, perhaps in confusion or sorrow, believing that their Lord had been moved, went home.

Mary, who stayed behind, was the first to behold the risen Jesus, her teacher. But even she first mistook him for the gardener. How often do we have to look beyond appearances or first impressions to discover the truth?

PRACTICE OF HOPE

GOD SHOWS NO PARTIALITY. Among the most hopeful words we hear today are from the Acts of the Apostles, "Anyone who is God-fearing and does what is right is acceptable to God." These were words of great joy and consolation to the Gentile members of the early church, and should be for us as well. Then, as now, there was heated debate about theological correctness and salvation. But Christ's sacrifice was not just for one small group of people, but for all. Every person of every nation, Jews, Gentiles, everyone is included in Christ's saving work.

When our hope is weak, when we feel unworthy of God's love, it is good to remember that God loved us first. It is especially good to remember God's all-embracing love when we are tempted to dismiss others as unacceptable to God. Jesus Christ "is Lord of all."

PRACTICE OF CHARITY

"WE ARE WITNESSES OF ALL THAT HE DID." Our belief that Jesus conquered death can give us the courage to profess all that he taught. Network, a national Catholic social justice lobby founded by a group of women religious, does this every day. They examine the work of Congress in light of Christian principles and lobby on behalf of legislation they support. Network and its 10,000 members believe that small victories can eventually lead to significant changes in federal law. Legislators who are friends of Network are grateful for receiving the facts they need to support their vote. Those who oppose policies supported by Network often change their minds as a result of the meticulous research the group provides. To learn more, contact Network, 801 Pennsylvania Ave. SE, Suite 460, Washington DC 20003-2167; 202-547-5556; e-mail network@ networklobby.org.

WEEKDAY READINGS (Mo)Acts 2:14, 22–33; (Tu)2:36–41; (We)3:1–10; (Th)3:11–26; (Fr)4:1–12; (Sat)4:13–21

READING I *Acts: 2:42–47*

Revised Common Lectionary: Acts 2:14, 22–32

The baptized devoted themselves to the apostles' teaching and common life, to the breaking of bread and the prayers. Awe came upon everyone, because many wonders and signs were being done by the apostles. All who believed were together and had all things in common; they would sell their possessions and goods and distribute the proceeds to all, as any had need. Day by day, as they spent much time together in the temple, they broke bread at home and ate their food with glad and generous hearts, praising God and having the goodwill of all the people. And day by day the Lord added to their number those who were being saved.

READING II *1 Peter 1:3–9*

Blessed be the God and Father of our Lord Jesus Christ, by whose great mercy we have been given a new birth into a living hope through the resurrection of Jesus Christ from the dead, and into an inheritance that is imperishable, undefiled, and unfading, kept in heaven for you, who are being protected by the power of God through faith for a salvation ready to be revealed in the last time. In this you rejoice, even if now for a little while you have had to suffer various trials, so that the genuineness of your faith—being more precious than gold that, though perishable, is tested by fire—may be found to result in praise and glory and honor when Jesus Christ is revealed.

Although you have not seen him, you love him; and even though you do not see him now, you believe in him and rejoice with an indescribable and glorious joy, for you are receiving the outcome of your faith, the salvation of your souls.

GOSPEL *John 20:19–31*

When it was evening on that day, the first day of the week, and the doors of the house where the disciples had met were locked for fear of the Judeans, Jesus came and stood among them and said, "Peace be with you." After he said this, he showed them his hands and his side. Then the disciples rejoiced when they saw the Lord. Jesus said to them again, "Peace be with you. As the Father has sent me, so I send you." When he had said this, he breathed on them and said to them, "Receive the Holy Spirit. If you forgive the sins of any, they are forgiven them; if you retain the sins of any, they are retained."

But Thomas (who was called the Twin), one of the twelve, was not with them when Jesus came. So the other disciples told him, "We have seen the Lord." But he said to them, "Unless I see the mark of the nails in his hands, and put my finger in the mark of the nails and my hand in his side, I will not believe."

A week later his disciples were again in the house, and Thomas was with them. Although the doors were shut, Jesus came and stood among them and said, "Peace be with you." Then he said to Thomas, "Put your finger here and see my hands. Reach out your hand and put it in my side. Do not doubt but believe." Thomas said to Jesus, "My Lord and my God!" Jesus said to him, "Have you believed because you have seen me? Blessed are those who have not seen and yet have come to believe."

Now Jesus did many other signs in the presence of his disciples, which are not written in this book. But these are written so that you may come to believe that Jesus is the Messiah, the Son of God, and that through believing you may have life in his name.

Monday, April 8, 2002

ANNUNCIATION OF THE LORD

Isaiah 7:10–14 *A virgin will bear a child.*

Hebrews 10:4–10 *I come to do God's will.*

Luke 1:26–38 *Rejoice, O highly favored daughter!*

Because pregnancy outside of marriage was punishable by death, Mary's "yes" to the angel was an acceptance of death. But in this death, the risen Spirit conquers death. Mary's mortal body conceives the Immortal One. The paschal victory is won.

REFLECTION

Even after the resurrection, John reminds us, those who had watched Jesus hang from a cross lived in fear and doubt. The hope that had flowered for a little while as Jesus preached the reign of God and healed the sick and lame withered in the face of his death. Moreover, no one but Mary Magdalene had reported seeing Jesus. So when Jesus came and stood in the midst of the disciples, the very sight of him renewed their hope.

Thomas was no different. He too wanted to see the Lord and had the courage to say so. Ever after, he has been known as "Doubting Thomas." The epithet has some shame attached to it. We are told not to be like him. But what Jesus said to Thomas might be addressed to all disciples: "Have you believed because you have seen me?" Thomas is the one who had the courage to touch the wounds. Thomas confronted physically the worst the world could do, and at the same time he realized the miracle of resurrection

Did Jesus' gentle scolding cause the other disciples to look deeply into their belief or doubt? Had Thomas doubted more than the others? We don't know. But from this disciple who doubted comes the simplest statement of faith: "My Lord and my God." Perhaps the greatest doubt does lead to the greatest faith, yet we remember Thomas for his doubt. In doing so we remind ourselves that God is revealed in ways we might not understand.

Peter preaches the resurrection of Jesus and those who heard were so transformed that they changed the way they lived. They began to learn together, and to break bread and pray in common. None of these people saw Jesus, but they took to heart the stories they heard and the example of other followers of Christ. Thomas's words, "My Lord and my God" expressed the indescribable presence of someone they loved even without having seen him.

■ We too believe in someone we have not seen. What is the source of your faith? What helps you to keep believing that Jesus is Lord?

■ Doubt is part of the human condition. Have you ever doubted God's presence or ability to transform a situation? What was helpful to you at that time?

PRACTICE OF FAITH

WATER, OIL, BREAD. The newest Catholics among us offer us glorious joy. We have urged them on and given them what we have faithfully received. Their reception of baptism, confirmation and eucharist recalls our own participation in these sacraments. Their visible joy echoes the moments when we have been able to say: "We have seen the Lord!"

Now our lives must continue to express this joy and conviction, so that as we believe we may also live.

PRACTICE OF HOPE

A NEW BIRTH, A LIVING HOPE. We have been given a new birth through the resurrection of Christ. With that new birth we receive new life and an inheritance as children of God.

As the Easter season progresses, we, like the early disciples, experience our *mystagogia,* that is, our experience of "indescribable and glorious" joy which can only be known through living it. This special time offers us the opportunity to see with new eyes, to re-vision our lives and our attitudes toward the world. Reach out in love and faith to another this week, and offer some of that hope and joy.

PRACTICE OF CHARITY

A PLEDGE OF PEACE. Three times in John's account of Jesus' appearance to the disciples, Jesus says, "Peace be with you." No doubt he knew how frightened they must be. So often fear is what underlies violence. One group is certain that if they do not attack first, they will be defeated. You can support Jesus' wish for peace today by supporting the International Peace Academy, founded by Ruth Forbes Young in 1970. It is dedicated to finding peaceful solutions to conflicts between and within nations. This non-profit group has brought innovative approaches to conflicts all over the world. Learn more: International Peace Academy, 777 United Nations Plaza, 4th floor, New York NY 10017-3521.

WEEKDAY READINGS (Mo)Annunciation of the Lord, see box; (Tu)Acts 4:32–37; (We)5:17–26; (Th)5:27–33; (Fr)5:34–42; (Sa)6:1–7

READING I *Acts 2:14, 22–24*

Roman Catholic complete reading: Acts 2:14, 22–33
Revised Common Lectionary: Acts 2:14, 36–41

Peter, standing with the eleven, raised his voice and addressed the people:

"You who are Israelites, listen to what I have to say: Jesus of Nazareth, a man attested to you by God with deeds of power, wonders, and signs that God did through him among you, as you yourselves know—this Jesus, handed over to you according to the definite plan and foreknowledge of God, you crucified and killed by the hands of those outside the law. But God raised him up, having freed him from death, because it was impossible for him to be held in its power."

READING II *1 Peter 1:17–21*

If you invoke as Father the one who judges all people impartially according to their deeds, live in reverent fear during the time of your exile. You know that you were ransomed from the futile ways inherited from your ancestors, not with perishable things like silver or gold, but with the precious blood of Christ, like that of a lamb without defect or blemish. Christ was destined before the foundation of the world, but was revealed at the end of the ages for your sake. Through Christ you have come to trust in God, who raised him from the dead and gave him glory, so that your faith and hope are set on God.

GOSPEL *Luke 24:13–23, 25–35*

Now on that same day when Jesus had appeared to Mary Magdalene, two of them were going to a village called Emmaus, about seven miles from Jerusalem, and talking with each other about all these things that had happened. While they were talking and discussing, Jesus himself came near and went with them, but their eyes were kept from recognizing him. And Jesus said to them, "What are you discussing with each other while you walk along?" They stood still, looking sad. Then one of them, whose name was Cleopas, answered him, "Are you the only stranger in Jerusalem who does not know the things that have taken place there in these days?" He asked them, "What things?" They replied, "The things about Jesus of Nazareth, who was a prophet mighty in deed and word before God and all the people, and how our chief priests and leaders handed him over to be condemned to death and crucified him. But we had hoped that he was the one to redeem Israel. Yes, and besides all this, it is now the third day since these things took place. Moreover, some women of our group astounded us. They were at the tomb early this morning, and when they did not find his body there, they came back and told us that they had indeed seen a vision of angels who said that he was alive."

Then Jesus said to them, "Oh, how foolish you are, and how slow of heart to believe all that the prophets have declared! Was it not necessary that the Messiah should suffer these things and then enter into his glory?" Then beginning with Moses and all the prophets, he interpreted to them the things about himself in all the scriptures.

As they came near the village to which they were going, he walked ahead as if he were going on. But they urged him strongly, saying, "Stay with us, because it is almost evening and the day is now nearly over." So he went in to stay with them. When Jesus was at the table with them, he took bread, blessed and broke it, and gave it to them. Then their eyes were opened, and they recognized him; and he vanished from their sight. They said to each other, "Were not our hearts burning within us while he was talking to us on the road, while he was opening the scriptures to us?"

That same hour they got up and returned to Jerusalem; and they found the eleven and their companions gathered together. They were saying, "The Lord has risen indeed, and has appeared to Simon!" Then they told what had happened on the road, and how Jesus had been made known to them in the breaking of the bread.

REFLECTION

Luke's story of what happened on the road to Emmaus is a paradigm for our own journeys. It begins with the disciples describing what happened that has set them on their way. They talk about everything, including their crushed hopes and the mystery of the empty tomb. They continue to talk even after the stranger joins them, because they are trying to make sense out of the events of the last three days. The disciples fall silent to listen to the stranger as he calls them "slow of heart." They wonder what they have missed and hear the scripture with fresh ears.

When they arrive at Emmaus, they know it was Jesus who called to their hearts. The English word "recognize" is a good one here, for its Latin root means "to know again." They recognize Jesus when he takes bread, blesses and breaks it, and gives it to them. Jesus vanishes, but they recall their experience: "Were not our hearts burning within us"?

We journey through these same movements. We move from talking to listening to recognizing to opening our hearts to what we have experienced. We come to know that it is with the heart that we see rightly, but we also know that the heart is slow. We too must talk and listen in order to know what burns in our hearts. The disciples recognized Jesus in the breaking of the bread, but they knew him in the breaking open of their hearts.

■ **Recount your journey of faith. Have you been slow of heart? What transformed you?**

■ **New insights lead to new actions. What new actions will you take because of what Jesus has taught you?**

PRACTICE OF FAITH

"LET GOD BE GOD." A friend in recovery recently reaffirmed the importance of these words. Although she had heard them many times before, it was as if she understood them for the first time.

Perhaps this was how the disciples on the road felt when they realized who was walking with them. What are those moments of recognition in your life, when you have been able to see God, and to let God be God?

PRACTICE OF HOPE

BUT WE HAD HOPED. Is there anything sadder than dashed hopes? If we lose what we have hoped for, we are devastated. To lose hope is to be tempted by despair. But Jesus appears to the disciples on the road to Emmaus and speaks to their hearts, which were "burning within." When they recognize him, the spark of new life rekindles their hope. Energized, they get up and immediately go back to Jerusalem.

What words make your heart burn within? What energizes your faith and rekindles hope? Share that lovingly with another this week.

PRACTICE OF CHARITY

IN THE BREAKING OF THE BREAD. In a land rich in resources, there are still those who go hungry. There are many who will never be able to support themselves. Some of these are the mentally ill, who in years past would have been cared for in an institution, but now are on the streets. Others are addicted to alcohol or other drugs. Many who work for minimum wage or survive on a fixed income must choose whether to buy food or pay the rent. As when the disciples on the road to Emmaus recognized Jesus in the breaking of the bread, many hungry people experience Jesus in the Christian service of Second Harvest, a network of more than 200 feeding programs around the United States. They supply food to soup kitchens, shelters and food pantries. To learn more, contact America's Second Harvest, 116 S. Michigan Ave., Chicago IL 60603; 800-771-2303 or 312-263-2303.

WEEKDAY READINGS (Mo)Acts 6:8–15; (Tu)7:51—8:1a; (We)8:1b–8; (Th)Acts 8:26–40; (Fr)9:1–20; (Sa)9:31–42

READING I *Acts 2:14, 36–47*

Peter, standing with the eleven, raised his voice and addressed the people:

"Therefore let the entire house of Israel know with certainty that God has made this Jesus whom you crucified to be both Lord and Messiah."

Now when they heard this, they were cut to the heart and said to Peter and to the other apostles, "Brothers, what should we do?" Peter said to them, "Repent, and be baptized every one of you in the name of Jesus Christ so that your sins may be forgiven; and you will receive the gift of the Holy Spirit. For the promise is for you, for your children, and for all who are far away, everyone whom the Lord our God calls." And Peter testified with many other arguments and exhorted them, saying, "Save yourselves from this corrupt generation."

So those who welcomed his message were baptized, and that day about three thousand persons were added.

The baptized devoted themselves to the apostles' teaching and common life, to the breaking of bread and the prayers. Awe came upon everyone, because many wonders and signs were being done by the apostles. All who believed were together and had all things in common; they would sell their possessions and goods and distribute the proceeds to all, as any had need. Day by day, as they spent much time together in the temple, they broke bread at home and ate their food with glad and generous hearts, praising God and having the goodwill of all the people. And day by day the Lord added to their number those who were being saved.

READING II *1 Peter 2:19–25*

It is a credit to you if, being aware of God, you endure pain while suffering unjustly. If you endure when you are beaten for doing wrong, what credit is that? But if you endure when you do right and suffer for it, you have God's approval. For to this you have been called, because Christ also suffered for you, leaving you an example, so that you should follow in his steps.

"He committed no sin, and no deceit was found in his mouth." When abused, Christ did not return abuse; when suffering, he did not threaten; but he entrusted himself to the one who judges justly. Christ himself bore our sins in his body on the tree, so that, free from sins, we might live for righteousness; by his wounds you have been healed. For you were going astray like sheep, but now you have returned to the shepherd and guardian of your souls.

GOSPEL *John 10:1–10*

Jesus said: "Very truly, I tell you, anyone who does not enter the sheepfold by the gate but climbs in by another way is a thief and a bandit. The one who enters by the gate is the shepherd of the sheep. The gatekeeper opens the gate for the shepherd, and the sheep hear his voice. He calls his own sheep by name and leads them out. When he has brought out all his own, he goes ahead of them, and the sheep follow him because they know his voice. They will not follow a stranger, but they will run away because they do not know the voice of strangers."

Jesus used this figure of speech with them, but they did not understand what he was saying to them. So again Jesus said to them, "Very truly, I tell you, I am the gate for the sheep. All who came before me are thieves and bandits; but the sheep did not listen to them. I am the gate. Whoever enters by me will be saved, and will come in and go out and find pasture. The thief comes only to steal and kill and destroy. I came that they may have life, and have it abundantly."

REFLECTION

Peter preached a frightening message to the people of Jerusalem. The Lord and Messiah was the very Jesus they had crucified. For the ones who listened, their immediate response was repentance. They wanted to transform their lives. Peter told them: Reform and be baptized. On the Sunday after Easter we heard the description of common meals and prayers as well as the distribution of goods according to need. It seems both simplistic and idealistic, yet this is the way Luke, the writer of the Acts of the Apostles, described the radical way these early Christians understood the gospel. Today's reading from Acts emphasizes the spiritual effects of faith in Jesus—forgiveness of sins and the gifts of the Holy Spirit. Peter's many arguments are effective, particularly when he said the entire generation had gone astray. Peter also anticipates how society would resist the new ways of living Christians espoused, and challenges them to see their suffering as pleasing to God.

It is still an idealistic picture, we might even say naïve. Yet we read in the gospel that Jesus came that we may have life, and have it abundantly. The generosity of God in sending the Son, who is at once the gate through which we walk and the shepherd who guides us, makes us desire to be generous. Can we do less than live as though Jesus' life, death and resurrection has made a difference? It is, after all, in the sharing of companionship, prayer, food, possessions and daily kindness that we live in the image of God. It is in the willingness to embrace suffering that we understand in some small measure what Jesus has done for us.

■ What does it mean "to have life, and have it abundantly"? For you as an individual? For the community?

■ Today is Good Shepherd Sunday. What does this image tell us about God and about God's relationship with us?

PRACTICE OF FAITH

EASTER PASSION. I attended a funeral last week. The deceased had lived a long life with his spouse; many noble things were said about him. His widow said at the cemetery, "Everyone spoke the truth about my dear husband," and weeping, she choked, "I will miss him so."

At times of such great sorrow, can we recall that we have a Shepherd who was no stranger to suffering and pain? Can we endure our suffering and still believe that Jesus came to give us abundant life?

PRACTICE OF HOPE

ABUNDANT LIFE. Many good people worry that they won't know in their hearts what comes from God and what doesn't. Some people are even afraid of silent prayer and contemplation because they don't want to be confused by conflicting inner voices. Today's gospel should reassure us greatly. The sheep know the shepherd's voice, and they will not follow a stranger.

How do we recognize the voice of the Good Shepherd when we hear so many inner voices? Familiarity. As a mother knows her child's cry above the cries of other children, so we come to know God's loving words to us by dwelling in closeness to God. Silent listening helps us learn to distinguish the voice of God in all the noise that distracts us. A good spiritual director can help, too. Have no fear. The Shepherd calls and the sheep hear his voice.

PRACTICE OF CHARITY

ALL THINGS IN COMMON. Eighty years ago, Dorothy Day and Peter Maurin began a newspaper called the Catholic Worker. In this daily paper, which still sells for one penny, they attacked those responsible for the abject poverty in which some men and women in New York lived. They also opened a home where all lived with everything in common. Those with jobs contributed their salaries so that the needs of all could be met. I suspect that their lives together went about as smoothly as the lives of the early Christians described in the Acts of the Apostles. It is never easy for a disparate group of people to occupy the same living space. In both cases, it was only their belief in the risen Lord which sustained them. Perhaps the guests of the Catholic Worker House did not always share that belief. Dorothy is alleged to have said, "Don't call me a saint; I won't be dismissed that easily."

WEEKDAY READINGS (Mo)Acts 11:1–18; (Tu)11:19–26; (We)12:24—13:5a; (Th)1 Peter 5:5b–14; (Fr)Acts 13:26–33; (Sa)13: 44–52

READING I *Acts 6:1–7*

Revised Common Lectionary: Acts 5:55–60

Now during those days, when the disciples were increasing in number, the Hellenists complained against the Hebrews because their widows were being neglected in the daily distribution of food. And the twelve called together the whole community of the disciples and said, "It is not right that we should neglect the word of God in order to wait on tables. Therefore, friends, select from among yourselves seven men of good standing, full of the Spirit and of wisdom, whom we may appoint to this task, while we, for our part, will devote ourselves to prayer and to serving the word." What they said pleased the whole community, and they chose Stephen, a man full of faith and the Holy Spirit, together with Philip, Prochorus, Nicanor, Timon, Parmenas, and Nicolaus, a proselyte of Antioch. They had these men stand before the apostles, who prayed and laid their hands on them.

The word of God continued to spread; the number of the disciples increased greatly in Jerusalem, and a great many of the priests became obedient to the faith.

READING II *1 Peter 2:2–10*

Like newborn infants, long for the pure, spiritual milk, so that by it you may grow into salvation—if indeed you have tasted that the Lord is good.

Come to the Lord, a living stone, though rejected by mortals yet chosen and precious in God's sight, and like living stones, let yourselves be built into a spiritual house, to be a holy priesthood, to offer spiritual sacrifices acceptable to God through Jesus Christ. For it stands in scripture: "See, I am laying in Zion a stone, a cornerstone chosen and precious; and whoever has faith in it will not be put to shame." To you then who believe, it is precious; but for those who do not believe, "The stone that the builders rejected has become the very head of the corner," and "A stone that makes them stumble, and a rock that makes them fall." They stumble because they disobey the word, as they were destined to do.

But you are a chosen race, a royal priesthood, a holy nation, God's own people, in order that you may proclaim the mighty acts of the one who called you out of darkness into the marvelous light of God. Once you were not a people, but now you are God's people; once you had not received mercy, but now you have received mercy.

GOSPEL *John 14:1–14*

Jesus said: "Do not let your hearts be troubled. Believe in God, believe also in me. In my Father's house there are many dwelling places. If it were not so, would I have told you that I go to prepare a place for you? And if I go and prepare a place for you, I will come again and will take you to myself, so that where I am, there you may be also. And you know the way to the place where I am going."

Thomas said to Jesus, "Lord, we do not know where you are going. How can we know the way?" Jesus said to him, "I am the way, and the truth, and the life. No one comes to the Father except through me. If you know me, you will know my Father also. From now on you do know and have seen my Father."

Philip said to him, "Lord, show us the Father, and we will be satisfied." Jesus said to him, "Have I been with you all this time, Philip, and you still do not know me? Whoever has seen me has seen the Father. How can you say, 'Show us the Father'? Do you not believe that I am in the Father and the Father is in me? The words that I say to you I do not speak on my own; but it is the Father who dwells in me who does these works. Believe me that I am in the Father and the Father is in me; but if you do not, then believe me because of the works themselves.

"Very truly, I tell you, the one who believes in me will also do the works that I do and, in fact, will do greater works than these, because I am going to the Father. I will do whatever you ask in my name, so that the Father may be glorified in the Son. If in my name you ask me for anything, I will do it."

REFLECTION

The prophet Hosea told Israel that the nation that had been named "Not my people" was to be called "My people," and that which had been named "Not pitied" was to be called "Pitied." Although Israel had been destroyed for sin, Hosea expressed God's compassion for the people. Peter believes that God's comfort and compassion are fully realized in Jesus, and so he echoes the words of Hosea when he preaches to the newly formed Christian community. He even assigns to them the ancient identity that Moses, at God's command, first gave to the Israelites—a chosen race, a royal priesthood, a holy nation. Jews and Christians understood God's choice as a sign of love. It was not a boast of pride, but a humble acceptance. It did not mean that God did not or could not choose anyone else, but was an affirmation of God's love and compassion for them.

What did it mean to be a royal priesthood? Both kings and priests had particular jobs in the Jewish community. Priests were servants and ministers to God; kings were to be an example of what it meant of follow the law of God and to walk in righteousness. As a holy nation, Israel was a nation set apart, a nation that did not follow the ways of the world but acted according to God's commands.

The early Christian church took on these titles from their Jewish ancestry. They saw in Jesus both the destination they sought and the path to follow. When they entered relationship with him, they became servants and children of God. This new awareness of their identity made the followers of Jesus bold and courageous. They showed the world and one another what it meant to follow the Lord who was the way, the truth and the light.

■ **The Second Vatican Council echoed the words of Moses and Peter, that everyone in the community of faith is part of a priestly people. Our call to service and the world grows out of that common priesthood. How is your work a sign of your participation in the priesthood of all believers? How is it the same and how is it different from the ordained priesthood?**

■ **Does being a Christian mean being counter-cultural? If so, in what ways?**

PRACTICE OF FAITH

RECKONING TIME. The Acts of the Apostles portrays the infant church in steady growth yet replete with human struggles. We read that opposition has become internal: Greek-speakers complained against the Hebrew-speakers because their widows were being neglected in the daily distribution of food.

Church enemies would have been pleased, and cynics today would shrug, "Isn't that always the way?" Yet do we not all struggle with neglecting one thing for another? Unrelenting activity denies us needed rest and distracts us from relationships at home and with God.

This week, assess how much time you spend on each phase of life. What do you need to restore a rhythm and balance to your spirit?

PRACTICE OF HOPE

ASK ME FOR ANYTHING. What an offer! Does Jesus really mean "anything"? Is this like the genie and the lamp, only without the three-wish limit? It's not magic, and it's not about personal riches. This promise is about faith, hope and love, and what will further the Reign of God. Jesus promises his help to those who are already faith-filled and hopeful. He promises his help to those who ask in love, in his name, for whatever they need. It is a promise of a lover; one who listens to the needs of the beloved and grants their requests. If we are afraid, we ask for peace. If we are weak, we ask for strength. If another is suffering or in need, we ask for help for that person. What do you need? Go ahead: ask!

PRACTICE OF CHARITY

STONES FOR LIVING. People of faith have taken stones and bricks and by working together, made them into houses for those who had none. One group of high school students traveled to Kentucky and spent a week building a house. At night they all bedded down in sleeping bags in one large room. These students went back home with some new skills of wielding hammer and saw, but they also brought home something more valuable—a sense of community and an appreciation of people much poorer than themselves. One girl remarked on how happy the people were even though they lacked material goods that the teens took for granted. Habitat for Humanity International has built houses all over the world (121 Habitat St., Americus, GA 31709-3498).

WEEKDAY READINGS (Mo)Acts 14:5–18; (Tu)14:19–28; (We)15:1–6; (Th)15:7–21; (Fr)1 Corinthians 15:1–8; (Sa)Acts 16:1–10

READING I *Acts 8:5–8, 14–17*

Revised Common Lectionary: Acts 17:22–31

Philip went down to the city of Samaria and proclaimed the Messiah to them. The crowds with one accord listened eagerly to what was said by Philip, hearing and seeing the signs that he did, for unclean spirits, crying with loud shrieks, came out of many who were possessed; and many others who were paralyzed or lame were cured. So there was great joy in that city.

Now when the apostles at Jerusalem heard that Samaria had accepted the word of God, they sent Peter and John to them. The two went down and prayed for them that they might receive the Holy Spirit (for as yet the Spirit had not come upon any of them; they had only been baptized in the name of the Lord Jesus). Then Peter and John laid their hands on them, and they received the Holy Spirit.

READING II *1 Peter 3:13–22*

Who will harm you if you are eager to do what is good? But even if you do suffer for doing what is right, you are blessed. Do not fear what they fear, and do not be intimidated, but in your hearts sanctify Christ as Lord. Always be ready to make your defense to anyone who demands from you an accounting for the hope that is in you; yet do it with gentleness and reverence. Keep your conscience clear, so that, when you are maligned, those who abuse you for your good conduct in Christ may be put to shame. For it is better to suffer for doing good, if suffering should be God's will, than to suffer for doing evil. For Christ also suffered for sins once for all, the righteous for the unrighteous, in order to bring you to God. Christ was put to death in the flesh, but made alive in the spirit, in which also he went and made a proclamation to the spirits in prison, who in former times did not obey, when God waited patiently in the days of Noah, during the building of the ark, in which a few, that is, eight persons, were saved through water.

And baptism, which this prefigured, now saves you—not as a removal of dirt from the body, but as an appeal to God for a good conscience, through the resurrection of Jesus Christ, who has gone into heaven and is at the right hand of God, with angels, authorities, and powers made subject to him.

GOSPEL *John 14:15–21*

Jesus said: "If you love me, you will keep my commandments. And I will ask the Father, who will give you another Advocate, to be with you forever. This is the Spirit of truth, whom the world cannot receive, whom the world neither sees nor knows. You know the Spirit, because the Spirit abides with you, and will be in you.

"I will not leave you orphaned; I am coming to you. In a little while the world will no longer see me, but you will see me; because I live, you also will live. On that day you will know that I am in my Father, and you in me, and I in you. They who have my commandments and keep them are those who love me; and those who love me will be loved by my Father, and I will love them and reveal myself to them."

REFLECTION

Philip's proclamation of the gospel and his miracles of healing contributed powerfully to the spread of Christianity in the early first century. Samaria was the name of both the capital of the ancient northern kingdom and the region around the city. An old dispute between Samaritans and Jews caused a rift that Jesus used to his advantage in several parables. To depict Philip preaching the good news to these disputed neighbors was to capture the essence of Jesus' ministry to the outcast and the stranger. It also underscored the gospel mission to teach all nations.

The reading from the Acts of the Apostles includes a brief description of the ritual of confirmation in which the faith of the newly baptized converts is confirmed by the laying on of hands and the invocation of the Holy Spirit. Philip calls on Peter and John, leaders of the community, to perform this ceremony and to pray for the Spirit to come. In much the same way, we call on bishops to confirm those who have been baptized into the faith of the church today.

The confirmation and outpouring of the Holy Spirit in the first reading demonstrates the truth of Jesus' claim that he will not leave his followers orphans. The Samaritan converts were among the first outside Jerusalem to receive the revelation of God's word. Speaking from the conviction of his own heart, Philip was able to persuade his audience of God's truth.

■ **How would you describe your understanding of God to someone outside the Christian tradition or your cultural background? What insights about God have you received from someone outside your tradition?**

■ **What evidence do you have that Jesus has not left you orphaned?**

PRACTICE OF FAITH

MUTUAL HONOR. "New evangelization" is a favorite theme of Pope John Paul II. To witness to Jesus' good news we must see the world as open and responsive. In John's gospel, the world symbolizes those realms estranged from God. Yet we know that God sent Jesus because God so loved the world.

The attitude of the first gospel-bearers imitated Christ's: Honor everyone—without exception. To honor everyone is the attitude of Christ. Through us Christ gathers others: I will love them and reveal myself to them. Honor everyone, beginning nearby.

PRACTICE OF HOPE

THE HOPE THAT IS IN YOU. What helps us nurture the hope that we have in God? "Do not fear . . . and do not be intimidated." "Keep your conscience clear. . . . Make your defense . . . yet do it with gentleness and reverence." "The Spirit abides with you."

This reassurance of the presence of the Trinity in the hearts of those who believe is the ground of our hope. If we keep the word of Jesus, that is, love one another, we know that Christ is with us and in us, and that we are one in the love of God. The presence of God in our lives enables us to live as people of faith. We are empowered to love and to be strong, even in times of testing. This hope in us is the work of the Holy Spirit.

PRACTICE OF CHARITY

THE SPIRIT OF TRUTH. Truth is in peril in the modern world. The distinction between news reports and dramas based on news is blurry. Politicians seem to say what they think will attract contributions rather than what is true. If candidates campaign more for contributors than for voters, our votes count for less. In fact, many citizens are so convinced that their vote does not count that they have stopped voting. Common Cause has been working to do something about this for 32 years. This nonpartisan citizens' lobby is dedicated to real campaign finance reform. Contact Common Cause at 1250 Connecticut Ave. NW, Washington DC 20036.

WEEKDAY READINGS (Mo)Acts 16:11–5; (Tu)16:22–34; (We)17:15, 22—18:1; (Th)Ascension of the Lord: see Sunday, May 12; (Fr)18:9–18; (Sa)18:23–28

READING I *Acts 1:1–11*

Luke writes: In the first book, Theophilus, I wrote about all that Jesus did and taught from the beginning until the day when he was taken up to heaven, after giving instructions through the Holy Spirit to the apostles whom he had chosen. After his suffering Jesus presented himself alive to them by many convincing proofs, appearing to them during forty days and speaking about the dominion of God. While staying with them, Jesus ordered them not to leave Jerusalem, but to wait there for the promise of the Father. "This," he said "is what you have heard from me; for John baptized with water, but you will be baptized with the Holy Spirit not manly days from now."

"So when they had come together, they asked him, "Lord, is this the time when you will restore the dominion to Israel?" He replied, "It is not for you to know the times or the periods that the Father has set by divine authority. But you will receive power when the Holy Spirit has come upon you and you will be my witnesses in Jerusalem, in all Judea and Samaria, and to the ends of the earth." When Jesus had said this, as they were watching, he was lifted up, and a cloud took him out of their sight.

While he was going and they were gazing up toward heaven, suddenly two men in white robes stood by them. They said, "You Galileans, why do stand looking up toward heaven? This Jesus, who has been taken up from you into heaven will come in the same way as you saw him go into heaven."

READING II *Ephesians 1:15–23*

I have heard of your faith in the Lord Jesus and your love toward all the saints, and for this reason I do not cease to give thanks for you as I remember you in my prayers. I pray that the God of our Lord Jesus Christ, the Father of glory, may give you a spirit of wisdom and revelation, as you come to know God, so that, with the eyes of your heart enlightened, you may know what is the hope to which God has called you, what are the riches of God's glorious inheritance among the saints, and what is the immeasurable greatness of God's power for us who believe, according to the working of God's great power.

God put this power to work in Christ when God raised him from the dead and seated him at the right hand of Power in the heavenly places, far above all rule and authority and power and dominion, and above every name that is named, not only in this age but also in the age to come. And God has put all things under the feet of Christ and has made him the head over all things for the church which is the body of Christ, the fullness of the one who fills all in all.

GOSPEL *Matthew 28:16–20*

Now the eleven disciples went to Galilee, to the mountain to which Jesus had directed them. When they saw him, they worshipped him; but some doubted. And Jesus came and said to them, "All authority in heaven and on earth has been given to me. Go therefore and make disciples of all nations, baptizing them in the name of the Father and of the Son and of the Holy Spirit, and teaching them to obey everything that I have commanded you. And remember, I am with you always, to the end of the age."

R E F L E C T I O N

Jesus' promise to send the Holy Spirit to his followers is an integral part of his resurrection appearances. The Holy Spirit, variously called the Advocate, Comforter or Helper, is the felt presence of God after Jesus is no longer with the disciples. Through the Spirit, the followers of Jesus receive power to give witness to God's reign on earth. Surprisingly, Luke records two different reactions to Jesus' ascension. In the gospel, the disciples return to Jerusalem to bless God continually in the temple. In the Acts of the Apostles, the disciples are caught staring up into heaven as though they can't believe their eyes. Amazement and worship are reactions to the power of God. In the Hebrew scriptures, we read about believers like Abraham who fall to the ground when they encounter the Holy One. In a different experience, Elisha watches in awe and anguish as Elijah is taken up to heaven in a flaming chariot and a whirlwind. All the gospels tell of the crowds and the followers of Jesus who are amazed at his miracles. Amazement signals that those experiencing the event do not fully understand what is happening. Worship is a response of adoration and gratitude to the presence of God.

The disciples teach us to open ourselves to the possibility of being amazed by the power of God and to give thanks and praise to God.

■ **When Jesus ascends he sends his disciples to preach repentance and the forgiveness of sins. How are these important for you?**

■ **What experiences evoke amazement and awe for you? How do you act on that response?**

PRACTICE OF

FAITH

"WHY?" "BECAUSE." Like children, when it comes to faith adults often long for clear-cut answers. We want to understand and know rather than accept.

Yet Jesus entrusts us with something greater than knowledge: "You will be my witnesses." Not our knowledge but the Holy Spirit's power in our lives makes us witnesses.

After Jesus' resurrection the disciples worshiped him, but some doubted. Still Jesus commanded them to go forth and make disciples of all nations. How do we witness to our faith?

PRACTICE OF

HOPE

THAT YOU MAY KNOW. The letter to the Ephesians speaks of "the hope that belongs to [God's] call." That hope is for a share in the glory of Christ, to be filled with "the fullness of the one who fills all things in every way." The call to be a member of the Body of Christ came to us in our baptism, in which we became children of God and heirs with Christ. Christ has commissioned us, his disciples, to baptize "in the name of the Father, and of the Son, and of the Holy Spirit." We have the comfort of knowing that Christ is with us always, as he promised, until the end of time. Our prayer is that we will know, not just with our minds, but with our hearts and souls, how blessed we are.

PRACTICE OF

CHARITY

THE EYES OF YOUR HEART. Many of us read *The Little Prince* by Antoine Saint-Exupery and fondly remember the fox's wise words to the Little Prince: It is only with the heart that one sees rightly, for what is essential is invisible to the eye. This week, pay attention to your heart's vision. How differently do you see people or view events in your life with the eyes of your heart?

WEEKDAY READINGS (Mo)Acts 19:1–8; (Tu)1:15–17, 20–26; (We)20:28–38; (Th)22:30, 23:6–11; (Fr)25:13b–21; (Sa)28:16–20, 30–31

READING I *Acts 1:6–14*

Roman Catholic: Acts 1:12–14

When the apostles had come together, they asked Jesus, "Lord, is this the time when you will restore dominion to Israel?" He replied, "It is not for you to know the times or periods that the Father has set by divine authority. But you will receive power when the Holy Spirit has come upon you; and you will be my witnesses in Jerusalem, in all Judea and Samaria, and to the ends of the earth."

When he had said this, as they were watching, he was lifted up, and a cloud took him out of their sight. While he was going and they were gazing up toward heaven, suddenly two men in white robes stood by them. They said, "You Galileans, why do you stand looking up toward heaven? This Jesus, who has been taken up from you into heaven, will come in the same way as you saw him go into heaven."

Then they returned to Jerusalem from the mount called Olivet, which is near Jerusalem, a sabbath day's journey away. When they had entered the city, they went to the room upstairs where they were staying, Peter, and John, and James, and Andrew, Philip and Thomas, Bartholomew and Matthew, James son of Alphaeus, and Simon the Zealot, and Judas son of James. All these were constantly devoting themselves to prayer, together with certain women, including Mary the mother of Jesus, as well as his brothers.

READING II *1 Peter 4:12–14; 5:6–11*

Roman Catholic: 1 Peter 4:13–16

Beloved, do not be surprised at the fiery ordeal that is taking place among you to test you, as though something strange were happening to you. But rejoice insofar as you are sharing Christ's sufferings, so that you may also be glad and shout for joy when his glory is revealed. If you are reviled for the name of Christ, you are blessed, because the spirit of glory, which is the Spirit of God, is resting on you.

Humble yourselves therefore under the mighty hand of God, so that God may exalt you in due time. Cast all your anxiety on God, because God cares for you. Discipline yourselves, keep alert. Like a roaring lion your adversary the devil prowls around, looking for someone to devour. Resist the devil, steadfast in your faith, for you know that your brothers and sisters in all the world are undergoing the same kinds of suffering.

And after you have suffered for a little while, that very God of all grace, who has called you into eternal glory in Christ, will restore, support, strengthen, and establish you. To God be the power forever and ever. Amen.

GOSPEL *John 17:1–11*

After Jesus had spoken these words, he looked up to heaven and said, "Father, the hour has come; glorify your Son so that the Son may glorify you, since you have given him authority over all people, to give eternal life to all whom you have given him. And this is eternal life, that they may know you, the only true God, and Jesus Christ whom you have sent. I glorified you on earth by finishing the work that you gave me to do. So now, Father, glorify me in your own presence with the glory that I had in your presence before the world existed.

"I have made your name known to those whom you gave me from the world. They were yours, and you gave them to me, and they have kept your word. Now they know that everything you have given me is from you; for the words that you gave to me I have given to them, and they have received them and know in truth that I came from you; and they have believed that you sent me. I am asking on their behalf; I am not asking on behalf of the world, but on behalf of those whom you gave me, because they are yours. All mine are yours, and yours are mine; and I have been glorified in them.

"And now I am no longer in the world, but they are in the world, and I am coming to you. Holy Father, protect them in your name that you have given me, so that they may be one, as we are one."

REFLECTION

Jesus' prayer of protection for the disciples shows the care of a brother. Particularly telling is his recognition that although he is no longer in the world, they are. First-century Palestine was no easy place for Jew or Christian. The Romans saw both groups as troublemakers who worshiped God instead of Caesar. In the years before John's gospel, the Romans had destroyed the Jewish temple and begun full-scale persecution of the Christians. John's emphasis on spirit rather than flesh and knowledge of God as the path to eternal life reveal his theology of hope.

The prayer of Jesus also points out his hope that his followers would know the same unity with the Father and with one another that he himself enjoyed. For the disciples and the members of the early church, this meant sharing in the suffering of Jesus through persecution. In spite of "the fiery ordeal," Peter preaches confidence because the spirit of God rests on the people. He proclaims that after this small suffering, God will restore and establish God's people forever. There must have been times when the message seemed absurd; when it seemed easier and far more prudent to renounce faith in Jesus and save one's own life. The disciples of Jesus heard a deeper call to glory in Christ and a share in his resurrection. They heard it together and knew they were not alone. It is not an accident that Luke records the names of all those who gathered in the upper room after the ascension. Mary, Peter, John, James and their companions knew the presence of Jesus in their midst and their bond with one another. Jesus' prayer that they may be one was already taking effect.

■ **The church has always held that prayer has both a personal and a communal dimension. We listen and talk to God in private; we gather as a people to worship. Why are both important?**

■ **Jesus glorified God by finishing the work God had given him to do. It is no different for us. What is the proper work of a Christian? How does it help complete God's work?**

PRACTICE OF FAITH

BLESS THESE SEEDS I SOW. This Wednesday is the feast of Saint Isidore the farmer. The Catholic Rural Life Conference sponsors blessings of farmers and their fields on this day. Traditionally the days before the feast of the Ascension were a time for planting crops. Say this prayer from *Catholic Household Blessings and Prayers:* "O God, from the very beginning of time you commanded the earth to bring forth vegetation and fruit of every kind. You provide the sower with seed and give bread to eat. Grant, we pray, that this land, enriched by your bounty and cultivated by human hands, may be fertile with abundant crops. Then your people, enriched by the gifts of your goodness, will praise you unceasingly now and for ages unending. Grant this through Christ our Lord. Amen."

PRACTICE OF HOPE

YOU ARE BLESSED. In times of trouble, when we suffer for our belief in the gospel, it is hard to think of that suffering as a blessing. When we and others we know are persecuted for following Christ, it is easy to become discouraged and disillusioned. But we have hope in the One who loves us and suffered for our sake.

"Rejoice insofar as you are sharing Christ's sufferings." It is logical to suffer for doing bad things, but when we suffer for the good we do, it just doesn't make sense, especially when the suffering comes from within our own churches. Have courage, like the early Christians before you, for "if you are reviled for the name of Christ, you are blessed."

PRACTICE OF CHARITY

THAT THEY MAY BE ONE. In 1998, a group of young white men tied a black man to the back bumper of their truck and drove away, dragging him for miles. The saddest thing is that they did not seem to appreciate the horror of their action. Somehow they were able to convince themselves that this African American man was not equal to them in his humanity and that they did not need to respect his basic human dignity. Cornel West and Henry Louis Gates, both distinguished professors at Harvard University, have joined their considerable knowledge in a recent book, *The African American Century: How Black Americans Have Shaped Our Country.* This book chronicles 100 black leaders who have made important contributions to American history and culture. Perhaps if more of us were aware of the achievements of these men and women, tragedies involving racism would become rare.

WEEKDAY READINGS (Mo)Acts 19:1–8; (Tu)1:15–17, 20–26; (We)20:28–38; (Th)22:30, 23:6–11; (Fr)25:13b–21; (Sa)28:16–20, 30–31

READING I *Acts 2:1–11*

When the day of Pentecost had come, they were all together in one place. And suddenly from heaven there came a sound like the rush of a violent wind, and it filled the entire house where they were sitting. Divided tongues, as of fire, appeared among them, and a tongue rested on each of them. All of them were filled with the Holy Spirit and began to speak in other languages, as the Spirit gave them ability.

Now there were devout Jews from every nation under heaven living in Jerusalem. And at this sound the crowd gathered and was bewildered, because each one heard them speaking in the native language of each. Amazed and astonished, they asked, "Are not all these who are speaking Galileans? And how is it that we hear, each of us, in our own native language? Parthians, Medes, Elamites, and residents of Mesopotamia, Judea and Cappadocia, Pontus and Asia, Phrygia and Pamphylia, Egypt and the parts of Libya belonging to Cyrene, and visitors from Rome, both Jewish-born and proselytes, Cretans and Arabs—in our own languages we hear them speaking about God's deeds of power."

READING II *1 Corinthians 12:3–13*

No one can say "Jesus is Lord" except by the Holy Spirit. Now there are varieties of gifts, but the same Spirit; and there are varieties of services, but the same Lord; and there are varieties of activities, but it is the same God who activates all of them in everyone. To each is given the manifestation of the Spirit for the common good. To one is given through the Spirit the utterance of wisdom, and to another the utterance of knowledge according to the same Spirit, to another faith by the same Spirit, to another gifts of healing by the one Spirit, to another the working of miracles, to another prophecy, to another the discernment of spirits, to another various kinds of tongues, to another the interpretation of tongues. All these are activated by one and the same Spirit, who allots to each one individually just as the Spirit chooses.

For just as the body is one and has many members, and all the members of the body, though many, are one body, so it is with Christ. For in the one Spirit we were all baptized into one body—Jews or Greeks, slaves or free—and we were all made to drink of one Spirit.

GOSPEL *John 20:19–23*

When it was evening on that day, the first day of the week, and the doors of the house where the disciples had met were locked for fear of the Judeans, Jesus came and stood among them and said, "Peace be with you." After he said this, he showed them his hands and his side. Then the disciples rejoiced when they saw the Lord. Jesus said to them again, "Peace be with you. As the Father has sent me, so I send you."

When he had said this, he breathed on them and said to them, "Receive the Holy Spirit. If you forgive the sins of any, they are forgiven them; if you retain the sins of any, they are retained."

Saturday night through Sunday dawn, May 18–19

PENTECOST VIGIL

Genesis 11:1–19 *At Babel the Lord confused their speech.*

or

Exodus 19:3–8, 16–20 *Fire and wind descended on Sinai.*

or

Ezekiel 37:1–14 *O spirit, breathe on the dead!*

or

Joel 2:28–32 *On the Day of the Lord I will impart my own spirit.*

Romans 8:22–27 *We have the Spirit as first fruits.*

John 7:37–39 *Let the thirsty come to drink of living waters.*

We end Eastertime the way we began it, with a nighttime vigil, poring over the scriptures. We keep watch on Mount Sinai, where we meet God face to face, where we receive the life-giving Spirit. Our paschal journey, begun so long ago in ashes, is finished in fire.

REFLECTION

Breath, wind and fire provide contrasting images in the different stories about the coming of the Holy Spirit into the world. In the gospel, the moment is a private one between Jesus and his disciples. He breathes the Spirit into them, preparing them to be sent forth. He empowers them to forgive sin by this same Spirit. This will be part of their mission in the world. In the Acts of the Apostles, the Spirit does not come in a soft breath but in a violent wind and the appearance of fire. The presence of the Spirit is not private but public. The disciples begin to preach out of the fullness in their hearts in languages that bring the assembled crowd together. The Spirit comes not only on those gathered in the name of Jesus, but on those who hear them speaking in their own languages. The Spirit comes, bringing a unity that has not been witnessed since the tower of Babel. In the prophetic tradition of Israel, the Spirit comes on young and old, slave and free, male and female.

Pentecost is both a private and public event. The Spirit is breathed into us and blown into the world. Like the disciples we are sent out to preach, teach, heal, prophesy, and use our gifts to renew the earth.

The Spirit does not belong to any one people or group, but has come for all and works through all for the peace and justice of God.

■ We do not bring the Spirit. We point to it and get out of the way. How do we develop the humility to recognize the Spirit at work through others, especially those who are different than us?

■ What do the images of breath, wind and fire tell us about the Spirit? What other metaphors do we have?

PRACTICE OF FAITH

A VIOLENT WIND. How often do we think that the spiritual life is serene, without distress or disturbances? Do we believe that the Spirit is at work when there is wind, flame and many voices all talking at once? The Spirit has a boisterous side too!

This week see how the Spirit is trying to work in situations that seem conflicting or confusing. Elijah heard God in the still, small voice; at Pentecost God's presence was like the "rush of a violent wind."

PRACTICE OF HOPE

MANY GIFTS. It is easy to be discouraged when we see all the work there is to be done. We see our own limits and feel overwhelmed. Today is a day to refocus our attention on the work of the Spirit.

We forget that one person or one church cannot do it all. There are many gifts so that many services can be given. That is why we are "one body." One may be talented in running a shelter; another has the gift of a listening ear for those who need someone to listen. Another has the gift of saying just the right thing when someone needs words that comfort or words that challenge. Another has the gift of deep prayer and intercession. We all pray, encourage each other and help others, but not in the same way. Today is the day to listen to the Spirit of God, and to discern what the Lord is inviting each of us to do as a member of the one body.

PRACTICE OF CHARITY

VARIETIES OF GIFTS BUT THE SAME SPIRIT. We share the same Holy Spirit that came to abide with us after the resurrection. And we all share the same human spirit that makes us sons and daughters of the Creator. It seems so strange, then, that we can allow the children of migrant workers in the United States to live in deplorable conditions and not cry out in outrage for our young sisters and brothers. There are approximately 800,000 of these children working in our country, subjected to pesticides, which can harm their young brains and bodies, and to inadequate drinking water and sanitary facilities. According to a report by Human Rights Watch, "Agricultural work is the most hazardous and grueling area of employment open to children in the United States. It is also the least protected." Contact Human Rights Watch, 350 Fifth Ave., New York NY 10118-3299; 212-290-4700.

WEEKDAY READINGS (Mo)James 3:13–18; (Tu)4:1–10; (We)4:13–17; (Th)5:1–6; (Fr)5:9–12; (Sa)5:13–20

SUMMER ORDINARY TIME

Give us care like yours for this earth.

Praise is due to you,
O God in Zion.

You visit the earth and water it,
you greatly enrich it;
the river of God is full of water.
You provide its grain,
for so you have prepared it.

You water its furrows abundantly,
settling its ridges,
softening it with showers,
and blessing its growth.
You crown the year with your bounty.

The hills gird themselves with joy,
the meadows clothe themselves with flocks,
the valleys deck themselves with grain,
they shout and sing together for joy.

—Psalm 65:1a, 9–11a, 12b–13

God who called each day's creation good,
all we have for our food
and shelter and clothing
are the crust and air, the light and water
    of this planet.
Give us care like yours for this earth:
to share its bounty
with generations to come
and with all alike in this generation,
to savor its beauty and respect its power,
to heal what greed and war and foolishness
have done to your earth and to us.
Bring us finally to give thanks,
always and everywhere.

—Prayer of the Season

READING I *Exodus 34:4–6, 8–9*

Revised Common Lectionary: Genesis 1:1—2:4

Moses rose early in the morning and went up on Mount Sinai, as the LORD had commanded him, and took in his hand the two tablets of stone. The LORD descended in the cloud and stood with him there, and proclaimed the name, "The LORD." The LORD passed before him, and proclaimed,

> "The LORD, the LORD,
> a God merciful and gracious,
> slow to anger,
> and abounding in steadfast love and faithfulness."

And Moses quickly bowed his head toward the earth, and worshiped. He said, "If now I have found favor in your sight, O LORD, I pray, let the LORD go with us. Although this is a stiff-necked people, pardon our iniquity and our sin, and take us for your inheritance."

READING II *2 Corinthians 13:11–13*

Paul writes: Finally, brothers and sisters, farewell. Put things in order, listen to my appeal, agree with one another, live in peace; and the God of love and peace will be with you. Greet one another with a holy kiss. All the saints greet you.

The grace of the Lord Jesus Christ, the love of God, and the communion of the Holy Spirit be with all of you.

GOSPEL *John 3:16–18*

Revised Common Lectionary: Matthew 28:16–20

For God so loved the world that he gave his only Son, so that everyone who believes in him may not perish but may have eternal life.

Indeed, God did not send the Son into the world to condemn the world, but in order that the world might be saved through him. Those who believe in him are not condemned; but those who do not believe are condemned already, because they have not believed in the name of the only Son of God.

REFLECTION

We have been baptizing children and adults in the name of the Father and of the Son and of the Holy Spirit since the earliest days of the church. But the reality of a God who is three and one at the same time is a mystery we are still trying to unfold. The names we use tell us something of the intimate inner relationship of God. Phrases like "lover, beloved and love itself," "source, wellspring and fountain of living water," or "creator, redeemer and sustainer of the world" try to capture something of the unity and the complexity. We celebrate the generative and familial aspects of Father, Son and Spirit, and attempt to articulate the motherhood of God, the child Jesus, and the Spirit that proceeds from that holy bond. Symbols like three-leaf clovers and triangles provide visual cues for reflection, and yet we struggle to understand the depths of the mystery.

In the end we are left with a story, a promise and a letter. God reveals the divine name to a prophet on a mountain and thus receives a stubborn people into a relationship unlike any other in creation. Jesus, God's self-giving Word made human, comes in love to the world, promising eternal life in the compassion of God. Paul writes of the love of God that manifests itself in the way the members of the Christian community love and are related to one another. In the end we are left with the gift, that is, the grace of Jesus Christ, the love of God and the communion of the Holy Spirit; each of them drawing us closer to one another and to the mystery that is God. It may be that in the unity and relationship we experience together as a people of God we can best understand the Trinity that is God.

■ Following Jesus' words, the church named its understanding and experience of God as Father, Son and Holy Spirit. How do these words help explain Trinity? How do they hinder understanding? What are some other images that can help us envision the reality of the Trinity?

■ We are made in the image of God. How do we reveal the trinitarian relationship in our lives as people of God?

PRACTICE OF FAITH

DIVINE COMPANY. On most Sundays when we gather around the eucharistic table we focus on events of Jesus' life. Today is an exception. The Feast of the Holy Trinity belongs to a category sometimes called "idea feasts." "Idea" means "belief." Today we celebrate our belief in the three persons in one God.

We can understand the mystery of the Trinity as "divine action." It is divine love turned toward the world: God so loved the world that he gave his only Son. After Jesus ascended to the Father, he sent the Spirit. We acknowledge our faith in the Trinity each time we make the sign of the cross.

PRACTICE OF HOPE

ENCOURAGE ONE ANOTHER. The Holy Trinity is our model for our human community. Centuries ago, arguments over the nature of the Trinity divided Christians. The Holy Trinity is a profound mystery. It is a great gift to us that Christ has revealed something of that mystery for our contemplation. But contemplation is not definition or theological argument: It is faith, hope and love at work in us.

Perhaps it is time to "mend [our] ways" and be at peace with each other. May the grace of the Lord Jesus Christ, and the love of God and the fellowship of the Holy Spirit be with all of us.

PRACTICE OF CHARITY

BROTHERS AND SISTERS, REJOICE. Our belief in a trinitarian God points the way to our belief that we are to live in community. Paul tell us, "Mend your ways, encourage one another, agree with one another, live in peace . . ." We celebrate the feast this year one day before Memorial Day. Many people used to visit cemeteries on this day to remember those who preceded them, especially those who served their country during war. On this holiday we might consider the debt of gratitude we owe our ancestors. They believed in the importance of community enough that the generations after them have enjoyed rich blessings of prosperity and pluralism. There are not many countries where different ethnic groups live in peace and agree on basic rights as citizens.

WEEKDAY READINGS: (Mo)1 Peter 1:3–9; (Tu)1:10–16; (We)1:18–25; (Th)2:2–5, 9–12; (Fr)Zephaniah 3:14–18; (Sa)Jude 17:20–25

READING I *Deuteronomy 8:2–3, 14–16*

Moses said to the people: "Remember the long way that the LORD your God has led you these forty years in the wilderness, in order to humble you, testing you to know what was in your heart, whether or not you would keep his commandments. He humbled you by letting you hunger, then by feeding you with manna, with which neither you nor your ancestors were acquainted, in order to make you understand that one does not live by bread alone, but by every word that comes from the mouth of the LORD.

"Do not exalt yourself, forgetting the LORD your God, who brought you out of the land of Egypt, out of the house of slavery, who led you through the great and terrible wilderness, an arid wasteland with poisonous snakes and scorpions. He made water flow for you from flint rock, and fed you in the wilderness with manna that your ancestors did not know, to humble you and to test you, and in the end to do you good."

READING II *1 Corinthians 10:16–17*

Brothers and sisters: The cup of blessing that we bless, is it not a sharing in the blood of Christ? The bread that we break, is it not a sharing in the body of Christ? Because there is one bread, we who are many are one body, for we all partake of the one bread.

GOSPEL *John 6: 51–59*

Jesus said to the people: "I am the living bread that came down from heaven. Whoever eats of this bread will live forever; and the bread that I will give for the life of the world is my flesh.

The Judeans then disputed among themselves, saying, "How can this man give us his flesh to eat?" So Jesus said to them, "Very truly, I tell you, unless you eat the flesh of the Son-of-Man and drink his blood, you have no life in you. Those who eat my flesh and drink my blood have eternal life, and I will raise them up on the last day; for my flesh is true food and my blood is true drink. Those who eat my flesh and drink my blood abide in me, and I in them. Just as the living Father sent me, and I live because of the Father, so whoever eats me will live because of me. This is the bread that came down from heaven, not like that which your ancestors ate, and they died. But the one who eats this bread will live forever."

He said these things while he was teaching in the synagogue at Capernaum.

Friday, June 7, 2002

SACRED HEART OF JESUS

Deuteronomy 7:6–11 *The Lord loves you.*

1 John 4:7–16 *God is love.*

Matthew 11:25–30 *I am gentle and humble of heart.*

Today is an echo of Good Friday, a reminder that every Friday is kept with renewed efforts to understand and to share the compassion of God. If Christ lives in our hearts, we bear the love of God in our own bodies.

REFLECTION

How strange it must have seemed to the crowd listening to Jesus to hear him talk about himself as the living bread that came down from heaven. After all, manna, which had fed the Jews on their desert journey, was miraculous food—always enough, never too much. It was a gift from God, a sign of God's care. Jesus claimed to be all that and more. He said that those who eat his flesh and drink his blood would have eternal life and would be one with him. It sounds foreign to our ears, even barbaric. How are we to understand such words?

Jesus says something profound about what becomes heart of our hearts and flesh of our flesh. In a very real way, we are what we eat. Food gives us energy and growth. It allows us to survive. It delights us with taste, texture and smell. In the Lord's Prayer, we ask for food before we ask for forgiveness, because our daily bread is what keeps us going. When we understand Jesus as the daily bread that feeds us and becomes part of us, we are closer to understanding that we become a part of Jesus as well. We share in his life and death, his baptism and resurrection. We share in his eternal life before God.

As a community, the church gathers around a table every week, even every day, to remember what real food is like. As church, we gather in thanksgiving because Jesus gave himself wholly to us and invited us to become wholly a part of him. In that wholeness, we find our life.

■ **Food was a common metaphor in the early Christian community. What does food mean to us? How does the idea of food clarify our understanding of Jesus?**

■ **What is the significance of the table in the home? What does the image of gathering around the table tell us about the eucharist?**

PRACTICE OF FAITH

BEING CHRIST. Saint Augustine exhorted Christians "to become what you receive." Communion prepares us to "be Christ." When we receive communion we are nourished and transformed in Christ.

Meditate on how your life is different because you partake in the Body and Blood of Christ.

PRACTICE OF HOPE

ONE BREAD, ONE BODY. We Christians, though professing belief in the same Lord Jesus Christ, have different understandings and different beliefs about the eucharist, the Lord's supper, holy communion. Our deepest hope should be that we may one day break this bread together as one people, not necessarily in uniformity of theology, but in the unity of love. As brothers and sisters, we often engage in a kind of sibling rivalry rather than embrace each other in mutual respect and love.

While the theologians and church leaders are talking (and sometimes arguing), we who are God's people, the Body of Christ, can be embracing each other, respecting each other, accepting our differences and rejoicing in our common belief in the Lord. Do you have any friends or family members who belong to another Christian church? Share a meal with them this week, and rejoice in the gift of the Lord's presence in our lives. Pray that we all may be one.

PRACTICE OF CHARITY

BREAD FOR THE WORLD. Bread is the staple food for most of the world. It symbolizes that which is necessary to maintain human life. How fitting the name "Bread for the World" is for the dedicated people, people of faith, who work on so many fronts to combat hunger among the world's poorest. One of their main tools to help the hungry is to draft congressional legislation to address some of the underlying causes of hunger. In recent years they have worked for passage of bills concerning aid to Africa, increasing WIC funds (Women, Infants and Children) and forgiving the debt of the poorest developing countries. They focus their energy on a specific issue for the year, use experts to help draft the legislation, and provide materials to educate congregations about the issue BFW is addressing. For more information, contact Bread for the World, 50 F St., NW, Suite 500, Washington DC 20001-1565, 800-822-7323.

WEEKDAY READINGS: (Mo)2 Peter 1:2–7; (Tu)3:12–15a, 17–18; (We)2 Timothy 1:1–3, 6–12; (Th)2:8–15; (Fr)Sacred Heart of Jesus, see box; (Sa)4:1–8

READING I *Deuteronomy 11:18–21, 26–28*

Moses said to all Israel: You shall put these words of mine in your heart and soul, and you shall bind them as a sign on your hand, and fix them as an emblem on your forehead. Teach them to your children, talking about them when you are at home and when you are away, when you lie down and when you rise. Write them on the doorposts of your house and on your gates, so that your days and the days of your children may be multiplied in the land that the LORD swore to your ancestors to give them, as long as the heavens are above the earth.

See, I am setting before you today a blessing and a curse: the blessing, if you obey the commandments of the LORD your God that I am commanding you today; and the curse, if you do not obey the commandments of the LORD your God, but turn from the way that I am commanding you today, to follow other deities that you have not known.

READING II *Romans 1:16–17; 3:22b–28*

I am not ashamed of the gospel; it is the power of God for salvation to everyone who has faith, to the Jew first and also to the Greek. For in it the righteousness of God is revealed through faith for faith; as it is written, "The one who is righteous will live by faith."

For there is no distinction, since all have sinned and fall short of the glory of God; they are now justified by God's grace as a gift, through the redemption that is in Christ Jesus, whom God put forward as a sacrifice of atonement by his blood, effective through faith. This was to show God's righteousness, because in divine forbearance God had passed over the sins previously committed; and that God justifies the one who has faith in Jesus. Then what becomes of boasting? It is excluded. By what law? By that of works? No, but by the law of faith. For we hold that a person is justified by faith apart from works prescribed by the law.

GOSPEL *Matthew 7:21–29*

Jesus said: "Not everyone who says to me, 'Lord, Lord,' will enter the dominion of heaven, but only the one who does the will of my Father in heaven. On that day many will say to me, 'Lord, Lord, did we not prophesy in your name, and do many deeds of power in your name?' Then I will declare to them, 'I never knew you; go away from me, you evildoers.'

"Everyone then who hears these words of mine and acts on them will be like a wise man who built his house on rock. The rain fell, the floods came, and the winds blew and beat on that house, but it did not fall, because it had been founded on rock. And everyone who hears these words of mine and does not act on them will be like a foolish man who built his house on sand. The rain fell, and the floods came and the winds blew and beat against that house, and it fell—and great was its fall!"

Now when Jesus had finished saying these things, the crowds were astounded at his teaching, for Jesus taught them as one having authority, and not as their scribes.

REFLECTION

There is no room for indecision at the end of the Sermon on the Mount. One chooses either to do the will of God or not. Good results achieved without true conversion of heart do not bring life. Jesus offers no loopholes, no gray areas, no fence on which to sit. The true disciple is not content to say one thing and do another, or to be satisfied with the mere appearance of holiness.

The metaphor of a house built on rock or sand is apt. The way of God protects the disciple from destruction because it is solid and strong. "The Lord is my Rock," sang the psalmist, and a better foundation for life cannot be found. This was a comforting message for the early church, which endured alienation and persecution. For us, who face the challenges of an increasingly pluralistic and secular society as well as the temptations of consumerism, economic demands and social injustice, a rock-solid foundation in Jesus' message provides a basis for response. There is no foundation apart from God that is strong enough to withstand the forces of nature or the temptations of the world. In the desert of Israel, sand was constantly in motion at the mercy of the wind. Every desert dweller knew the folly of building on sand that might not be there tomorrow. Jesus spoke truth that they knew in their lives.

Jesus was not the first to face the question. In the stories the Jews told around their dinner tables, they remembered that Moses had set life and death before them in similar terms. Life was God; death was anything that was not God. Moses spoke with the authority of God himself. In Jesus, that authority was made manifest again and more profoundly than even Moses had known it.

■ **The decision for or against God is up to each one who hears Jesus' message and takes it to heart. We are accustomed to the idea that nothing is absolute. How does our choice as Christians to obey God's law affect our choices as children of a culture that sees many sides of the same coin?**

■ **Moses commanded that the words of God be placed where the Jews could see them the first thing in the morning and the last thing at night. Which of God's commands would you keep before you? What words of God would you want to remember morning and night?**

PRACTICE OF FAITH

LIVING FAITH. Not long after our father's heart attack, my sister went for a health screening. We were surprised to learn that this slender and energetic woman had high cholesterol. We knew intellectually that there is no direct relationship between body weight and cholesterol levels, yet our surprise showed us that we did not really believe it.

True faith surpasses knowledge about faith. The experience of being in a relationship gives us an understanding about love far more real than reading about others' relationships. Faith is lived with body, mind and spirit. When have you experienced your faith as a living flesh-and-blood reality, not an idea or abstraction?

PRACTICE OF HOPE

NO DISTINCTION. We can identify with the faith/good works debate in today's readings. We deeply believe that what we do affects the outcome of our lives. Eat right, exercise, don't smoke, and you can avoid an array of deadly diseases. But down deep we know that we cannot control everything, and that no matter how healthful a life we lead, we will someday die. This truth can lead us to despair if we do not have hope.

God has freely bestowed eternal life, forgiveness and grace on everyone, without exception, without having to earn it, while we were still in sin. It is God who saves, not the law or our works. We pin our hopes on God's goodness, not our own.

PRACTICE OF CHARITY

ACT ON HIS WORDS. The United States declares itself a peace-loving nation. Yet how can any peace-loving nation oppose a worldwide treaty to ban landmines? Many innocent civilians, even children, have been maimed or killed by stepping on a buried landmine, because they are impossible to see. Can we not decide that some weapons should be outlawed? The Campaign for a Landmine-Free World has heard God's word and is acting on it. They have joined an international effort to remove the millions of these deadly weapons, which especially endanger farmers. They also aid those who require reconstructive surgery and prostheses. Campaign for a Landmine-Free World, c/o VVAF, P.O. Box 96713, Washington DC 20090-6713.

WEEKDAY READINGS: (Mo)1 Kings 17:1–6; (Tu)Acts 11:21b–26; 13:1–3; (We)1 Kings 18:20–39; (Th)18:41–46; (Fr)19:9a, 11–16; (Sa)19:19–21

READING I *Hosea 5:15—6:6*

Roman Catholic: Hosea 6:3–6

I will return again to my place until they acknowledge their guilt and seek my face. In their distress they will beg my favor: "Come, let us return to the LORD; for having torn, the LORD will heal us; having struck us down, the LORD will bind us up. After two days the LORD will revive us, and on the third day will raise us up, that we may live before the face of the LORD. Let us know, let us press on to know the LORD, whose appearing is as sure as the dawn; the LORD will come to us like the showers, like the spring rains that water the earth."

What shall I do with you, O Ephraim? What shall I do with you, O Judah? Your love is like a morning cloud, like the dew that goes away early. Therefore I have hewn them by the prophets, I have killed them by the words of my mouth, and my judgment goes forth as the light. For I desire steadfast love and not sacrifice, the knowledge of God rather than burnt offerings.

READING II *Romans 4:13–25*

Roman Catholic: Romans 4:18–25

The promise that Abraham would inherit the world did not come to him or to his descendents through the law but through the righteousness of faith. If it is the adherents of the law who are to be heirs, faith is null and the promise is void. For the law brings wrath; but where there is no law, neither is there violation.

For this reason it depends on faith, in order that the promise may rest on grace and be guaranteed to all Abraham's descendents, not only to the adherents of the law but also to those who share the faith of Abraham (for he is the father of all of us, as it is written, "I have made you the father of many nations")—in the presence of the God in whom Abraham believed, who gives life to the dead and calls into existence the things that do not exist.

Hoping against hope, Abraham believed that he would become "the father of many nations," according to what was what was said, "So numerous shall your descendants be." He did not weaken in faith when he considered his own body, which was already as good as dead (for he was about a hundred years old), or when he considered the barrenness of Sarah's womb. No distrust made Abraham waver concerning the promise of God, but he grew strong in his faith as he gave glory to God, being fully convinced that God was able to do what God had promised. Therefore his faith "was reckoned to him as righteousness," Now the words, "it was reckoned to him," were written not for his sake alone, but for ours also. It will be reckoned to us who believe in the one who raised Jesus our Lord from the dead, who was handed over to death for our trespasses and was raised for our justification.

GOSPEL *Matthew 9:9–13*

Revised Common Lectionary: Matthew 9:9–13, 18–26

As Jesus was walking along, he saw a man called Matthew sitting at the tax booth and he said to him, "Follow me." And he got up and followed him.

And as Jesus sat at dinner in the house, many tax collectors and sinners came and were sitting with him and his disciples. When the Pharisees saw this, they said to his disciples, "Why does your teacher eat with tax collectors and sinners?" But when he heard this, he said, "Those who are well have no need of a physician, but those who are sick. Go and learn what this means, 'I desire mercy, not sacrifice.' For I have come to call not the righteous but sinners."

REFLECTION

The apostles were called at the beginning of Jesus' ministry to become fishers of all people. They were to use their honorable means of making a living in a new way. Peter, Andrew and the rest of the disciples left their families and livelihoods, but continued to use their talents and skill as fishers.

The tax collector Matthew is the last to be called. Unlike fishing, tax collecting was a despised, hated profession. The early rabbis considered tax collectors to be traitors who robbed their own people for the conquering Romans and got rich on their ill-gotten gains. The gospels frequently place tax collectors in the same category as sinners, prostitutes and Gentiles who do not follow the law.

But Jesus asks a tax collector to follow him; he even eats at Matthew's house, and furthermore, not alone, but with other notorious sinners. In those days, to associate with outcasts like these was to become like them.

Jesus' choice of Matthew sends a clear signal about his ministry. Jesus will not be bound by social or religious conventions. In fact, he quotes a familiar proverb to the onlooking Pharisees that it is the sick, not the well, who need a physician. Thus Jesus indirectly identifies himself as a healer for those in need. In the same way that a doctor must talk with and touch a patient in order to heal, Jesus must spend time with sinners and outcasts. How else could he reveal God's love for all creation, God's desire for mercy and kindness, not sacrifice?

■ Who are outcasts in our society? In what ways are we like the Pharisees? What do we need to do to change?

■ The gospel implies that Jesus helped Matthew move into a new way of life. Has there been an instance in your life when you changed because of God's mercy?

PRACTICE OF FAITH

NO COMPROMISE. "I desire mercy, not sacrifice." Jesus was not merely echoing Hosea. He was commanding those who claimed to know the prophets to recognize that the law alone cannot save. Mercy and compassion save. Where does adherence to "law" get in the way of living with mercy and compassion for you? Examine your attitudes to see what informs them. How does "law" help and how does it hinder your following Jesus?

PRACTICE OF HOPE

HOPING AGAINST HOPE. Abraham believed in God's promise, and had hope that the One who promised would fulfill that promise. His faith was credited to him as good works. Steadfast love nourishes that faith in God. Abraham and Sarah knew that God is greater than the law, even the laws of nature; only God can save and not law alone. Jesus points this out to the Pharisees when he tells them, "Go and learn what this means, 'I desire mercy, not sacrifice.'"

Hope is inextricably bound up with faith and love. If we could be saved only by following the law, "faith is null and the promise is void." No one can call themselves righteous. We are all sinners. So then, if salvation comes from the law, we are doomed; there is no hope. But our hope is in God, who loves us and gave us our Lord Jesus Christ to fulfill the promises made to our ancestors in faith.

PRACTICE OF CHARITY

"MERCY, NOT SACRIFICE." There is no one more deserving of our mercy than Mother Earth. Many groups are committed to environmental causes, seeking to heal the planet's hurts, and their myriad suggestions can be almost overwhelming. Mothers and Others publishes a monthly newsletter with concrete suggestions on what you can do to help the environment. The newsletter is short and simple: One subject per issue, printed on one sheet of paper. That's not overwhelming. Their suggestions are based on solid research and are thoroughly worthwhile. *The Green Guide* can be obtained from Mothers and Others, 40 W. 20th St., New York NY 10011-4211; 212-242-0010; www.mothers.org.

WEEKDAY READINGS (Mo)1 Kings 17:1–6; (Tu)Acts 11:21b–28; 13:1–3; (We)1 Kings 18:20–39; (Th)18:41–46; (Fr)19:9a, 11–16; (Sa)19:19–21

READING I *Exodus 19:2–8*

The Israelites had journeyed from Rephidim, entered the wilderness of Sinai, and camped in the wilderness; Israel camped there in front of the mountain. Then Moses went up to God; the LORD called to him from the mountain, saying, "Thus you shall say to the house of Jacob, and tell the Israelites: You have seen what I did to the Egyptians, and how I bore you on eagles' wings and brought you to myself. Now therefore, if you obey my voice and keep my covenant, you shall be my treasured possession out of all the peoples. Indeed, the whole earth is mine, but you shall be for me a realm of priests and a holy nation. These are the words that you shall speak to the Israelites."

So Moses came, summoned the elders of the people, and set before them all these words that the LORD had commanded him. The people all answered as one: "Everything that the LORD has spoken we will do."

READING II *Romans 5:1–11*

Since we are justified by faith, we have peace with God through our Lord Jesus Christ, through whom we have obtained access to this grace in which we stand; and we boast in our hope of sharing the glory of God. And not only that, but we also boast in our sufferings, knowing that suffering produces endurance, and endurance produces character, and character produces hope, and hope does not disappoint us, because God's love has been poured into our hearts through the Holy Spirit that has been given to us.

For while we were still weak, at the right time Christ died for the ungodly. Indeed, rarely will anyone die for a righteous person—though perhaps for a good person someone might actually dare to die. But it is proof of God's own love for us in that while we still were sinners Christ died for us.

Much more surely then, now that we have been justified by his blood, will we be saved through him from the wrath of God. For if while we were enemies, we were reconciled to God through the death of the Son of God, much more surely, having been reconciled, will we be saved by the life of the Son of God. But more than that, we even boast in God through our Lord Jesus Christ, through whom we have now received reconciliation.

GOSPEL *Matthew 9:35—10:8*

Jesus went about all the cities and villages, teaching in their synagogues, and proclaiming the good news of the dominion of heaven, and curing every disease and every sickness. When he saw the crowds, he had compassion for them, because they were harassed and helpless, like sheep without a shepherd. Then he said to his disciples, "The harvest is plentiful, but the laborers are few; therefore ask the Lord of the harvest to send out laborers for the harvesting." Then Jesus summoned his twelve disciples and gave them authority over unclean spirits, to cast them out, and to cure every disease and every sickness.

These are the names of the twelve apostles: first, Simon, also known as Peter, and his brother Andrew; James son of Zebedee, and his brother John; Philip and Bartholomew; Thomas and Matthew the tax collector; James son of Alphaeus, and Thaddaeus; Simon the Cananaean, and Judas Iscariot, the one who betrayed him. These twelve Jesus sent out with the following instructions: "Go nowhere among the Gentiles, and enter no town of the Samaritans, but go rather to the lost sheep of the house of Israel. As you go, proclaim the good news, 'The dominion of heaven has come near.' Cure the sick, raise the dead, cleanse those with leprosy, cast out demons. You received without payment; give without payment."

REFLECTION

The compassion of God brought the Jews to the foot of Mount Sinai to receive the Ten Commandments. That same compassion brought Christ to preach the good news to the children of Israel. In both Old and New Testaments, God reaches out to God's people.

The gospel story demonstrates the generosity of divine love in the naming of the twelve disciples who share in Jesus' authority to cast out demons and heal the sick. For the first time, we are introduced to a group that includes a tax collector, a sinner by his community's standards, who will develop into a faithful disciple, as well as a betrayer who will hand Jesus over. The description of the twelve and Jesus' solemn instructions show us how the kingdom is meant to advance through human strengths and frailties.

In our own world, we dismiss what is broken or obsolete. Weakness is to be overcome and perfection attained. But Jesus counted among his followers two people who even in our culture might be shunned. When we think of our own failings and imperfections, we would do well to remember that in the dominion of heaven good comes from the most unexpected places.

■ **What is the work of God that needs to be done in today's world? How can the church promote and support that work among all its members?**

■ **How do we as individuals hear and respond to the call of Jesus to follow him? How do we discern our particular path?**

PRACTICE OF FAITH

CHOSEN. God chose Israel to be God's treasured possession; Jesus chose the apostles "to go, proclaim the good news." We too have been chosen to participate in God's plan for salvation. No less than Jesus' first followers, we too are commissioned to proclaim the kingdom of God by our actions as well as our words. Pray that Christians everywhere will take seriously their responsibility to be Christ in the world.

PRACTICE OF HOPE

LIKE SHEEP WITHOUT A SHEPHERD. In troubling times, it's always the poor who suffer the most. Struggling to make a living and keep their families together, they don't have time to fight for their rights. They are dependent on good leaders who will advocate for them. Christ offers hope. He sends out his disciples with a commission to cure disease and drive out demons. He is very clear about their mission: "You received without payment; give without payment." These gifts of leadership are given for the good of the people of God, not for the apostles' own benefit. Paul understood this well. "While we were still sinners, Christ died for us." We must place our hope in the God who loves us, and pray for good leaders who will selflessly and generously serve.

PRACTICE OF CHARITY

HEAVEN IS AT HAND. If you want to feed people, give them fish; but if you want to end their hunger, teach them to fish. This is the guiding principle of Oxfam America. One way they do this is to support fledgling NGOs (non-government organizations) in developing countries. In addition to giving people the opportunity to help themselves, supporting new NGOs is a way to break through the rigidity and frequent corruption of the governments in these countries. Oxfam has supported NGOs in El Salvador, Guatemala, Cambodia, Vietnam, Senegal, Mozambique, Ecuador and Peru. To learn more about their work, contact Oxfam America, 26 West St., Boston MA 02111-1206; www.oxfamamerica.org.

WEEKDAY READINGS (Mo)1 Kings 21:1–16; (Tu)21:17–29; (We)2 Kings 2:1, 6–14; (Th)Sirach 48:1–14; (Fr)2 Kings 11:1–4, 9–18, 20; (Sa)2 Chronicles 24:17–25

READING I *Jeremiah 20:7, 10–13*

O LORD, you have enticed me, and I was enticed;
you were too powerful for me, and you have
    prevailed.
I have become a laughing stock all day long;
everyone mocks me.
I hear many whispering: "Terror is all around!
Denounce him! Let us denounce him!"
All my close friends are watching for me to stumble.
"Perhaps Jeremiah can be enticed,
and we can prevail against him,
    and take our revenge on him."

But the LORD is with me like a dread warrior;
therefore my persecutors will stumble,
    and they will not prevail.
They will be greatly shamed,
    for they will not succeed.
Their eternal dishonor will never be forgotten.
O LORD of hosts, you test the righteous,
you see the heart and the mind;
let me see your retribution upon them,
for to you I have committed my cause.

Sing to the LORD; praise the Lord!
For the LORD has delivered the life of the needy
from the hands of evildoers.

READING II *Romans 5: 12–15*

Revised Common Lectionary: Romans 6:1b–11

Just as sin came into the world through one human
being, and death came through sin, and so death
spread to all because all have sinned — sin was
indeed in the world before the law, but sin is not
reckoned when there is no law. Yet death exercised
dominion from Adam to Moses, even over those
whose sins were not like the transgression of Adam,
who is a type of the one who was to come.

But the free gift is not like the trespass. For if the
many died through the trespass of one human,
much more surely have the grace of God and the
free gift in the grace of the one human, Jesus Christ,
abounded for the many.

GOSPEL *Matthew 10:26–33*

Revised Common Lectionary: Matthew 10:24–39

Jesus said: "So have no fear of them; for nothing is
covered up that will not be uncovered, and nothing
secret that will not become known. What I say to
you in the dark, tell in the light; and what you hear
whispered, proclaim from the housetops. Do not
fear those who kill the body but cannot kill the soul;
rather fear the one who can destroy both soul and
body in hell. Are not two sparrows sold for a penny?
Yet not one of them will fall to the ground apart
from your Father. And even the hairs of your head
are all counted. So do not be afraid; you are of more
value than many sparrows.

"Everyone therefore who acknowledges me
before others, I also will acknowledge before my
Father in heaven; but whoever denies me before others, I also will deny before my Father in heaven."

Monday, June 24, 2002

BIRTH OF JOHN THE BAPTIST

VIGIL

Jeremiah 1:4–10 *Before I formed you in the womb, I knew you.*

1 Peter 1:8–12 *Rejoice with inexpressible joy.*

Luke 1:5–17 *Many will rejoice at John's birth.*

DAY

Isaiah 49:1–6 *From my mother's womb I am given my name.*

Acts 13:22–26 *John's message is for all children of Abraham.*

Luke 1:57–66, 80 *What will the child be?*

John said, "I must decrease if Christ is to increase."
Today the daytime begins to decrease. It is the midsum-
mer nativity. John is born to be the best man of the
Bridegroom, the lamp of the Light and the voice of the
Word. Rejoice in John's birth!

REFLECTION

The coming of the Messiah was supposed to bring an era of peace and justice for Israel. How confusing it must have been to the early church to be rejected and persecuted by both the political and religious powers. Jesus offers words of encouragement and some challenging advice. "Do not fear," Jesus says, repeating a refrain that echoes throughout the scriptures. "Do not fear" tells the hearer that God has broken into human history again, just as God has done countless times in the past. What they have heard and taken to heart, they are not to keep to themselves but must shout to the world.

To the first-century Christians who faced death at the hands of their enemies, Jesus makes a profound observation. It is not the death of the body that kills; it is the death of the soul. And fear is what kills the soul. A proclamation of faith shouted from the rooftops would tell the world that Jesus' disciples will not cower in fear. They will not hide their faith but will live it openly. They who have experienced Jesus and his resurrection must share this good news with the world.

"The Lord is with me like a dread warrior," sings Jeremiah, who is besieged on every side. "God delivers the life of the needy from the hands of evildoers." Jesus reaffirms this message: God will be with God's people. They can find peace in the confidence that what they have experienced in Jesus is the will of God.

■ **We do not face persecution in the United States as the early Christians did. Yet even today, in other places in the world, people are persecuted, even killed because they dare to proclaim their faith. What could lead people to give up their lives for their faith?**

■ **Sometimes things do not work out even for those with strong faith. What does the church have to say to them? As a Christian, how do you respond to those who think God has abandoned them?**

PRACTICE OF FAITH

PROPHETS. Just as Jeremiah was mocked and persecuted, so John was ridiculed and imprisoned. Yet both were God's heralds and prophets. Why is the voice of the prophet so difficult to hear? Why is there so much resistance to the prophet's message? Who are the prophets of our time? Reflect on how you respond to their call for repentance and change. Does your response come from fear or faith? Monday is the feast of John the Baptist.

PRACTICE OF HOPE

FEAR NOT. We are not to fear, we are to live in the light of hope, for the One who went before us leads us and will not abandon us.

Our prayer this week can be simple meditation, perhaps contemplation. In silence, we learn to listen for the voice of the Holy Spirit, who teaches us how to pray. As we learn to distinguish the voice of God from the noise of our lives and from all the other voices, we will grow deeper in faith and in love, and our hope will greatly nourished. The voice of God is a quiet voice, gently urging us toward the good. Spend some time each day in silent prayer, listening, discerning, hoping for the gift.

PRACTICE OF CHARITY

FEAR NO ONE. After centuries of often brutal Spanish domination of the indigenous Mayan people, Guatemala experienced the "Ten Years of Spring" in 1944. Popularly elected President Arbenz legalized unions and diverse political parties, and implemented a land reform program to buy land from large landowners for peasant cooperatives. When the United Fruit Company had to sell its fallow acreage for the undervalued amount it had declared on its tax returns, management went to the U.S. government and the Guatemalan leaders were accused of Communism. As a result, the CIA initiated a clandestine campaign to train and equip the Guatemalan military to make war against the Guatemalan people. In March 1999, after peace finally came to Guatemala, the United Nations declared that the Guatemalan military had committed 93% of the war crimes there, committing genocide against the Mayan people. See www.globalexchange.org/campaigns/guatemala/history.html.

WEEKDAY READINGS (Mo)Birth of John the Baptist, see box; (Tu)2 Kings 19:9b–11, 31–36; (We)22:8–13; 23:1–3; (Th)24:8–17; (Fr)25:1–12; (Sa)Peter and Paul, see box, page 108.

READING I *2 Kings 4:8–12, 14–17*

Revised Common Lectionary: Jeremiah 28:5–9

One day Elisha was passing through Shunem, where a wealthy woman lived, who urged him to have a meal. So whenever he passed that way, he would stop there for a meal. She said to her husband, "Look, I am sure that this man who regularly passes our way is a holy man of God. Let us make a small roof chamber with walls, and put there for him a bed, a table, a chair, and a lamp, so that he can stay there whenever he comes to us."

One day when he came there, he went up to the chamber and lay down there. He said to his servant Gehazi, "Call the Shunammite woman."

He said, "What then may be done for her?" Gehazi answered, "Well, she has no son, and her husband is old." He said, "Call her." When he had called her, she stood at the door. He said, "At this season, in due time, you shall embrace a son." She replied, "No, my lord, O man of God; do not deceive your servant."

The woman conceived and bore a son at that season, in due time, as Elisha had declared to her.

READING II *Romans 6:3–4, 8–11*

Revised Common Lectionary: Romans 6:12–23

Do you not know that all of us who have been baptized into Christ Jesus were baptized into his death? Therefore we have been buried with him by baptism into death, so that, just as Christ was raised from the dead by the glory of the Father, so we too might walk in newness of life.

But if we have died with Christ, we believe that we will also live with him. We know that Christ, being raised from the dead, will never die again; death no longer has dominion over him. The death he died, he died to sin, once for all; but the life he lives, he lives to God.

So you also must consider yourselves dead to sin and alive to God in Christ Jesus.

GOSPEL *Matthew 10:37–42*

Jesus said: "Whoever loves father or mother more than me is not worthy of me; and whoever loves son or daughter more than me is not worthy of me; and whoever does not take up the cross and follow me is not worthy of me. Those who find their life will lose it, and those who lose their life for my sake will find it.

"Whoever welcomes you welcomes me, and whoever welcomes me welcomes the one who sent me. Whoever welcomes a prophet in the name of a prophet will receive a prophet's reward; and whoever welcomes a righteous person in the name of a righteous person will receive the reward of the righteous; and whoever gives even a cup of cold water to one of these little ones in the name of a disciple— truly I tell you, none of these will lose their reward."

Saturday, June 29, 2002

PETER AND PAUL, APOSTLES

VIGIL

Acts 3:1–10 *Peter cried, "Look at us!"*

Galatians 1:11–20 *God chose to reveal Christ to me.*

John 21:15–19 *Simon Peter, do you love me?*

DAY

Acts 12:1–11 *The chains dropped from Peter's wrists.*

2 Timothy 4:6–8, 17–18 *I have kept the faith.*

Matthew 16:13–19 *I entrust to you the keys of the kingdom.*

Today we keep a festival in honor of the two apostles who began the harvest of God's reign. They preached from Jerusalem to Rome, keeping the Easter commandment to bring the good news to the ends of the earth.

REFLECTION

Prophets, servants and children all had the power to speak for the one who had sent them. Prophets spoke for God, or, more properly, allowed God to speak through them. Because servants did the bidding of their master or mistress, to insult or injure the servant was to insult or injure the sender. To hear a child delivering a parent's message was equal to hearing the parent.

Jesus draws on this understanding of relationships to encourage the disciples as they move into a world that will not always welcome them. The experience of Jesus was so unlike anything anyone had ever known that even members of the same family often opposed one another. Into this situation, the disciples are sent with only their faith and understanding that they preach in the name of Jesus. But just like prophets, servants and children, the disciples carry Jesus' presence with them. Thus Jesus could tell the disciples that those who oppose them oppose him, and those who welcome even the least of them welcome him and God who had sent them.

Jesus' definition of welcome, however, calls us to look carefully at the responses we give and expect. The least gesture of kindness or compassion welcomes both the disciples and Jesus. A cup of cool water in the heat of the day is as good as a feast. The care of one human being for another means that God is at work in a world of division and hurt. The disciples are not to hold out for big signs and many conversions. They are to look for the smallest indication of acceptance from a people afraid to believe that their hopes could be realized.

In our journey in the world, we minister to one another by doing the little things that provide comfort to those on the road. We never know if we are entertaining a prophet or an angel or just another person trying to make their way. But Jesus is present in all of them.

■ **The saying goes that it is better to give than receive. How does the example of Jesus help us to understand both giving and receiving as part of our mission as disciples?**

■ **If we were getting a room ready for a holy person, what things would we put in it? How do we prepare for the coming of the Holy One?**

PRACTICE OF FAITH

WIDE OPEN. Jesus taught that hospitality to anyone is hospitality to him. This is a blessing for us because it opens wide the possibilities for welcoming Jesus in everyone we encounter. How often do we recognize, as the poet Gerard Manley Hopkins wrote, that Christ plays in ten thousand places, "lovely in arms and limbs not his," visible in human faces? Open wide your eyes and see Christ.

PRACTICE OF HOPE

HOSPITALITY. Jesus presents us with some disturbing paradoxes. Don't love anyone or anything more than Christ; take up your cross; save your life and lose it; lose your life and save it. What are we to make of all this? It gets a little clearer in the second part.

We are to be open to others for Jesus' sake. To welcome a prophet, a good person, a child, for his sake, is to begin to live the Reign of God. In other words, in thinking of others, we begin to find our true selves. Our hospitality is to be generous with attentiveness as well as with food and drink. Have lunch with someone new this week, and listen with an open heart. You may hear some surprising wisdom.

PRACTICE OF CHARITY

WHOEVER RECEIVES YOU RECEIVES ME. Susan, age 6, was moved to use all of her personal savings to buy flowers for all the "grandmas and grandpas" at the nursing home she regularly passed in the car with her family. She and her mother went to the supermarket and bought $44 worth of flowers to distribute to the nursing home residents. When Susan gave out the flowers, the old people were deeply touched. Her mother said she had no idea where Susan got the notion to do this. She had no elderly relatives who lived in a nursing home. Susan's parents had given her the money to buy something for herself. She said she couldn't wait to buy flowers for people in other nursing homes. Think about this little girl and what she did.

WEEKDAY READINGS (Mo)Amos 2:6–10, 13–16; (Tu)3:1–8; 4:11–12; (We)Ephesians 2:19–22; (Th)Amos 7:10–17; (Fr) 8:3–6, 9–12; (Sa)9:11–15

READING I *Zechariah 9:9–12*

Rejoice greatly, O daughter Zion!
Shout aloud, O daughter Jerusalem!
Lo, your king comes to you;
triumphant and victorious is he,
humble and riding on a donkey,
on a colt, the foal of a donkey.
The king will cut off the chariot from Ephraim
and the war horse from Jerusalem;
and the battle bow shall be cut off,
and he shall command peace to the nations;
his dominion shall be from sea to sea,
and from the River to the ends of the earth.

As for you also, because of the blood
of my covenant with you,
I will set your prisoners free from the waterless pit.
Return to your stronghold, O prisoners of hope;
today I declare that I will restore to you double.

READING II *Romans 8:9, 11–13*

Revised Common Lectionary: Romans 7:15–25

But you are not in the flesh; you are in the Spirit, since the Spirit of God dwells in you. Anyone who does not have the Spirit of Christ does not belong to Christ. If the Spirit of the one who raised Jesus from the dead dwells in you, the one who raised Christ from the dead will give life to your mortal bodies also through this Spirit dwelling in you.

So then, brothers and sisters, we are debtors, not to the flesh, to live according to the flesh—for if you live according to the flesh, you will die; but if by the Spirit you put to death the deeds of the body, you will live.

GOSPEL *Matthew 11:16–19, 25–30*

Roman Catholic: Matthew 11:25–30

Jesus said: "To what will I compare this generation? It is like children sitting in the marketplaces and calling to one another, 'We played the flute for you, and you did not dance; we wailed, and you did not mourn.' For John came neither eating nor drinking, and they say, 'He has a demon'; the Son-of-Man came eating and drinking, and they say, 'Look, a glutton and a drunkard, a friend of tax collectors and sinners!' Yet wisdom is vindicated by wise deeds."

At that time Jesus said, "I thank you, Father, Lord of heaven and earth, because you have hidden these things from the wise and the intelligent and have revealed them to infants; yes, Father, for such was your gracious will. All things have been handed over to me by my Father; and no one knows the Son except the Father, and no one knows the Father except the Son and anyone to whom the Son chooses to reveal the Father.

"Come to me, all you that are weary and are carrying heavy burdens, and I will give you rest. Take my yoke upon you, and learn from me; for I am gentle and humble in heart, and you will find rest for your souls. For my yoke is easy, and my burden is light."

REFLECTION

Many of us learned in school that God is omnipotent, eternal and never-changing. Contrast and paradox had no part in God, yet it is contrast and paradox that confront us in the readings today. The all-powerful God is triumphant and victorious in Zechariah's prophecy, just as we might expect. But God is also humble and comes riding on a donkey. No one who rides on a mere donkey can defeat the instruments of war—warhorses, chariots and battle bows wielded by soldiers. Yet God somehow does it, stretching the divine dominion from sea to sea.

Jesus came to proclaim release to prisoners, to free the oppressed, to redeem us from sin and to show us what it means to be children of God. Jesus is humble, but he also brings a yoke to replace the one he is removing. He reassures his followers that his yoke is easy and his burden is light, unlike the world's oppression. But even an easy yoke and a light burden are unexpected from the one who has said he will free us from the things that weigh us down. How are we to think of these contrasts? What do they tell us about this God in whom we believe?

First we learn that the power of God is so great that God does not need to rule the world by force—the instruments of war. What is weak in the world can be strong with God, and God's thoughts and visions are not the world's thoughts and visions. Secondly, the freedom that truly frees us does not mean abandoning our relationships so that we live for ourselves alone. Rather, freedom is the choice to do the will of God, to become a disciple of Jesus Christ, to be yoked to the Holy One so that we may become instruments through which God works in the world. If we accept these two ways of thinking about God, we too become paradoxes in a world that loves consistency and reason. What better way can we witness to a God of surprise?

■ A yoke both harnesses an animal and allows the animal to carry heavy burdens with ease. In what way do you experience Christian life as a yoke? What is the light burden that Jesus asks us to take on?

■ How does the image of a crucified God connect with that of the all-powerful God? What is your experience of that paradox?

PRACTICE OF FAITH

HIDDEN AND REVEALED. This Saturday we celebrate the memorial of Kateri Tekakwitha. Kateri was a member of the Mohawk nation who became a Christian. Because her family objected to her conversion, she left her home in what is now upstate New York and fled to Montréal. There she continued to do her beadwork and care for the children and the sick of her community.

Kateri Tekakwitha was beatified in 1980. She is the first Native American to be so recognized.

PRACTICE OF HOPE

PRISONERS OF HOPE. These words from Zechariah 9:12 are not the only paradoxical ones in today's readings. A humble king riding on a donkey; things hidden from the intelligent and revealed to infants; an easy yoke and a light burden: Such are the seeming contradictions of the Reign of God. It is just such paradoxes that Jesus uses to teach us the value of hope. Hope is nourished by the possibility of the impossible. Things that are certain are not the objects of hope. Hope is directed toward things that are future and uncertain.

We place all our hopes on a humble king, who promises rest for the weary and relief for the burdened. Not a bad paradox, that.

PRACTICE OF CHARITY

YOU WILL DIE. Paul reminds us that if we live according to the flesh we will die. Deaths from automobile accidents caused by drunk driving continue to haunt our country. The 1999 toll was 15,794. Some states have enacted stiff penalties for anyone caught with a blood alcohol level over .08%. What some people don't seem to be aware of is just how few drinks it takes to achieve that level. Even when state law requires someone charged with DUI to face a bench trial, often the judge is too lenient. Someone who has caused a fatal accident and has a record of previous violations can be given a sentence that involves taking a driver's education course and losing his or her driver's license for as little as 2 months. Urge your legislators to make sure that the laws on the books are carried out and that appropriate sentences are given. Of course, one other thing you can do is never drive when you've had one too many, and don't let an intoxicated friend drive either. Also support MADD, Mothers Against Drunk Driving, 511 E. John Carpenter Freeway, Suite 700, Irving TX 75062; 214-744-6233; www.madd.org.

WEEKDAY READINGS (Mo)Hosea 2:16, 17b–18, 21–22; (Tu) 8:4–7, 11–13; (We)10:1–3, 7–8, 12; (Th)11:1–4, 8c-9; (Fr)14:2–10; (Sa)Isaiah 6:1–8

READING I *Isaiah 55:10–13*

For as the rain and the snow come down
   from heaven,
and do not return there until they have watered
   the earth,
making it bring forth and sprout,
giving seed to the sower and bread to the eater,
so shall my word be that goes out from my mouth;
it shall not return to me empty,
but it shall accomplish that which I purpose,
and succeed in the thing for which I sent it.

For you shall go out in joy,
and be led back in peace;
the mountains and the hills before you
shall burst into song,
and all the trees of the field shall clap their hands.
Instead of the thorn shall come up the cypress;
instead of the brier shall come up the myrtle;
and it shall be to the LORD for a memorial,
for an everlasting sign that shall not be cut off.

READING II *Romans 8:18–23*

Revised Common Lectionary: Romans 8:1–11

I consider that the sufferings of this present time are not worth comparing with the glory about to be revealed to us. For the creation waits with eager longing for the revealing of the children of God; for the creation was subjected to futility, not of its own will but by the will of the one who subjected it, in hope that the creation itself will be set free from its bondage to decay and will obtain the freedom of the glory of the children of God. We know that the whole creation has been groaning in labor pains until now; and not only the creation, but we ourselves, who have the first fruits of the Spirit, groan inwardly while we wait for adoption, the redemption of our bodies.

GOSPEL *Matthew 13:1–9, 18–23*

That same day Jesus went out of the house and sat beside the sea. Such great crowds gathered around him that he got into a boat and sat there, while the whole crowd stood on the beach. And he told them many things in parables, saying: "Listen! A sower went out to sow. And in the sowing, some seeds fell on the path, and the birds came and ate them up. Other seeds fell on rocky ground, where they did not have much soil, and they sprang up quickly, since they had no depth of soil. But when the sun rose, they were scorched; and since they had no root, they withered away. Other seeds fell among thorns, and the thorns grew up and choked them. Other seeds fell on good soil and brought forth grain, some a hundredfold, some sixty, some thirty. Let anyone with ears listen!

"Hear then the parable of the sower. When anyone hears the word of the dominion of heaven and does not understand it, the evil one comes and snatches away what is sown in the heart; this is what was sown on the path. As for what was sown on rocky ground, this is the one who hears the word and immediately receives it with joy; yet such a person has no root, but endures only for a while, and when trouble or persecution arises on account of the word, that person immediately falls away. As for what was sown among thorns, this is the one who hears the word, but the cares of the world and the lure of wealth choke the word, and it yields nothing. But as for what was sown on good soil, this is the one who hears the word and understands it, who indeed bears fruit and yields, in one case a hundredfold, in another sixty, and in another thirty."

REFLECTION

One interpretation of the parable of the sower forces us to reflect on how we hear God's word. We ask questions about the preparation, nurture and care of the soil of our lives that allow the divine message to yield a fruitful harvest. In this interpretation, we are responsible for the abundance of the holy harvest that was begun when God spoke the first word of creation.

But what if we are the seed, sown by God with great and generous abandon into the world? Do we not then reflect on the way God works in and through our lives? Do we not wonder how fruitful we will be as we make our way? We watch for the temptations that can make us less than we were intended to be. We seek places where we can take root and nurture our seedling souls. We find people whose care, compassion and direction make our growth possible. We learn to trust in God, who gives rain in due season and warmth to tender shoots, and, finally, gives fullness of life. Here, we are responsible for our lives as gifts of God to be returned to God at season's end, wheat sprouted green in God's field and leaving the promise of future harvests.

Can we imagine ourselves as the sower, with the seed as the message of Jesus Christ and the soil as those who hear it? It is our task to scatter the seed far and wide so that it might take root in the unlikeliest of spots. It is not our job—and we might pay attention to this—to cultivate one small field so that the seeds may grow only there. Rather we allow every part of the earth the opportunity to grow the word of God. We become the image of the Divine Sower whose word was sent forth into the world to accomplish the purpose of the One who sent it.

Soil, seed, and sower—in the many facets of our lives, we are all of these. In each part of the story, we help to nurture and spread the word of God. We become the word of God.

■ **Of the three parts of this story, which do you feel most in touch with? With which image do you identify the church as a whole?**

■ **How do you go about sowing the word of God every day? What part does evangelization play in the life of a Catholic Christian?**

PRACTICE OF FAITH

HOW DOES YOUR GARDEN GROW? Today's scriptures present a mosaic of garden conditions: seeds and rain and sowers. Just as precipitation soaks the earth to promote green growth, God's word nurtures us. Yet we experience not just pristine, weed-free growth, for good and evil grow together. Paul describes this human reality in terms of the arduous, agonizing labor pains that all creation, including ourselves, experiences. Think about these earth images. How do they ground our faith?

PRACTICE OF HOPE

WHICH KIND OF SOIL AM I? Ever wonder, when you hear the parable of the sower, which kind of ground in you the seed is falling on? Are we weighted down and packed tight, like the footpath? Or are we hard of heart, like the rocky ground, suffering from "empathy burnout"? It is very easy to see ourselves as overwhelmed by worldly cares. It seems we hardly have time to think, so bombarded are we with constant media barrages urging us to consume more and more. But we *hope* we are like the good ground.

Trouble is, we never know for sure which one we are consistently. The truth is, we are all of these at various times, and our progress toward the Reign of God is propelled by the hope of doing better. Our hope is in God, the Sower of the Word in our hearts. God, like a good farmer, will help the seed along. Count on it.

PRACTICE OF CHARITY

I SPEAK IN PARABLES. In today's gospel reading, Jesus ends the parable with a detailed interpretation of what kind of person the different soils represent. Scripture scholars do not believe that this explanation was given by Jesus. That would take away from the purpose of a story. The beauty of any good story—and Jesus was an excellent storyteller—is that every reader will relate it to his or her personal experience to understand its meaning. The story gains in richness with each retelling as the reader sees it in a new, different light. A good story is one that can be told over and over without exhausting its meaning. Visit someone in a hospital or nursing home and share one of your favorite stories or books.

WEEKDAY READINGS (Mo)Isaiah 1:10−17; (Tu)7:1−9; (We)10:5−7, 13−16; (Th)26: 7−9, 12, 16−19; (Fr)38:1−6, 21−22, 7−8; (Sa)Micah 2:1−5

READING I *Wisdom 12:13, 16–19*

Revised Common Lectionary: Isaiah 44:6–8

There is no deity besides you,
    whose care is for all people,
to whom you should prove
    that you have not judged unjustly.

For your strength is the source of righteousness,
and your sovereignty over all
    causes you to spare all.
For you show your strength when people doubt
    the completeness of your power,
and you rebuke any insolence
    among those who know it.
Although you are sovereign in strength,
    you judge with mildness,
and with great forbearance you govern us;
for you have power to act whenever you choose.

Through such works you have taught your people
that the righteous must be kind,
and you have filled your children with good hope,
because you give repentance for sins.

READING II *Romans 8:12–14, 18–27*

So then, brothers and sisters, we are debtors, not to the flesh, to live according to the flesh—for if you live according to the flesh, you will die; but if by the Spirit you put to death the deeds of the body, you will live. For all who are led by the Spirit of God are children of God.

I consider that the sufferings of this present time are not worth comparing with the glory about to be revealed to us. For the creation waits with eager longing for the revealing of the children of God; for the creation was subjected to futility, not of its own will but by the will of the one who subjected it, in hope that the creation itself will be set free from its bondage to decay and will obtain the freedom of the glory of the children of God. We know that the whole creation has been groaning in labor pains until now; and not only the creation, but we ourselves, who have the first fruits of the Spirit, groan inwardly while we wait for adoption, the redemption of our bodies.

For in hope we were saved. Now hope that is seen is not hope. For who hopes for what is seen? But if we hope for what we do not see, we wait for it with patience.

Likewise the Spirit helps us in our weakness; for we do not know how to pray as we ought, but that very Spirit intercedes with sighs too deep for words. And God, who searches the heart, knows what is the mind of the Spirit, because the Spirit intercedes for the saints according to the will of God.

GOSPEL *Matthew 13:24–30*

Complete reading: Matthew 13:24–43

Jesus put before the crowds another parable: "The dominion of heaven may be compared to a man who sowed good seed in his field; but while everybody was asleep, an enemy came and sowed weeds among the wheat, and then went away. So when the plants came up and bore grain, then the weeds appeared as well. And the slaves of the householder came and said to him, 'Master, did you not sow good seed in your field? Where, then, did these weeds come from?' He answered, 'An enemy has done this.' The slaves said to him, 'Then do you want us to go and gather them?' But he replied, 'No; for in gathering the weeds you would uproot the wheat along with them. Let both of them grow together until the harvest; and at harvest time I will tell the reapers, Collect the weeds first and bind them in bundles to be burned, but gather the wheat into my barn.'"

Thursday, July 22, 2002

MARY MAGDALENE

Exodus 19:1–2, 9–11, 16–20 *On the third day the Lord will come.*

John 20:1–2, 11–18 *I have seen the Lord!*

This loving woman of the gospels was faithful to Jesus to his death and was the first messenger of his resurrection.

REFLECTION

"Listen!" Jesus' command at the end of the gospel makes the hearer acutely aware that something important has been said. After "Remember" and "Do not be afraid," the command to listen may be the most important in the scriptures. When we listen, we learn something of the way God sees the world. Jesus' and Matthew's concern grows out of the possible discouragement the disciples will face when confronted with evil in the world. It leads to an age-old question. "Why do the wicked prosper and the righteous suffer?" The psalmist often sang this despair when witnessing the situation in the world. The Wisdom writers commented on the seeming futility of working for good since both the wicked and the righteous would die. Jesus is not unaware that his followers live in a world that does not see as they do. The vision of a world filled with the justice and mercy of God is often counter to the way the world sees itself.

As the disciples live and work in this situation, Jesus offers them an insight into the mind of God. The world began in goodness. What was intended to be a bountiful harvest was threatened by the appearance of weeds among wheat. Yet God does not despair. God does not indiscriminately tear up the weeds, lest the wheat be torn away as well. The inborn goodness of the field and of the wheat, which is to say the world, is not spoiled simply because weeds exist in it. Rather, God's patient care allows wheat and weeds, good and bad, to grow up together. At the end, the weeds will be easily separated from the wheat. The wicked will be taken away and those who shine like the sun will be gathered to God. This vision of redemption and the coming justice of God is graceful hope to those who wait for the Lord.

■ **What are the situations of despair in today's world? What hope do we hold for those?**

■ **Is there anything we can do to confront evil in our time? Should we do nothing and wait for God?**

PRACTICE OF FAITH

THE GIFT OF REPENTANCE. Most of us think that repentance is something that we do. Yet this week's reading from the book of Wisdom suggests that God gives us repentance, and therefore we can have hope. This is a different way to appreciate this possibility for growth and change in our lives. Be mindful this week of where you harbor feelings of guilt, of resentment. Bring them before God in your prayer and ask for this gift.

PRACTICE OF HOPE

IN HOPE WE WERE SAVED. In today's second reading, the Revised Common Lectionary ends where the Roman Catholic lectionary begins. If we rejoin the fragments (Romans 8:24–27) we see the connection between the virtue of hope and our prayer in the Spirit of God. "Hope that is seen is not hope . . . if we hope for what we do not see, we wait for it with patience"(24–25). We wait and we pray, but we are not alone, even though we do not see where we are going. But "the Spirit comes to the aid of our weakness; for we do not know how to pray as we ought. . . . The Spirit . . . intercedes . . . and the one who searches hearts knows what is the intention of the Spirit."

Try to hold these two truths in your heart this week: we hope and pray, and the Spirit of God helps us. The Reign of God unfolds in ways we cannot see, while we wait in patient and joyful hope and, with the Spirit's help, pray for its fulfillment.

PRACTICE OF CHARITY

A CHRISTIAN LEADER. Monday, July 22, we honor Mary Magdalene, a saint who has been misunderstood and poorly represented for many years. Most of us grew up thinking of her as a prostitute on whom Jesus took pity. She has always been a symbol of the sinner who repents, is forgiven and leads a life of faith. But in recent years, there has been a strong movement to rediscover and honor the real Mary Magdalene. Nowhere in the scriptures is there an indication that she was a prostitute. In fact, there is considerable evidence that she was an important leader of the Christian community in Jerusalem.

WEEKDAY READINGS (Mo)Mary Magdalene, see box; (Tu)Micah 7:14–15, 18–20; (We)Jeremiah 1:1, 4–10; (Th)2 Corinthians 4:7–15; (Fr)Jeremiah 3:14–17; (Sa)7:1–11

READING I   *1 Kings 3:5–12*

At Gibeon the LORD appeared to Solomon in a dream by night; and God said, "Ask what I should give you." And Solomon said, "You have shown great and steadfast love to your servant my father David, because he walked before you in faithfulness, in righteousness, and in uprightness of heart toward you; and you have kept for him this great and steadfast love, and have given him a son to sit on his throne today. And now, O LORD my God, you have made your servant king in place of my father David, although I am only a little child; I do not know how to go out or come in. And your servant is in the midst of the people whom you have chosen, a great people, so numerous they cannot be numbered or counted. Give your servant therefore an understanding mind to govern your people, able to discern between good and evil; for who can govern this your great people?"

It pleased the LORD that Solomon had asked this. God said to him, "Because you have asked this, and have not asked for yourself long life or riches, or for the life of your enemies, but have asked for yourself understanding to discern what is right, I now do according to your word. Indeed I give you a wise and discerning mind; no one like you has been before you and no one like you shall arise after you."

READING II   *Romans 8:26–34*

The Spirit helps us in our weakness; for we do not know how to pray as we ought, but that very Spirit intercedes with sighs too deep for words. And God, who searches the heart, knows what is the mind of the Spirit, because the Spirit intercedes for the saints according to the will of God.

We know that all things work together for good for those who love God, who are called according to God's purpose. For those whom God foreknew God also predestined to be conformed to the image of the Son of God, in order that the Son might be the firstborn within a large family. And those whom God predestined God also called; and those whom God called God also justified; and those whom God justified God also glorified.

What then are we to say about these things? If God is for us, who is against us? The very Son of God was not withheld, but was given up for all of us; will God not along with the son also give us everything else? Who will bring any charge against God's elect? It is God who justifies. Who is to condemn? It is Christ Jesus, who died, yes, who was raised, who is at the right hand of God, who indeed intercedes for us.

GOSPEL   *Matthew 13:44–52*

Jesus told them another parable: "The dominion of heaven is like treasure hidden in a field, which a man found and hid; then in his joy he goes and sells all that he has and buys that field.

"Again, the dominion of heaven is like a merchant in search of fine pearls; on finding one pearl of great value, he went and sold all that he had and bought it.

"Again, the dominion of heaven is like a net that was thrown into the sea and caught fish of every kind; when it was full, they drew it ashore, sat down, and put the good into baskets but threw out the bad. So it will be at the end of the age. The angels will come out and separate the evil from the righteous and throw them into the furnace of fire, where there will be weeping and gnashing of teeth.

"Have you understood all this?" They answered, "Yes." And Jesus said to them, "Therefore every scribe who has been trained for the dominion of heaven is like a householder who brings out of the household treasure what is new and what is old."

REFLECTION

Jesus has been speaking in parables about the reign of God. By using what is familiar and ordinary, Jesus sparks his listeners' imagination and challenges them to break out of conventional ways of thinking about the reign of God.

The dominion of heaven is the treasure for which we search. When we find it, we are not content to have only that treasure, we also desire the field in which it was buried. For this field we would gladly sell everything.

The dominion of heaven is like a merchant who searches for the finest pearl. He, too, sells all that he has in order to possess this one gem. What is the pearl that is worth all that the merchant has?

The dominion is also like a net that gathers in every kind of fish. There is the possibility of finding some use for the fish—there is a last chance for redemption.

What do these mean? Parables are never exhausted by one interpretation, but we can make a start. These call to mind the commandment to love the Lord God with our whole heart, our whole soul. As the poet T.S. Eliot writes, it requires that "condition of complete simplicity, (Costing not less than everything)."

God's dominion is all-inclusive; it is the net that gathers in all the fish. In the end, God will gather us all up in a last moment of saving grace. Might this be worth selling everything we have? No doubt the dominion of God will surprise us!

■ **What do you think it means to "sell all that one has"?**

■ **Jesus gave his life for us "while we were yet sinners." What does that tell us about God? What does it tell us about us?**

PRACTICE OF FAITH

SOLD ALL THAT HE HAD. We've all heard the saying, "where your heart is, there your treasure lies." Is there anything for which you would sell everything you have? Probe your heart to see what you value most. And like Solomon, pray for the wisdom to discern what is good and what is evil, what serves life and what hinders it.

PRACTICE OF HOPE

THE REIGN OF GOD IS LIKE...Stories told around a campfire, each one revealing a small part of the great reality of life. In parables, Jesus reveals glimpses of the reign of God that enable us to intuit a greater picture. As each of us imagines the wonderful whole of which these stories are a part, our hope takes flight. Moreover, we begin to create that reign of God by our own appropriation of the stories. Each of us has a different view of the meaning of these parables, and when we begin to put them into practice, we discover even more ways to be God's people!

In communion with Christ and each other, we weave a rich tapestry of hope in the things to come, and it begins to come to life before our very eyes. The reign of God is like...

PRACTICE OF CHARITY

AN UNDERSTANDING HEART. King Solomon, famous for wisdom, comes to mind when impossible decisions must be made. In these times of rapid growth in medical technology, it is important to pray for compassion as well as wisdom. Not long ago, a couple in England was faced with deciding whether to allow one of their conjoined twin daughters to survive by separating her from her sister, who would inevitably die. The twins had lived for three months joined together at the abdomen. The Roman Catholic parents believed that their faith required them to let both girls live without surgery until God took them. The state, however, intervened and insisted that they be separated. The parents sadly acquiesced, the operation took place, and one of the daughters lived at the expense of her sister's life. What an awesome responsibility our capabilities inflict on us. We must pray for the wisdom of Solomon and the guidance of our loving and merciful God.

WEEKDAY READINGS (Mo)Jeremiah 13:1–11; (Tu)14:17–22; (We)15:10, 16–21; (Th)18:1–6; (Fr)26:1–9; 26:11–16, 24; (Sa)Jeremiah 26:11–16, 24

READING I *Isaiah 55:1–5*

Ho, everyone who thirsts, come to the waters;
and you that have no money, come, buy and eat!
Come, buy wine and milk
     without money and without price.
Why do you spend your money
     for that which is not bread,
and your labor for that which does not satisfy?
Listen carefully to me, and eat what is good,
and delight yourselves in rich food.

Incline your ear, and come to me;
listen, so that you may live.
I will make with you an everlasting covenant,
my steadfast, sure love for David.
See, I made him a witness to the peoples,
a leader and commander for the peoples.
See, you shall call nations that you do not know,
and nations that do not know you shall run to you,
because of the LORD your God,
     the Holy One of Israel,
for the LORD has glorified you.

READING II *Romans 8:35, 37–39*

Revised Common Lectionary: Romans 9:1–5

Who will separate us from the love of Christ? Will hardship, or distress, or persecution, or famine, or nakedness, or peril, or sword?

No, in all these things we are more than conquerors through the one who loved us. For I am convinced that neither death, nor life, nor angels, nor rulers, nor things present, nor things to come, nor powers, nor height, nor depth, nor anything else in all creation, will be able to separate us from the love of God in Christ Jesus our Lord.

GOSPEL *Matthew 14:13–21*

Now when Jesus heard about the beheading of John the Baptist, he withdrew from there in a boat to a deserted place by himself. But when the crowds heard it, they followed him on foot from the towns. When he went ashore, he saw a great crowd; and he had compassion for them and cured their sick.

When it was evening, the disciples came to Jesus and said, "This is a deserted place, and the hour is now late; send the crowds away so that they may go into the villages, and buy food for themselves." Jesus said to them, "They need not go away; you give them something to eat." They replied, "We have nothing here but five loaves and two fish." And he said, "Bring them here to me." Then he ordered the crowds to sit down on the grass. Taking the five loaves and the two fish, Jesus looked up to heaven, and blessed and broke the loaves, and gave them to the disciples, and the disciples gave them to the crowds. And all ate and were filled; and they took up what was left over of the broken pieces, twelve baskets full. And those who ate were about five thousand men, besides women and children.

Tuesday, August 6, 2002

THE TRANSFIGURATION OF THE LORD

Daniel 7:9–10, 13–14 *I saw the Man of Heaven on the clouds.*

2 Peter 1:16–19 *We are eyewitnesses to God's glory.*

Matthew 17:1–9 *How good it is to be here!*

At the peak of the glory of summer, the Lord shines on the holy mountain. With the law and the prophets, we gaze face to face on God. Yet which mountain is it—Calvary or Tabor? Perhaps they are one and the same.

REFLECTION

What does it mean to feed someone? It is to show care and nurture, to help a person grow, and even prevent that person from dying of hunger. To feed someone is to enter into his or her life at the fundamental point of need, and become intimate with what it means to be human and weak. Jesus' disciples must learn to embrace with compassion all who hunger.

Nowhere is this more apparent than in the feeding of the five thousand that Matthew tells briefly. The details stand out. Crowds follow Jesus to a deserted place. Some are sick. They do not ask for help, but Jesus' compassion spills forth into healing. They do not ask for food, but the disciples, perhaps aware of their own hunger, become more aware of the crowd's need to be fed. Jesus invites them to act on this, but they feel helpless.

Jesus uses this opportunity to show the disciples what their mission will be. He invites them to act in response to the need, the hunger, they see before them. With their tentative offering of a few loaves, they are empowered to feed a multitude. Their sharing of bread under Jesus' leadership also suggests the eucharist we share now and the heavenly banquet that is to come.

In the face of such a challenge, we, too, might do as the disciples did. We might look at our inadequacies, how little we have to offer, and fear that it will not be enough. But the gospel teaches that if we take what we have, offer it to God for a blessing, and then share it, we will have enough, even more than enough.

■ **What gift do you bring to your work as a Christian? How is that gift blessed, broken and shared with others?**

■ **Matthew does not count the women and the children, but Jesus and the disciples did and fed them until they were full. Who, in the world today, remains uncounted? How do we feed them until they are full?**

PRACTICE OF FAITH

THIS TUESDAY WE CELEBRATE THE FEAST OF THE TRANSFIGURATION. We also remember that nuclear weapons were first used in war on this date, August 6, 1945, on Hiroshima, Japan. When he visited Hiroshima Pope John Paul II said, "In the past it was possible to destroy a village, a town, a region, even a country. Now the whole planet has come under threat." Pray for peace, work for justice.

PRACTICE OF HOPE

THE EYES OF ALL LOOK HOPEFULLY TO YOU. These words from Psalm 145 express our stance toward God's great generosity and hospitality. Isaiah assures us of God's hospitality, and Jesus extends it to thousands of hungry people who have sought nourishing words, and are fed generously, body and soul. Our hope is justified, for God is compassionate to all (not just some, but all). Look to God and ask for what you need. As the psalmist says to God, "You open your hand and satisfy the desire of every living thing."

Turn to God with an expectant hopefulness. You will not be disappointed.

PRACTICE OF CHARITY

THE LOVE OF JESUS. Paul tells us that nothing can separate us from the love of God in Christ. This week we remember the atomic bombing of Hiroshima and Nagasaki 57 years ago. If you are concerned about the continued growth in defense spending, support the Center for Defense Information. This organization has several experienced military men on its staff and board. The fact that these people, who know the importance of a strong military, believe that our defense budget is unjustifiably large might cause us to question how our national revenue is used. To find out more, contact the Center for Defense Information, 1779 Massachusetts Avenue NW, Washington DC 20036; 202-332-0600.

WEEKDAY READINGS (Mo)Jeremiah 28:1–17; (Tu) Transfiguration, see box; (We)Jeremiah 31:1–7; (Th)31:31–34; (Fr)Nahum 2:1, 3; 3:1–3, 6–7; (Sa)2 Corinthians 9:6–10

READING I   *1 Kings 19:9,11–13*

Elijah came to a cave, and lodged there. And the LORD said, "Go forth, and stand upon the mount before the LORD." And behold, the LORD passed by, and a great and strong wind rent the mountains, and broke in pieces the rocks before the LORD, but the LORD was not in the wind; and after the wind an earthquake, but the LORD was not in the earthquake; and after the earthquake a fire, but the LORD was not in the fire; after the fire a still small voice. And when Elijah heard it, he wrapped his face in his mantle and went out and stood at the entrance of the cave.

READING II   *Romans 9:1–5*

Revised Common Lectionary: Romans 10:5–15

I am speaking the truth in Christ, I am not lying; my conscience bears me witness in the Holy Spirit, that I have great sorrow and unceasing anguish in my heart. For I could wish that I myself were accursed and cut off from Christ for the sake of my people, my kin by race. They are Israelites, and to them belong the adoption, the glory, the covenants, the giving of the law, the worship, and the promises; to them belong the patriarchs, and of their race, according to the flesh, comes the Messiah, who is over all, God be blessed forever. Amen.

GOSPEL   *Matthew 14:22–33*

Jesus made the disciples get into the boat and go before him to the other side, while he dismissed the crowds. And having dismissed the crowds, Jesus went up on the mountain by himself to pray. When evening came, he was there alone, but the boat by this time was many furlongs distant from the land, beaten by the waves; for the wind was against them. And in the fourth watch of the night Jesus came to them, walking on the sea. But when the disciples saw Jesus walking o the sea, they were terrified, saying, "It is a ghost!" And they cried out for fear. But immediately Jesus spoke to them, saying, "Take heart, it is I; have no fear."

And Peter answered Jesus, "Lord, if it is you, bid me come to you on the water." Jesus said, "Come." So Peter got out of the boat and walked on the water and came to Jesus; but when he saw the wind, he was afraid, and beginning to sink he cried out, "Lord, save me." Jesus immediately reached out his hand and caught him, saying to him, "O you of little faith, why did you doubt?" And when they got into the boat, the wind ceased. And those in the boat worshipped Jesus, saying, "Truly you are the Son of God."

Thursday, August 15, 2002

THE ASSUMPTION OF MARY INTO HEAVEN

VIGIL

1 Chronicles 15:3–4, 15–16; 16:1–2 *David before the ark.*
1 Corinthians 15:54–57 *God gave us victory over death.*
Luke 11:27–28 *Blessed is the womb that bore you!*

DAY

Revelation 11:19; 12:1–6, 10 *A woman clothed in the sun.*
1 Corinthians 15:20–26 *Christ is the firstfruits of the dead.*
Luke 1:39–56 *He has raised the lowly to the heights.*

Now we keep the festival of Mary's passover. In time, each one of us will be gathered into the reign of God, shining like the sun with the moon at our feet.

REFLECTION

There is something of Elijah in all of us—we hide in a cave while the most awesome displays take place and we still hide when we realize that God is so powerful he controls even the silence. We hide when the voice of God is drowned out in the winds of violence and hatred, the fires of racism and ethnic cleansing, or the storms that shake our individual lives—death and illness and poverty. But God will not be pushed away. We are called to stand boldly in the face of the world's power and believe that God is the One before whom everything else falls silent.

Jesus, too, had to leave his mountaintop and enter the heart of what frightened the apostles so badly. He walked on water. For the Jews, Sheol, the realm of the dead, was under the earth. No wonder the disciples thought Jesus was a ghost. Yet his calm and insistent voice gave Peter the courage to step out of the only security he knew—a tiny boat—and begin to walk. As long as his focus was on Jesus, Peter didn't falter. It was only when he was distracted that Peter slipped beneath the waves, sure that the hand of death had reached up to grasp him. He was sure until that other strong hand pulled him to safety. When Peter recovered enough to notice, the wind and sea were calm—the power of God in Jesus so great that even the most powerful of storms became nothing in the face of it.

The most profound question we can ask is: Who is this that would come through a life-threatening storm to find us? Who would step on the threshold of death itself to be with his friends? God does this for each and every one of us to show that real power lies not in the things that destroy, but in love that challenges death and brings new life.

Like Elijah, Peter and even Jesus, we must leave our safe places, believing that God's love can still every fear. If we do not leave cave or boat, we cannot give witness to God who left heaven to become one of us, sharing storms and quiet.

■ **The still, small voice of God (better translated as the sound of sheer silence) can be overwhelming in its power. Where do you find time to be silent and listen for God? Where does the church invite silence in its liturgy? Why?**

PRACTICE OF FAITH

WITHOUT SAYING. After church one Sunday when these readings had been proclaimed, my nephew asked, "Why did Elijah go to the cave and spend the night there?" His question reminds us that the scripture passages before and after the excerpts chosen for the lectionary are very important. Elijah had run for his life. Could hiding in the cave suggest that Elijah was fleeing God? The tumult outside the cave may have frightened him more, until he heard the "sound of sheer silence." Be still and silent for a time each day.

PRACTICE OF HOPE

"WHY DID YOU DOUBT?" In today's gospel, Jesus resumes his solitude on the mountain after the death of John the Baptist. He had gone there to pray, but his prayer is interrupted by thousands of people who sought his wisdom and compassion. After he responds to their needs, Jesus resumes his search for silent communion with God.

Strengthened by that prayer, Jesus once again reaches out, this time to sustain a doubting Peter. Peter wants to believe. But strong winds and weak faith take their toll and he sinks. The powerful image of Jesus' outstretched arm saving Peter from the water can sustain us when we are troubled and in turmoil.

PRACTICE OF CHARITY

LORD, SAVE ME. The modern plague of HIV/AIDS continues to affect millions of our brothers and sisters around the world. The countries hardest hit are also among the poorest. The medications used to treat the symptoms of the disease are too expensive for wide distribution in Third World countries, even at the reduced prices offered by pharmaceutical firms. You can lobby your legislators to increase the budget of the World Health Organization. You can also contact a local HIV/AIDS program and offer your help to its work.

WEEKDAY READINGS (Mo–We, Fr–Sa)Ezekiel, chapters 1, 2, 9, 16, 18; (Th)Assumption of Mary, see box.

READING I *Isaiah 56:1, 6–8*

Thus says the LORD:
Maintain justice, and do what is right,
for soon my salvation will come,
and my deliverance be revealed.

And the foreigners who join themselves to the LORD,
to minister to the LORD,
    to love the name of the LORD,
and to be the LORD's servants,
all who keep the sabbath, and do not profane it,
and hold fast my covenant—
these I will bring to my holy mountain,
and make them joyful in my house of prayer;
their burnt offerings and their sacrifices
    will be accepted on my altar;
for my house shall be called a house of prayer
    for all peoples.
Thus says the Lord GOD,
who gathers the outcasts of Israel,
I will gather others to them
besides those already gathered.

READING II *Romans 11:1–2, 29–32*

Paul writes: I ask, then, has God rejected the chosen people? By no means! I myself am an Israelite, a descendant of Abraham, a member of the tribe of Benjamin. God has not rejected the people whom ages ago God chose.

For the gifts and the calling of God are irrevocable. Just as you were once disobedient to God but have now received mercy because of their disobedience, so they have now been disobedient in order that, by the mercy shown to you, they too may now receive mercy. For God has imprisoned all in disobedience in order to be merciful to all.

GOSPEL *Matthew 15:10–28*

Jesus called the crowd to him and said to them, "Listen and understand: it is not what goes into the mouth that defiles a person, but it is what comes out of the mouth that defiles." Then the disciples approached and said to him, "Do you know that the Pharisees took offense when they heard what you said?" Jesus answered, "Every plant that my heavenly Father has not planted will be uprooted. Let them alone; they are blind guides of the blind. And if one blind person guides another, both will fall into a pit." But Peter said to him, "Explain this parable to us." Then Jesus said, "Are you also still without understanding? Do you not see that whatever goes into the mouth enters the stomach, and goes out into the sewer? But what comes out of the mouth proceeds from the heart, and this is what defiles. For out of the heart come evil intentions, murder, adultery, fornication, theft, false witness, slander. These are what defile a person, but to eat with unwashed hands does not defile."

Jesus left that place and went away to the district of Tyre and Sidon. Just then a Canaanite woman from that region came out and started shouting, "Have mercy on me, Lord, Son of David; my daughter is tormented by a demon." But he did not answer her at all. And his disciples came and urged him, saying, "Send her away, for she keeps shouting after us." Jesus answered, "I was sent only to the lost sheep of the house of Israel." But she came and knelt before him, saying, "Lord, help me." Jesus answered, "It is not fair to take the children's food and throw it to the dogs." She said, "Yes, Lord, yet even the dogs eat the crumbs that fall from their masters' table." Then Jesus answered her, "Woman, great is your faith! Let it be done for you as you wish." And her daughter was healed instantly.

REFLECTION

In several prophecies of Israel, God welcomes foreign nations and people who "love the name of the Lord" to gather in the heavenly city or at the holy banquet. At a time when Israel was trying to understand its place among other nations and the extent to which God could love others when God had "chosen" Israel, the problem of foreigners was a struggle. Prophets like Isaiah and Jonah showed God's care for all of creation and every people, even though God had chosen one in particular.

Out of this background of questions and reflections, the Canaanite woman approaches Jesus in prayer and supplication. Her concern for her possessed daughter motivates her to try even this Jew whose reputation for casting out demons is well known. She does not profess faith in the God of Israel, but she believes that Jesus can help her if he wishes to do so. The disciples, caught up in their own questions about the worthiness of foreigners, urge Jesus to send her away. It seems odd that Jesus says nothing at first and then seems to echo the sentiments of the disciples: "I was sent only to the lost sheep of Israel." His words seem strangely out of place for one whose life was spent reaching out to the outcast from society. They seem strange until we realize that he is saying them for the benefit of the disciples and everything in us that is like them. In our zeal to make God our personal property, we would send the outcast away; we would claim God as our own; we, too, would consider others as less than human and unworthy. The woman seizes the opportunity to show her faith once, twice, three times in the face of silence, adversity, insult.

Her courage and belief in Jesus keep her insistent in her prayer and sure that even his smallest attention will effect the cure she seeks. The woman is not interested in keeping the divine miracle for herself; she does not need to own God. Out of that ability to let go, she is able to show the disciples that true faith consists in trusting that God will find a way to share grace no matter whose table one sits at or under. She also reminds us that even the smallest crumb contains the whole of God's presence and mercy.

■ **Many people are comfortable with helping the outcasts of our society as long as it isn't done too close to home, a phemonenon known as NIMBY, for "not in my back yard." What can churches do to counteract this feeling?**

PRACTICE OF FAITH

RIPPLE EFFECT. Jesus said he came for "the lost tribes of Israel," but his message cannot be contained or limited. Jesus' embrace of the stranger, the outcast, the victim has transformed the way we view the "other." We can no longer define ourselves as better than anyone else because of our religion, race or status. What does it mean when we say "We believe in one holy catholic and apostolic church?"

PRACTICE OF HOPE

CRUMBS THAT FALL. My dog used to sit near the table during meals, every nerve attentive for a dropped morsel. Once, when a hotdog slipped from someone's bun, it never made it to the floor! He caught it in midair! That is the kind of attentiveness to the word of God that we need to have.

The hope that springs from the promises of God is for all, not just for those who are the chosen few. In Jesus, God extends salvation to everyone, even those who cannot keep the laws of the First Testament. Jesus puts back into perspective the real reason for all the ritual laws: holiness. It is what comes from the heart that makes a person clean or unclean, not what he or she eats. Holiness is attentively waiting for the Word of Life, and eagerly catching it when it comes.

PRACTICE OF CHARITY

KEEP THE SABBATH. In our secular culture, it can be difficult to observe religious precepts that everyone followed in years gone by. It is especially difficult to convince our children that Sunday should be set aside as somehow different from the rest of the week. From Monday through Friday they are busy with school, and weekends are for getting together with friends. But perhaps you can make an effort to spend time together as a family on Sunday, doing something special that all of you enjoy. The Jewish religion views the Sabbath as a *gift* from the Lord, a day when we are invited to stop our work and enjoy all the riches of creation. Why not discuss the idea of Sabbath with your family to see what is the best way for you to observe this day of the Lord.

WEEKDAY READINGS (Mo)Ezekiel 24:15–24; (Tu)28:1–10; (We)34:1–11; (Th)36:23–28; (Fr)37:1–14; (Sa)Revelation 21:9b–14

READING I *Isaiah 22:19–23*

Revised Common Lectionary: Isaiah 51:1–6

I will thrust you from your office, and you will be pulled down from your post. On that day I will call my servant Eliakim son of Hilkiah, and will clothe him with your robe and bind your sash on him. I will commit your authority to his hand, and he shall be a father to the inhabitants of Jerusalem and to the house of Judah. I will place on his shoulder the key of the house of David; he shall open, and no one shall shut; he shall shut, and no one shall open. I will fasten him like a peg in a secure place, and he will become a throne of honor to his ancestral house.

READING II *Romans 11:33–36; 12:1–8*

O the depth of the riches and wisdom and knowledge of God! How unsearchable are his judgments and how inscrutable his ways!

"For who has known the mind of the Lord?
Or who has been his counselor?
Or who has given a gift to him,
to receive a gift in return?"

For from him and through him and to him are all things. To him be the glory forever. Amen.

I appeal to you therefore, brothers and sisters, by the mercies of God, to present your bodies as a living sacrifice, holy and acceptable to God, which is your spiritual worship. Do not be conformed to this world, but be transformed by the renewing of your minds, so that you may discern what is the will of God—what is good and acceptable and perfect.

For by the grace given to me I say to everyone among you not to think of yourself more highly than you ought to think, but to think with sober judgment, each according to the measure of faith that God has assigned. For as in one body we have many parts, and not all the parts have the same function, so we, who are many, are one body in Christ, and individually we are parts one of another. We have gifts that differ according to the grace given to us: prophecy, in proportion to faith; ministry, in ministering; the teacher, in teaching; the exhorter, in exhortation; the giver, in generosity; the leader, in diligence; the compassionate, in cheerfulness.

GOSPEL *Matthew 16:13–20*

Now when Jesus came into the district of Caesarea Philippi, he asked his disciples, "Who do people say that the Son-of-Man is?" And they said, "Some say John the Baptist, but others Elijah, and still others Jeremiah or one of the prophets." Jesus said to them, "But who do you say that I am?" Simon Peter answered, "You are the Messiah, the Son of the living God."

And Jesus answered him, "Blessed are you, Simon son of Jonah! For flesh and blood has not revealed this to you, but my Father in heaven. And I tell you, you are Peter, and on this rock I will build my church, and the gates of Hades will not prevail against it. I will give you the keys of the dominion of heaven, and whatever you bind on earth will be bound in heaven, and whatever you loose on earth will be loosed in heaven." Then Jesus sternly ordered the disciples not to tell anyone that he was the Messiah.

REFLECTION

Peter and the disciples who follow Jesus do not often understand what Jesus is about. Today we are privileged to hear one of the few times they did. When Jesus asks them, "Who do you say I am," Peter answers from his heart. "You are the Messiah, the Son of the living God." Had he been able to see what was coming, who knows what he might have said? But the moment he opened himself to speak the truth about Jesus, he opened the door for Jesus to speak the truth about him. When Peter "gets it," he is, in a fundamental way, gotten as well. His name is changed; his job is changed; his life is changed. "You are Peter, and on this Rock I will build my church . . ." From that point, Peter takes up the work he is called to do.

So often we see this as a story about Peter rather than about us. But we are asked who Jesus is in every phase of our lives. Our greatest temptation is to answer: "John the Baptizer or Elijah, or Jeremiah, or one of the prophets," or maybe not to answer at all, because then we don't have to risk being named, being changed, becoming someone on whom a church is built.

Witnessing to God's presence in the world and building up the community of faith begins with searching our hearts and naming Jesus for who he is in our lives and in the life of the world. To answer with what we know to be the truth requires us to open the deepest part of ourselves, even if only for a moment, and become vulnerable to the grace of God. We, too, might suddenly find ourselves called and challenged to be rocks and role models for those who travel with us and come after us.

It is risky, because ultimately it is life-transforming. But we might keep Peter in mind on our journey. He continued to follow Jesus even when human reason might have told him to stop. Because, for one critical moment, he opened himself to the truth and was forever changed.

■ **Peter's confession, as this story is called, comes roughly in the middle of Matthew's gospel. It is a turning point. After this, events begin to move quickly toward the crucifixion. How has your faith in the Messiah changed your life?**

PRACTICE OF FAITH

CONVERSION. This week we celebrate the feasts of Saint Monica and her son, Augustine. Like many parents, Monica watched her brilliant child waste his talents, living a dissolute life. Unable to persuade him to change his ways, she entrusted him to God in her prayer. Eventually Augustine met Ambrose, the bishop of Milan, who guided him to conversion of heart. Read the compelling story of Augustine's struggles in his *Confessions*.

PRACTICE OF HOPE

ROCK, PAPER, SCISSORS. Remember that old children's game that is used to make choices? Rock wins over scissors, because rock breaks scissors. Scissors wins over paper, because scissors cut paper. Paper wins over rock, because paper covers rock. It's a sort of checks-and-balances system. Jesus, after receiving Peter's profession of faith, gives us another method for guiding the community called the church. Peter ("Rock") and later the other apostles (Matthew 18:18) will have authority to guide the church in its journey to God.

The hope and trust of the people of God rests in Christ's entrusting this important task to Peter and his successors. Pray for our shepherds, that their faith may be as strong as Peter's and that they will be as attentive to the voice of God as Peter was.

PRACTICE OF CHARITY

YOU ARE THE CHRIST. Over the centuries, this belief has been proclaimed all over the world. It is stated most clearly by the lives of Christians who live the teachings of Jesus. The Jesuit Volunteer Corp (JVC) is a program that was begun in the '50s when young adults were sent to Alaska for a year or two years to help in the missions there. From there it has spread across the United States and to some foreign countries. The four principles around which the program is structured are: community, spirituality, simple living, and social justice. Volunteers are assigned to work as teachers, parish workers, social workers; they help in soup kitchens and homeless shelters as well as in legal service clinics. These young people usually finish their volunteer service saying that they received much more than they gave. One of the special riches that JVC workers receive is lifelong friendships with people who believe with them that Jesus is the Christ, the Son of the living God. To learn more, visit their website at www.JesuitVolunteers.org.

WEEKDAY READINGS (Mo)2 Thessalonians 1:1–5, 11b–12; (Tu)2:1–3a, 14–17; (We)3:6–10, 16–18; (Th)1 Corinthians 1:1–9; (Fr)1:17–25; (Sa)1:26–31

READING I *Jeremiah 20:7–9*

Revised Common Lectionary: Jeremiah 15:15–21

O LORD, you have enticed me, and I was enticed;
you were too powerful for me,
   and you have prevailed.
I have become a laughingstock all day long;
everyone mocks me.
For whenever I speak, I must cry out,
I must shout, "Violence and destruction!"
For the word of the LORD has become for me
a reproach and derision all day long.
If I say, "I will not mention the LORD,
   or speak any more in the name of the LORD,"
then within me there is something like a burning fire
   shut up in my bones;
I am weary with holding it in, and I cannot.

READING II *Romans 12:1–2, 9–21*

I appeal to you therefore, brothers and sisters, by the mercies of God, to present your bodies as a living sacrifice, holy and acceptable to God, which is your spiritual worship. Do not be conformed to this world, but be transformed by the renewing of your minds, so that you may discern what is the will of God—what is good and acceptable and perfect.

Let love be genuine; hate what is evil, hold fast to what is good; love one another with mutual affection; outdo one another in showing honor. Do not lag in zeal, be ardent in spirit, serve the Lord. Rejoice in hope, be patient in suffering, persevere in prayer. Contribute to the needs of the saints; extend hospitality to strangers.

Bless those who persecute you; bless and do not curse them. Rejoice with those who rejoice, weep with those who weep. Live in harmony with one another; do not be haughty, but associate with the lowly; do not claim to be wiser than you are. Do not repay anyone evil for evil, but take thought for what is noble in the sight of all. If it is possible, so far as it depends on you, live peaceably with all.

Beloved, never avenge yourselves, but leave room for the wrath of God; for it is written, "Vengeance is mine, I will repay, says the Lord." No, "if your enemies are hungry, feed them; if they are thirsty, give them something to drink; for by doing this you will heap burning coals on their heads." Do not be overcome by evil, but overcome evil with good.

GOSPEL *Matthew 16:21–28*

From that time on, Jesus began to show his disciples that he must go to Jerusalem and undergo great suffering at the hands of the elders and chief priests and scribes, and be killed, and on the third day be raised. And Peter took Jesus aside and began to rebuke him, saying, "God forbid it, Lord! This must never happen to you." But he turned and said to Peter, "Get behind me, Satan! You are a stumbling block to me; for you are setting your mind not on divine things but on human things."

Then Jesus told his disciples, "If any want to become my followers, let them deny themselves and take up their cross and follow me. For those who want to save their life will lose it, and those who lose their life for my sake will find it. For what will it profit them if they gain the whole world but forfeit their life? Or what will they give in return for their life?

"For the Son-of-Man is to come with his angels in the glory of his Father, and then he will repay everyone for what has been done. Truly I tell you, there are some standing here who will not taste death before they see the Son-of-Man coming in his dominion."

REFLECTION

How can Peter be so insightful one moment and so dense the next? In his heart, he knows that Jesus is the Messiah. Yet he seems unable to remember and accept it. In frustration and anger, perhaps in sorrow, Jesus calls him by a different name—not Peter, but Satan. He is not the rock, but the tempter (the Hebrew word means accuser or the one who opposes, like a prosecuting attorney). In one name, Jesus shows us what temptation truly is—the human mind set on human things.

According to human hopes and dreams, the messiah of Israel was supposed to be victorious in battle, courageous in war, a liberator and savior for all time. The messiah was supposed to usher in the era of God's justice and peace. It was inconceivable that the messiah would be betrayed, would suffer and die. The very idea was unspeakable. And so Peter rebukes Jesus, tempting him to renounce what he had come to do, which is not rooted in human plans but in God's plan.

From a human perspective, Peter might have succeeded. But with divine imagination, Jesus takes the lead again, challenging Peter and all the disciples to get behind him, to get out of his way. The modern meaning of "to get behind" someone is to show support, but we can find a richer meaning. To follow behind Jesus is to believe that victory comes only in carrying the burden of love for one another and a passion for the things of God. To follow Jesus is to accept that God's Messiah does not live by the world's expectations, but takes up the suffering of creation and transforms it by laying down his life.

Jesus asks a haunting and insistent question: "What will it profit them if they gain the whole world but forfeit their life?" The world seems dedicated to acquiring more things at a faster pace, indulging self-desire and self-interest, chasing that shiny image of success and victory. Jesus challenges us with a different understanding that involves self-denial and a clear focus on the model of servanthood and selfless love represented by a cross.

■ **How do we try to find the path of least resistance and avoid taking up our crosses?**

■ **Have you, like Jeremiah, felt deceived by God? How did you achieve reconciliation with God?**

PRACTICE OF FAITH

NEW, CONTINUED. Today's gospel continues last Sunday's. Peter sees Jesus as the Messiah, and to him this means victory. Peter cannot fathom suffering or destruction as part of the Messiah's mission. Aware that he is God's Messiah and not Peter's, Jesus this time dubs Peter Satan.

It is tempting to doubt God when we experience suffering. The question of why God permits suffering challenges every age. How do you understand suffering in your life as a Christian?

PRACTICE OF HOPE

HOW DO YOU SPELL PROPHET/PROFIT? Jeremiah did some serious wrestling with God over proclaiming the word. He was a lonely and reluctant prophet, and no wonder! No one wants to hear bad news, and Jeremiah's message was full of exactly what they didn't want to hear. But God strengthened him and filled his mouth with God's word, and Jeremiah proclaimed it. Peter has the same struggle with the difficulties of suffering for God's Word. Jesus calls him a "Satan," which is pretty harsh. Where is the hope in this?

The hope is in the vision of the Reign of God; it's in the long view. If we only look at the short term, the "profits" are lousy. But if we look at the long term, God's time, the "prophets" are good. The message is filled with hope. God is in charge, and no matter how bleak things look, God will bring all things to fulfillment. Do you want in?

PRACTICE OF CHARITY

JUSTICE FOR JANITORS. Have you heard of two-parent families where both husband and wife work full-time, yet their combined income doesn't bring the family above the poverty level? There are millions. Many are these hardworking people are temporary workers who put in 40 hours a week but do not receive the benefits that go with full-time jobs. To understand their situation, contact the Service Employees International Union (SEIU), which has conducted a nationwide campaign called Justice for Janitors. They can arrange for a speaker to explain to parishioners why the union movement has been supported by religious leaders, and why it is still needed in our country. See their website: www.seiu.org.

WEEKDAY READINGS (Mo)1 Corinthians 2:1–5; (Tu)2:10b–16; (We)3:1–9; (Th)3:18–23; (Fr)4:1–5; (Sa)4:6b–15

READING I *Ezekiel 33:7–11*

So you, mortal, I have made a sentinel for the house of Israel; whenever you hear a word from my mouth, you shall give them warning from me. If I say to the wicked, "O wicked ones, you shall surely die," and you do not speak to warn the wicked to turn from their ways, the wicked shall die in their iniquity, but their blood I will require at your hand. But if you warn the wicked to turn from their ways, and they do not turn from their ways, the wicked shall die in their iniquity, but you will have saved your life.

Now you, mortal, say to the house of Israel, Thus you have said: "Our transgressions and our sins weigh upon us, and we waste away because of them; how then can we live?" Say to them, As I live, says the Lord GOD, I have no pleasure in the death of the wicked, but that the wicked turn from their ways and live; turn back, turn back from your evil ways; for why will you die, O house of Israel?

READING II *Romans 13:8–14*

Owe no one anything, except to love one another; for the one who loves another has fulfilled the law. The commandments, "You shall not commit adultery; You shall not murder; You shall not steal; You shall not covet"; and any other commandment, are summed up in this word, "Love your neighbor as yourself." Love does no wrong to a neighbor; therefore, love is the fulfilling of the law.

Besides this, you know what time it is, how it is now the moment for you to wake from sleep. For salvation is nearer to us now than when we became believers; the night is far gone, the day is near. Let us then lay aside the works of darkness and put on the armor of light; let us live honorably as in the day, not in reveling and drunkenness, not in debauchery and licentiousness, not in quarreling and jealousy. Instead, put on the Lord Jesus Christ, and make no provision for the flesh, to gratify its desires.

GOSPEL *Matthew 18:15–20*

Jesus said: "If another member of the church sins against you, go and point out the fault when the two of you are alone. If the member listens to you, you have regained that one. But if you are not listened to, take one or two others along with you, so that every word may be confirmed by the evidence of two or three witnesses. If the member refuses to listen to them, tell it to the church; and if the offender refuses to listen even to the church, let such a one be to you as a Gentile and a tax collector.

"Truly I tell you, whatever you bind on earth will be bound in heaven, and whatever you loose on earth will be loosed in heaven. Again, truly I tell you, if two of you agree on earth about anything you ask, it will be done for you by my Father in heaven.

"For where two or three are gathered in my name, I am there among them."

Saturday, September 14, 2002

HOLY CROSS

Numbers 21:4–9 *Whoever gazed on the serpent received life.*

Philippians 2:6–11 *He accepted death on a cross.*

John 3:13–17 *God so loved the world . . .*

As the darkness of another autumn lowers around us, we lift high the shining cross. The means of the execution of a criminal has become the means of entering into eternal life. The wood of the cross is the ark that rescues us and the tree that feeds us.

REFLECTION

How can Paul speak of love of neighbor and Matthew speak of banishing someone from the Christian community? Doesn't the law of love override the judgment of wrongdoing?

We must remember that both speak to a newborn church struggling with what it means to live as Jesus did and trying to put his words into practice. Jesus preached love of neighbor as one of the greatest of the commandments. For Paul, who wrote a few years before Matthew, love is foundational for Christian relationship. Someone who starts with a sense of love will never do wrong to a neighbor or to God. By the time Matthew wrote his gospel, community and the gathering of Christians for prayer and companionship had become crucially important. The great commandments, "love God" and "love your neighbor," still guided the lives of the early Christians, but they also needed to develop ways of living in community.

Matthew envisions what love tempered with justice and discipline can look like in a community of faith. Such compassion demands that members be given every opportunity to change their ways before being shunned as outsiders—Gentiles or tax collectors could not be part of the church at first. Yet such judgment carries awesome responsibility and cannot be taken lightly. Whatever is bound on earth is bound in heaven. The temptation to abuse that power must be compelling at times. The disciples had to remember that Jesus reached out to sinners, tax collectors and outsiders throughout his entire life. Following in his footsteps, with love as both ground and guide, the members of the early church were compelled to preach the gospel even—and maybe especially—to those they shunned, and invite them to know Christ. The love of God compels us to do no less.

■ **Many people believe that the God of the Old Testament is judging and the God of the New Testament is merciful. In reality, both parts of our Bible present both images. Why is it important to consider both as facets of God?**

PRACTICE OF FAITH

COMMUNICATION. We owe no one anything except to love one another. Commandments and church social teachings advise us how to fulfill our debt of love; they do not fulfill it for us. Genuine love is not silent. Its dynamics are interpersonal and social. Jesus knew that to love one another would entail conflicts. Conflicts do not themselves mean division. When we are not in the throes of one, we know they can lead to understanding and union. Jesus is not absent when we are in conflict; he is there among us as he promised.

PRACTICE OF HOPE

I AM THERE. At a time when there is so much contention and division in society and even in our churches, some of the most comforting and hopeful words appear in today's gospel. Here we have a method for helping each other grow closer to God, and for properly and lovingly correcting each other. Even at that, sometimes efforts fail and separation ensues. It is good to know that even two or three people, when gathered in faith and in hope, can count on the presence of the Lord in their midst.

Gather a few friends this week to pray for the needs of the church, the world and the community. And don't be afraid to ask for what you yourself need. As we hold each other lovingly in prayer, God is with us, and hears our prayer.

PRACTICE OF CHARITY

YOU SHALL LOVE YOUR NEIGHBOR. In urban and suburban areas, fewer and fewer people really know their neighbors. With more people working longer hours, time at home is scarce and usually devoted to household tasks, family doings or just "vegging out." Loneliness is a burden for older people whose families do not live close to them, for young mothers at home with their little ones, and for retired people with too much time on their hands. This week, think of one way you can reach out to a neighbor—someone on your block or in your parish. If you know of someone who is sick, bringing a pot of soup over might be welcome. There are young parents who would appreciate an offer of baby-sitting so they can have an evening to themselves. Be creative about how you can create community around you.

WEEKDAY READINGS (Mo)1 Corinthians 5:1–8; (Tu)6:1–11; (We)7:25–31; (Th)8:1b–7, 11–13; (Fr)9:16–19, 22b–27; (Sa)Holy Cross, see box.

READING I *Sirach 28:3–7*

Revised Common Lectionary: Genesis 50:15–21

Does anyone harbor anger against another,
    and expect healing from the Lord?
If one has no mercy toward another like himself,
    can he then seek pardon for his own sins?
If a mere mortal harbors wrath,
who will make an atoning for sacrifice for his sins?
Remember the end of your life, and set enmity aside;
remember corruption and death,
    and be true to the commandments.
Remember the commandments,
    and do not be angry with your neighbor;
remember the covenant of the Most High,
    and overlook faults.

READING II *Romans 14:1–12*

Roman Catholic: Romans 14:7–9

Welcome those who are weak in faith, but not for the purpose of quarreling over opinions. Some believe in eating anything, while the weak eat only vegetables. Those who eat must not despise those who abstain, and those who abstain must not pass judgment on those who eat; for God has welcomed them. Who are you to pass judgment on servants of another? It is before thir own lord that they stand or fall. And they will be upheld, for the Lord is able to make them stand.

Some judge one day to be better than another, while others judge all days to be alike. Let all be fully convinced in their own minds. Those who observe the day, observe it in honor of the Lord. Also, those who eat, eat in honor of the Lord, since they give thanks to God; while those who abstain, abstain in honor of the Lord and give thanks to God.

We do not live to ourselves, and we do not die to ourselves. If we live, we live to the Lord, and if we die, we die to the Lord; so then, whether we live or whether we die, we are the Lord's. For to this end Christ died and lived again, so that he might be Lord of both the dead and the living.

Why do you pass judgment on your brother or sister? Or you, why do you despise your brother or sister? For we will all stand before the judgment seat of God. For it is written, "As I live, says the Lord, every knee shall bow to me, and every tongue shall give praise to God." So then, each of us will be accountable to God.

GOSPEL *Matthew 18:21–35*

Peter came and said to Jesus, "Lord, if another member of the church sins against me, how often should I forgive? As many as seven times?" Jesus said to him, "Not seven times, but, I tell you, seventy-seven times.

"For this reason the dominion of heaven may be compared to a king who wished to settle accounts with his slaves. When he began the reckoning, one who owed him ten thousand talents was brought to him; and, as he could not pay, his lord ordered him to be sold, together with his wife and children and all his possessions, and payment to be made. So the slave fell on his knees before him, saying, 'Have patience with me, and I will pay you everything.' And out of pity for him, the lord of that slave released him and forgave him the debt.

"But that same slave, as he went out, came upon one of his fellow slaves who owed him a hundred denarii; and seizing him by the throat, he said, 'Pay what you owe.' Then his fellow slave fell down and pleaded with him, 'Have patience with me, and I will pay you.' But he refused; then he went and threw him into prison until he would pay the debt. When his fellow slaves saw what had happened, they were greatly distressed, and they went and reported to their lord all that had taken place. Then his lord summoned him and said to him, 'You wicked slave! I forgave you all that debt because you pleaded with me. Should you not have had mercy on your fellow slave, as I had mercy on you?' And in anger his lord handed him over to be tortured until he would pay his entire debt.

"So my heavenly Father will also do to every one of you, if you do not forgive your brother or sister from your heart."

REFLECTION

The idea of forgiveness as part of the relationship between God and God's people was familiar to the Jewish people. Prophet after prophet taught God's forgiveness of sin and promises to remember sin no more. Originally related to the forgiveness of a debt, forgiveness of sin meant to blot out sin altogether, to forget it, to start again.

Jesus uses both these meanings to make his point. Three details of the story are significant. The disciples ask specifically about a member of the church who sins. The members of the early church were a close-knit band, committed to the worship of God and the care of one another. A sin by one was a betrayal of trust.

The second detail is the number Peter asks and Jesus gives. Seven is a number of perfection. Peter was trying to be overwhelmingly generous in suggesting the perfect number. Jesus challenges him to expand his notion of generosity and perfection by suggesting a number that seems absurd. Who would keep allowing someone to sin against them like that?

The third detail is in the story itself when the lord of the slave not only releases him, but also forgives his debt. Jesus relies on the original meaning of the word to show the lord's compassion. The effect makes the slave's later treatment of another that much more barbaric.

Jesus' lesson is implicit. How can we put a limit on our forgiveness of another when God has not only released us, but also wiped away our debt? Paul is right. Christ is Lord over all things. Our concern is to understand God's forgiveness, for us and for everyone else.

■ **Studies on forgiveness indicate that forgiving is not forgetting the wrong as much as letting go of it. Discuss this distinction. Using your own experience, consider what may be involved in forgiving.**

■ **This week's gospel appears to conflict with the notion we heard last week of asking someone to leave the community of faith. Can both be true? If so, how?**

PRACTICE OF FAITH

FORGIVE US OUR TRESPASSES. We know what follows: "as we forgive those who trespass against us." Pray the Our Father each day this week and ask yourself what it means to forgive others. Why is there a connection between our forgiving others and being forgiven ourselves?

PRACTICE OF HOPE

BROTHERS AND SISTERS. "Sibling rivalry" seems to keep coming up in recent weeks. From Sirach to Paul to Matthew, we are constantly reminded that we are sinners, and we need forgiveness from God, and that God expects us to extend the same mercy to each other.

Nothing drags a person down faster than holding a grudge, or knowing that someone is holding a grudge against them. Some hurts are serious and cannot be forgotten, and certainly not excused. But they can be forgiven. Nothing gives hope to the heart like a fresh start, whether you are the offender or the one offended. Pray for someone this week who has hurt or offended you, and ask God for forgiveness for your own offenses. Then let them go. Pray for a blessing, and you will receive a blessing. Mercy and forgiveness are great blessings.

PRACTICE OF CHARITY

GREATEST CHARITY. A favorite topic among theologians has always been which kind of charity is of greatest merit. The word charity is derived from the Latin term *caritas,* which signifies the only form of love that is universal and unconditional. The person who gives such love does not desire anything back from the person to whom it is given. On the contrary, a person can bestow such love on an individual who is more than unlovable. Perhaps the people who most need *caritas* are those who are incarcerated for violent crimes.

Most nations and religious leaders believe that it is beyond the rights of any government to take a person's life. It is only the United States and South Africa that still exercise the death penalty. Let us pray and work so that our country may soon join the rest of the world.

WEEKDAY READINGS (Mo)1 Corinthians 11:17–26; (Tu) 12:12–14, 27–31a; (We)12:31—13:13; (Th)15:1–11; (Fr)15:12–20; (Sa)Ephesians 4:1–7, 11–13

AUTUMN ORDINARY TIME

Harvest us home to sing your praise!

When the Lord restored the fortunes
   of Zion,
we were like those who dream.
Then our mouth was filled with laughter,
and our tongue with shouts of joy.

Then it was said among the nations,
"The Lord has done great things for them."
The Lord has done great things for us,
and we are glad.

May those who sow in tears
reap with shouts of joy!
Those who go out weeping,
bearing the seed for sowing,
shall come home with shouts of joy,
carrying their sheaves.

—Psalm 126:1–3, 5–6

What tears you cry,
sower God, over us all.
But how you laugh in amazement
and what songs you sing
when there is some harvest.
Your saints from Adam and Eve,
from Moses and Miriam,
from Mary and Joseph,
until our own grandparents and parents,
and we too,
need your tears
and long to hear your laughter.
Harvest us home to sing your praise
forever and ever.

—Prayer of the Season

READING I *Isaiah 55:6–9*

Revised Common Lectionary: Jonah 3:10—4:11
Seek the LORD while the LORD may be found,
call upon God while God is near;
let the wicked forsake their way,
and the unrighteous their thoughts;
let them return to the LORD,
    who will have mercy on them,
and to our God, who will abundantly pardon.
For my thoughts are not your thoughts,
nor are your ways my ways, says the LORD.
For as the heavens are higher than the earth,
so are my ways higher than your ways
and my thoughts than your thoughts.

READING II *Philippians 1:20–30*

Christ will be exalted now as always in my body, whether by life or by death. For to me, living is Christ and dying is gain. If I am to live in the flesh, that means fruitful labor for me; and I do not know which I prefer. I am hard pressed between the two: my desire is to depart and be with Christ, for that is far better; but to remain in the flesh is more necessary for you. Since I am convinced of this, I know that I will remain and continue with all of you for your progress and joy in faith, so that I may share abundantly in your boasting in Christ Jesus when I come to you again.

Only, live your life in a manner worthy of the gospel of Christ, so that, whether I come and see you or am absent and hear about you, I will know that you are standing firm in one spirit, striving side by side with one mind for the faith of the gospel, and are in no way intimidated by your opponents. For them this is evidence of their destruction, but of your salvation. And this is God's doing. For God has graciously granted you the privilege not only of believing in Christ, but of suffering for Christ as well—since you are having the same struggle that you saw I had and now hear that I still have.

GOSPEL *Matthew 20:1–16*

Jesus said: "The dominion of heaven is like a landowner who went out early in the morning to hire laborers for his vineyard. After agreeing with the laborers for the usual daily wage, he sent them into his vineyard. When he went out about nine o'clock, he saw others standing idle in the marketplace; and he said to them, 'You also go into the vineyard, and I will pay you whatever is right.' So they went.

"When he went out again about noon and about three o'clock, he did the same. And about five o'clock he went out and found others standing around; and he said to them, 'Why are you standing here idle all day?' They said to him, 'Because no one has hired us.' He said to them, 'You also go into the vineyard.'

"When evening came, the owner of the vineyard said to his manager, 'Call the laborers and give them their pay, beginning with the last and then going to the first.' When those hired about five o'clock came, each of them received the usual daily wage. Now when the first came, they thought they would receive more; but each of them also received the usual daily wage. And when they received it, they grumbled against the landowner, saying, 'These last worked only one hour, and you have made them equal to us who have borne the burden of the day and the scorching heat.' But he replied to one of them, 'Friend, I am doing you no wrong; did you not agree with me for the usual daily wage? Take what belongs to you and go; I choose to give to this last the same as I give to you. Am I not allowed to do what I choose with what belongs to me? Or are you envious because I am generous?'

"So the last will be first, and the first will be last."

REFLECTION

Jesus could hardly have chosen a more provocative example of the reign of God than the landowner who pays the same amount to all the workers regardless how long they worked. It goes against every notion of just wages, fair treatment or business ethics.

What we get for our labor is a matter of personal interest. Even the disciples understand this. Just before Jesus tells them this parable, they ask Jesus what they might expect, since they have abandoned everything to follow him. Jesus' answer seems to reward their efforts—they will receive "a hundredfold." Then Jesus tells this parable.

Why is the reign of God like this landowner? What values does the landowner uphold? First, he cannot bear to see anyone idle. When he goes out even at the end of the day, he asks the people he meets about their idleness. Second, he believes he can do as he wishes with what belongs to him. Thus he chooses to give the same wage to all the workers.

The reign of heaven, like the landowner, has room for more workers. The invitation is constant; the reward is consistent. As workers in God's field, we agree to eternal life with God. How could there be more or less than that? Eternal life cannot be divided or diminished for those who work less than others.

But in our belief that our pay reflects our worth, we think that God's wage must conform to a human expectation of justice. Some workers must get less than others because they are not worth as much or have not worked as long. It is hard to grasp that our worth is shown in God's love for us, and not in our reward for anything we have done. "The last will be first and the first last" expresses our equality before God as we share in the work that needs to be done. When we are given eternal life, why would we think about what anyone else is getting at all?

■ **Have you ever felt that you did not get what you deserved? How did you respond to that feeling? Is God capable of giving you less than you deserve?**

■ **Can we use this story as an excuse to ignore God's call on the premise that it's never too late and we'll get the same reward anyway?**

PRACTICE OF FAITH

AUTUMNAL EQUINOX. Fall begins this week. In the north, the changing colors of the leaves herald the coming of cold and darkness. As we approach the end of the liturgical year the gospel readings are stern, reminding us that life is serious business. For many, fall is a time of reflection on the transitory nature of life. Use this time to take stock of your life and how your faith shapes the way you live.

PRACTICE OF HOPE

THE USUAL DAILY WAGE. The workers who worked for a full day in the heat had hoped for more than the agreed-upon wage, when they noticed that the last hired were getting the full amount. The daily wage was not great, but adequate. Those who had stood around in town all day were not idle by choice, and they certainly had the option to refuse the work offered so late in the day. After all, it would have yielded so little money, they might as well have gone home empty-handed. But through generosity, they went home with enough to buy food for their families. Greed can masquerade as hope when we "hope" for what we do not need or deserve, and when we are jealous of generosity shown to others. Gratitude is the antidote to greed. We need to look not at what others have been given through God's generosity, but what we have been given, also through God's generosity.

PRACTICE OF CHARITY

THE LAST WILL BE FIRST. The word *charity* has always carried a negative connotation for me. "She's a charity case." "Helping those people is a matter of charity." It has always struck me as an insipid word, with a hint of arbitrariness—you can practice it or not. It's above and beyond the call of duty; therefore it's optional. Justice, on the other hand, is a strong word. "Our God is a God of justice." "God will rain down justice on the earth." Justice sounds like something demanded by the Almighty as part of God's original plan of creation. It helps me understand the true meaning of charity when I hear this parable in which the landowner asks, "Are you envious because I am generous?" Charity surpasses justice *because* it goes beyond what is due. We must redefine charity so that it is just as strong a word as justice.

WEEKDAY READINGS (Mo)Proverbs 3:27–34; (Tu)21:1–6, 10–13; (We)30:5–9; (Th)Ecclesiastes 1:2–11; (Fr)3:1–11; (Sa)11:9—12:8

READING I *Ezekiel 18:1–4, 25–32*

The word of the LORD came to me: What do you mean by repeating this proverb concerning the land of Israel, "The parents have eaten sour grapes, and the children's teeth are set on edge"? As I live, says the Lord GOD, this proverb shall no more be used by you in Israel. Know that all lives are mine; the life of the parent as well as the life of the child is mine: it is only the person who sins that shall die. . . .

Yet you say, "The way of the Lord is unfair." Hear now, O house of Israel: Is my way unfair? Is it not your ways that are unfair? When the righteous turn away from their righteousness and commit iniquity, they shall die for it; for the iniquity that they have committed they shall die. Again, when the wicked turn away from the wickedness they have committed and do what is lawful and right, they shall save their life. Because they considered and turned away from all the transgressions that they had committed, they shall surely live; they shall not die. Yet the house of Israel says, "The way of the Lord is unfair." O house of Israel, are my ways unfair? Is it not your ways that are unfair?

Therefore I will judge you, O house of Israel, all of you according to your ways, says the Lord GOD. Repent and turn from all your transgressions; otherwise iniquity will be your ruin. Cast away from you all the transgressions that you have committed against me, and get yourselves a new heart and a new spirit! Why will you die, O house of Israel? For I have no pleasure in the death of anyone, says the Lord GOD. Turn, then, and live.

READING II *Philippians 2:1–11*

If then there is any encouragement in Christ, any consolation from love, any sharing in the Spirit, any compassion and sympathy, make my joy complete: be of the same mind, having the same love, being in full accord and of one mind. Do nothing from selfish ambition or conceit, but in humility regard others as better than yourselves. Let each of you look not to your own interests but to the interests of others.

Let the same mind be in you that was in Christ Jesus, who, although being in the form of God, did not regard equality with God as something to be exploited, but relinquished it all, taking the form of a slave, being born in human likeness. And being found in human form, he humbled himself and became obedient to the point of death—even death on a cross.

Therefore God also highly exalted him and gave him the name that is above every name, so that at the name of Jesus every knee should bend in heaven and on earth and under the earth, and every tongue should confess that Jesus Christ is LORD, to the glory of God, the Father.

GOSPEL *Matthew 21:28–32*

Jesus said to them, "What do you think? A man had two sons; he went to the first and said, 'Son, go and work in the vineyard today.' He answered, 'I will not'; but later he changed his mind and went. The father went to the second and said the same; and he answered, 'I go, sir'; but he did not go. Which of the two did the will of his father?" They said, "The first." Jesus said to them, "Truly I tell you, the tax collectors and the prostitutes are going into the dominion of God ahead of you. For John came to you in the way of righteousness and you did not believe him, but the tax collectors and the prostitutes believed him; and even after you saw it, you did not change your minds and believe him."

REFLECTION

Ezekiel's words resonate with last week's parable of the laborers in the vineyard. "God is unfair," the people say. The discovery that human notions of justice and fair play do not bind God is both surprising and disquieting. To embrace God's sense of justice means relinquishing our cherished notions of fairness and seeing the world as God sees it.

Ezekiel challenges the people of Israel to understand that even in exile, they cannot be less than faithful to the covenant of God. They must know that the most righteous ones among them are capable of sin, which will bring death, and that those most guilty of wrongdoing are capable of doing right, which will bring life.

God's question is a good one: "How am I unfair?"

We feel that something is unfair when the world or God is not playing by the rules that we assumed were in effect. The psalmist and those who wrote the wisdom literature were all acquainted with this human feeling and demanded that God rectify what they considered unjust. But the prophet Isaiah saw clearly that God's ways are not ours, and that we are not given the fullness of knowledge to understand the unfolding of God's plan. Entering into mystery was and is part of the human condition. Ezekiel fights against the assumption that sin will be overlooked in the lives of those who have been good most of their lives and that those who have done much evil can never return to the covenant love of God.

Matthew's parable of the two sons brings this home to the chief priests and elders. Bound by their own sense of what is fair, they admit that the son who looked bad actually did good, and the one who appeared righteous was disobedient. Jesus uses their answer to point out that tax collectors and prostitutes, whom they considered hopelessly lost to God, would come into God's dominion ahead of them. He opened their eyes to justice. It is not God who is unfair, but human beings who try to limit divine mercy and divine justice.

■ **The psalmists do their share of laying blame and taking blame for the evils of the world. How do we come to know the areas of our own sin and seek forgiveness?**

■ **Who does our society consider hopelessly lost or incapable of good? If these "lost" people performed an act of good, would we be able to see and acknowledge it, or would we be suspicious?**

PRACTICE OF FAITH

IN OCTOBER, A NUMBER OF IMPORTANT SAINTS ARE REMEMBERED. This week we celebrate the feasts of Saint Jerome, Saint Thérèse of Lisieux, the Guardian Angels, and Saint Francis of Assisi. Choose one of these to read about. There are many editions of the Lives of the Saints, and *The Companion to the Calendar: A Guide to the Saints and Mysteries of the Christian Calendar* by Mary Ellen Hynes, published by Liturgy Training Publications is a good resource.

PRACTICE OF HOPE

I SURE WON'T! The Pharisees and the elders are after Jesus again, and he is on to their game. They want to know where he gets his authority, and he turns it around on them, and asks them where they think John got his authority. They see the trap and won't answer. So Jesus tells them a parable. Which son did his father's will? The one who said "no" but then changed his mind, or the one who said "yes, sir" and ignored his duty?

Ordinary people who try to be faithful and truthful and yet suffer under bad management or bad leadership can take heart in this parable. For Jesus wryly shows that those who are sincere of heart and honest in their expression are closer to the reign of God than those who only pay lip service. Our hope is in God, who sees what it in the heart.

PRACTICE OF CHARITY

ALL GOD'S CREATURES. Saint Francis of Assisi, whose feast we celebrate on October 4, is known for his love of nature. He called the sun brother and the moon sister. He also spoke lovingly of all the animals God has created. For this reason, many parishes bless pets on October 4. Pets, especially dogs, are a blessing to us humans because of their loyalty and companionship. If you have a dog that is well-behaved and friendly (and up-to-date on his shots), consider taking your pet to a local nursing home to visit some of the elderly residents. Many retirement homes are happy to have dogs (with their owners) as visitors, because they recognize that one thing seniors miss is touching and being touched in friendly fashion. Petting your dog and getting a lick in return can be a source of great pleasure for someone who has little physical contact with others, human or canine.

WEEKDAY READINGS (Mo)Job 1:6–22; (Tu)3:1–3, 11–17, 20–23; (We)9:1–12, 14–16; (Th)19:21–27; (Fr)38:1, 12–21; 40:3–5; (Sa)42:1–3, 5–6, 12–17

READING I *Isaiah 5:1–7*

Let me sing for my beloved
my love-song concerning my beloved's vineyard:
"My beloved had a vineyard on a very fertile hill.
my beloved dug it and cleared it of stones,
and planted it with choice vines;
built a watchtower in the midst of it,
and hewed out a wine vat in it,
and expected it to yield grapes,
    but it yielded wild grapes."

And now, inhabitants of Jerusalem
    and people of Judah,
judge between me and my vineyard.
What more was there to do for my vineyard
    that I have not done in it?
When I expected it to yield grapes,
    why did it yield wild grapes?

And now I will tell you
    what I will do to my vineyard.
I will remove its hedge, and it shall be devoured;
I will break down its wall,
    and it shall be trampled down.
I will make it a waste; it shall not be pruned or hoed,
and it shall be overgrown with briers and thorns;
I will also command the clouds
    that they rain no rain upon it.

For the vineyard of the LORD of hosts
    is the house of Israel,
and the people of Judah are God's pleasant planting;
for the LORD expected justice, but saw bloodshed;
    righteousness, but heard a cry!

READING II *Philippians 4:6–9*

Revised Common Lectionary: Philippians 3:4–14

Do not worry about anything, but in everything by prayer and supplication with thanksgiving let your requests be made known to God. And the peace of God, which surpasses all understanding, will guard your hearts and your minds in Christ Jesus.

Finally, beloved, whatever is true, whatever is honorable, whatever is just, whatever is pure, whatever is pleasing, whatever is commendable, if there is any excellence and if there is anything worthy of praise, think about these things. Keep on doing the things that you have learned and received and heard and seen in me, and the God of peace will be with you.

GOSPEL *Matthew 21:33–41, 45–46*

Complete reading: Matthew 21:33–43

Jesus said: "Listen to another parable. There was a landowner who planted a vineyard, put a fence around it, dug a wine press in it, and built a watchtower. Then he leased it to tenants and went to another country. When the harvest time had come, he sent his slaves to the tenants to collect his produce. But the tenants seized his slaves and beat one, killed another, and stoned another. Again he sent other slaves, more than the first; and they treated them in the same way. Finally he sent his son to them, saying, 'They will respect my son.' But when the tenants saw the son, they said to themselves, 'This is the heir; come, let us kill him and get his inheritance.' So they seized him, threw him out of the vineyard, and killed him.

"Now when the owner of the vineyard comes, what will he do to those tenants?" They said to Jesus, "The owner will put those wretches to a miserable death, and lease the vineyard to other tenants who will give him the produce at the harvest time."

When the chief priests and the Pharisees heard his parables, they realized that he was speaking about them. They wanted to arrest him, but they feared the crowds, because the people regarded him as a prophet.

REFLECTION

The metaphor of God as divine gardener is deeply embedded in the prophetic books of the Old Testament. Isaiah's prophecy is filled with images of God who plants trees in a desert and makes flowers bloom in the wilderness. The passage we read today compares Israel to God's garden-vineyard which God expected to yield justice but instead yielded bloodshed and sorrow.

A song in the musical *The Fantasticks* celebrates the consistency of gardens over children. "Plant a turnip, get a turnip, not a Brussels sprout," it says. "But with children, you never know how it will turn out." God's planted people did not turn out the way God expected. They were wild and unyielding. Their fruit was sour. When a crop has gone bad, the only remedy is to uproot the garden and start over. With Israel lost in its own unfaithfulness, God had no choice but to clear the ground and begin again.

We are not much different today. As gardens go, we are an amazing variety of plants and flowers, each with its own goodnesses. The question remains, however: Are we what God wanted? Do we yield an abundant harvest or a few sour grapes? Do we withhold the produce from the One who planted the seeds in the first place? In what way are we the "pleasant planting" of God? These questions form the basis for a thorough examination of conscience as we look at how we live as disciples of Christ. Both Isaiah and Matthew speak of the care and affection with which God planted and tended the vineyard. But they also describe the anguish and the anger of God when his work is ruined. For Christians the challenge is in our acknowledgment that God has planted us and in our willingness to yield up the fruits of his harvest when he calls for them.

■ **The Bible begins with the garden of Eden in Genesis 2 and ends with a garden by the crystal river in Revelation 22. What is the significance of these two gardens in the story of salvation history?**

■ **What grows wild in you? What does God have to root out so that good seed can grow?**

PRACTICE OF FAITH

THE VINE. This is the third week in which Jesus echoes Isaiah's "vineyard song" in his parables. The image of Israel as the vineyard has deep roots in scripture (Noah was the first to plant a vineyard, Genesis 9:20). We are familiar with the image of Jesus as the vine, and we are the branches. Look at a vine plant. Can you distinguish between the vine and the branches?

PRACTICE OF HOPE

SOUR GRAPES. Today we have not one but two images of an unyielding vineyard. In Isaiah, it's the grapes that don't produce a yield, and in Matthew, it's the tenant farmers who are a bad lot. God, like the good landowner, does everything possible to nurture the vineyards, but no yield is forthcoming.

Like the vineyard in the gospel, we hope for good tending and nurturing. We know that God has provided every good thing for our growth and development, not for the enrichment of the selfish, but for the good of all. If we are suffering because of bad leadership, God will provide for our care. If we are flourishing under good leaders, thank God for the blessing, and, in turn, nurture others and care for their wellbeing. The word of God yields good fruit in those who nurture it.

PRACTICE OF CHARITY

LITERACY. As the school year starts up again, remember that there are many who were never able to finish their education. There are approximately 50 million illiterate adults in our country. They may manage to get by, but they are prevented from living fully. Think about how hard it would be if you could not read. For one thing, when letters and reports about your children were sent from their school you would not know what they said without asking your child's help. You would not be able to read instructions and warnings. You would not be able to read the Bible, God's word. Many adults in literacy programs want to learn to read so they can read the Bible. Find out more about literacy programs in your area and consider volunteering to help give this most precious gift.

WEEKDAY READINGS (Mo)Galatians 1:6–12; (Tu)1:13–24; (We)2:1–2, 7–14; (Th)3:1–5; (Fr)3:7–14; (Sa)3:22–29

READING I *Isaiah 25:6–10*

On this mountain the LORD of hosts
    will make for all peoples
a feast of rich food, a feast of well-aged wines,
of rich food filled with marrow,
    of well-aged wines strained clear.
And the LORD will destroy on this mountain
the shroud that is cast over all peoples,
the sheet that is spread over all nations;
the LORD will swallow up death forever.
Then the Lord GOD will wipe away
    the tears from all faces,
and the disgrace of the chosen people
    God will take away from all the earth,
for the LORD has spoken.
It will be said on that day,
Lo, this is our God, for whom we have waited
    so that God might save us.
This is the LORD for whom we have waited;
let us be glad and rejoice
    in the salvation of the LORD.
For the hand of the LORD
    will rest on this mountain.

READING II *Philippians 4:12–14, 19–20*

Revised Common Lectionary: Philippians 4:1–9

I know what it is to have little, and I know what it is to have plenty. In any and all circumstances I have learned the secret of being well-fed and of going hungry, of having plenty and of being in need. I can do all thing through him who strengthens me. In any case, it was kind of you to share my distress.

And my God will fully satisfy every need of yours according to his riches in glory in Christ Jesus. To our God and Father be glory forever and ever. Amen.

GOSPEL *Matthew 22:1–14*

Once more Jesus spoke to them in parables, saying: "The dominion of heaven may be compared to a king who gave a wedding banquet for his son. He sent his slaves to call those who had been invited to the wedding banquet, but they would not come. Again he sent other slaves, saying, 'Tell those who have been invited: Look, I have prepared my dinner, my oxen and my fat calves have been slaughtered, and everything is ready; come to the wedding banquet.' But they made light of it and went away, one to his farm, another to his business, while the rest seized his slaves, mistreated them, and killed them. The king was enraged. He sent his troops, destroyed those murderers, and burned their city.

"Then the king said to his slaves, 'The wedding is ready, but those invited were not worthy. Go therefore into the main streets, and invite everyone you find to the wedding banquet.' Those slaves went out into the streets and gathered all whom they found, both good and bad; so the wedding hall was filled with guests.

"But when the king came in to see the guests, he noticed a man there who was not wearing a wedding robe, and he said to him, 'Friend, how did you get in here without a wedding robe?' And he was speechless. Then the king said to the attendants, 'Bind him hand and foot, and throw him into the outer darkness, where there will be weeping and gnashing of teeth.'

"For many are called, but few are chosen."

REFLECTION

What would a party be without food? How could we celebrate a holiday with family and friends without the traditional ample food and drink? Sharing food brings people together. It should not come as a surprise that food figures prominently in Isaiah's prophecy about God's ultimate victory and in Matthew's story about the dominion of heaven. God's feast is the finest of all banquets. But today we see two very different sides of it.

At Isaiah's mountaintop banquet, God, the gracious host, provides the finest foods and sees to the guests' comfort in every way. Isaiah is describing a vision of hope for a people under attack, first from Assyria and then from Babylon. In this vision, God has only to speak and the sorrow and death will be taken away forever. God is the anticipated savior for whom Israel has waited in her siege and exile.

By contrast, Matthew's wedding feast features a king whose judgment seems, at best, harsh. First he invites a crowd of thugs, and when they not only refuse to come but continue their thuggery, he slays them and rounds up everyone in town to take their places. Then he throws out one poor neighbor because he didn't have the right clothes. Matthew is not comforting a people under siege or describing a vision of what is to come, but addressing the challenges of discipleship. True disciples of Jesus boldly respond to God's invitation. They are prepared, not tentative or hesitant when the invitation comes.

Matthew's parable takes aim at those who squander God's generosity and promise of faithfulness. They turn their backs; they abuse their relationship with God, believing that God will continue to ring the dinner bell for them. What host would invite such rude people? The successful banquet includes people who want to be there and who are willing to do their part to make it successful. The invitation goes out to everyone, but not everyone is willing or able to participate.

■ **What is the significance of eating together for our culture and for the Christian community?**

■ **Why do you think the master was so impatient with those unsuitably dressed? Why was it important to have the hall filled with guests before the feast?**

PRACTICE OF FAITH

IN ALL CIRCUMSTANCES. Two summers ago, an Olympic gold medal winner quoted Paul when a reporter asked how she felt about winning. The diver said, "I can do all things through Christ who strengthens me." No doubt she had invested years in training and practice. Yet in her moment of glory she recognized that her strength and ability was a gift.

Paul encourages us to see everything—whether abundance or deprivation—as an opportunity to acknowledge God's action in our lives. What are your strengths, talents, gifts? Give thanks to God for what you can do. What do you need? Trust that God will supply.

PRACTICE OF HOPE

"REGRETS ONLY." Sure, it's a pain when guests forget to respond to an invitation, especially for something as important as a wedding! But these invited guests went way beyond rude! They were not just "no-shows," but thugs and murderers! So the king fills his banquet with everyone he can find, bad and good alike.

God's invitation has been issued. Have we remembered to respond? All we need do is put on a wedding garment, provided by the host. Our lives have taken us down many highways and byways, but now we are invited to be gathered up, to be dressed in fine garments and to come to the feast! We are to put on Christ, and to be children of the one God. Don't forget to send in your RSVP.

PRACTICE OF CHARITY

THE FEAST IS READY. Autumn is a wonderful season. After a summer of watering and waiting, it is time to harvest my vegetables—especially the tomatoes, which take forever to ripen in our shady yard. It is also the time for picking apples and enjoying the beauty of leaves turning gold and red. It is a wonderful time to think about feasting. Any homegrown crop is meant to be shared. Make a pie, invite neighbors to come over for supper, take homemade soup to a shut-in. Paul tells us that he knows how to live in humble circumstances and also with abundance. We who have been so generously gifted by the Creator will find these fall days a good time to share the feast with others.

WEEKDAY READINGS (Mo)Galatians 4:22–24, 26–27, 31—5:1; (Tu)5:1–6; (We)5:18–25; (Th)Ephesians 1:1–10; (Fr)2 Timothy 4:10–17b; (Sa)Ephesians 1:15–23

READING I *Isaiah 45:1–7*

Thus says the LORD to Cyrus, the LORD'S anointed,
whose right hand I have grasped
    to subdue nations before him
and strip rulers of their robes,
to open doors before Cyrus—
and the gates shall not be closed:
I will go before you and level the mountains,
I will break in pieces the doors of bronze
and cut through the bars of iron,
I will give you the treasures of darkness
and riches hidden in secret places,
so that you may know that it is I, the LORD,
the God of Israel, who call you by your name.
For the sake of my servant Jacob,
    and Israel my chosen,
I call you by your name,
I surname you, though you do not know me.
I am the LORD, and there is no other;
besides me there is no god.
I arm you, though you do not know me,
so that they may know,
from the rising of the sun and from the west,
that there is no one besides me;
I am the LORD, and there is no other.
I form light and create darkness,
I make weal and create woe;
I the LORD do all these things.

READING II *1 Thessalonians 1:1–10*

Paul, Silvanus, and Timothy,
To the church of the Thessalonians
in God, the Father, and the Lord Jesus Christ:
Grace to you and peace.

We always give thanks to God for all of you and
mention you in our prayers, constantly remembering before our God and Father your work of faith
and labor of love and steadfastness of hope in our
Lord Jesus Christ. For we know, brothers and sisters
beloved by God, that God has chosen you, because
our message of the gospel came to you not in word
only, but also in power and in the Holy Spirit and
with full conviction; just as you know what kind of
persons we proved to be among you for your sake.
And you became imitators of us and of the Lord, for
in spite of persecution you received the word with
joy inspired by the Holy Spirit, so that you became
an example to all the believers in Macedonia and
in Achaia.

For the word of the Lord has sounded forth from
you not only in Macedonia and Achaia, but in every
place your faith in God has become known, so that
we have no need to speak about it. For the people of
those regions report about us what kind of welcome
we had among you, and how you turned to God
from idols, to serve a living and true God, and to
wait for God's Son from heaven, whom God raised
from the dead—Jesus, who rescues us from the
wrath that is coming.

GOSPEL *Matthew 22:15–22*

The Pharisees went and plotted to entrap Jesus in
what he said. So they sent their disciples to Jesus,
along with the Herodians, saying, "Teacher, we
know that you are sincere, and teach the way of God
in accordance with truth, and show deference to no
one; for you do not regard people with partiality.
Tell us, then, what you think. Is it lawful to pay taxes
to the emperor, or not?" But Jesus, aware of their
malice, said, "Why are you putting me to the test,
you hypocrites? Show me the coin used for the tax."
And they brought him a denarius. Then he said to
them, "Whose head is this, and whose title?" They
answered, "The emperor's."

Then Jesus said to them, "Give therefore to the
emperor the things that are the emperor's, and to
God the things that are God's." When they heard this,
they were amazed; and they left him and went away.

REFLECTION

Paying taxes is no more popular now than it was in Jesus' time. Every year someone keeps track of exactly how many workdays it takes to raise the money that will never be seen by the worker, but will go immediately to someone else, who will spend it, invest it or waste it. Every year people try to figure out how they can keep a little more of what seems rightfully theirs. Anyone who works, that is, all of us, might be forgiven if we joined the Pharisees on the question of payment of taxes. Their mistake was using the issue to trap Jesus. If Jesus answered "yes," he would be anti-religious. If he said "no," he would be a revolutionary. Rather than answer the question directly, Jesus uses the moment to teach a lesson in responsibility, not so much to Caesar, but to God.

We worry about our debt to credit card companies, banks and government agencies. When was the last time we worried about the debt to God? How much do we owe for redemption? The Jews believed that obedience to the Law was the natural response of a grateful heart. How could they do less? God had brought them out of Egypt and out of exile. God raised up a foreign messiah for them to rout the Babylonians and made sure that Cyrus knew that it was God who brought him the victory. To disobey God's law after such faithfulness would have been no less than rude.

Psalm 116 has it right. "How can I make a return for all the good that God has done to me?" It is Jesus who answers: "Render to God the things that are God's." We may owe the government money. After all, there are U.S. presidents' faces on our currency. But it is God who is inscribed on our souls. In our gratitude, we owe to God our very lives. Divine grace and steadfast love are things that money cannot buy.

■ **What are the things we owe God? How do we make that payment?**

■ **Should we pay taxes without question or can we withhold taxes because of moral or ethical stands? Is this an issue we need to spend time thinking about?**

PRACTICE OF FAITH

TO GOD AND TO CAESAR. Our political life is filled with conflicting opinions on the place of religion in the public realm. Issues of school prayer, vouchers for private schools, religious symbols in public places are lightning rods for people across the religious spectrum. Are these issues in your local community? In what ways do you think religion is a public matter? A private matter?

PRACTICE OF HOPE

ENDURANCE IN HOPE. Paul commends the church at Thessalonica for their work of faith and labor of love, and for their "endurance in hope." Hope does take endurance, for it can be sorely tested sometimes. God's ways are not our ways, and sometimes it is hard to see where the work is going, and whether it is accomplishing anything at all. That is where hope comes in. God makes use of the Persian King Cyrus to accomplish the restoration of Jerusalem and the return of the people to Israel. If God can call Cyrus "the Lord's anointed," anything can happen! God will restore the right balance and establish the Reign of God by whatever means God wills.

So our hope does not have to be based on what is logical or plausible or "do-able." Our hope has only to endure. We work in faith, and we labor in love, and hope will not disappoint. If our hope is in God, it will endure.

PRACTICE OF CHARITY

WHOSE TAXES ARE THEY? When we consider that we provide a large amount of money to the government, we might question more closely how it is put to use. Most of us do not want to sponsor any more wars or killing. Yet the School of the Americas is using our tax money to train member of various Central American military forces in the art of making war. There is clear evidence that some of the worst human rights violations of the last decades have been carried out under the direction of men trained at this American institution. In El Salvador and Nicaragua, priests and lay missionaries were killed by soldiers whose orders came from a graduate of the School of the Americas. Father Roy Bourgeois has led a crusade of non-violent civil disobedience for more than ten years to persuade our government that we taxpayers no longer want to support this school of death. Whose taxes are they anyway?

WEEKDAY READINGS (Mo)Ephesians 2:1–10; (Tu)2:12–22; (We)3:2–12; (Th)3:14–21; (Fr)4:1–6; (Sa)4:7–16

READING I *Exodus 22:20–26*

Revised Common Lectionary: Leviticus 19:1–2, 15–18
Whoever sacrifices to any god, other than the LORD alone, shall be devoted to destruction.

You shall not wrong or oppress a resident alien, for you were aliens in the land of Egypt. You shall not abuse any widow or orphan. If you do abuse them, when they cry out to me, I will surely heed their cry; my wrath will burn, and I will kill you with the sword, and your wives shall become widows and your children orphans.

If you lend money to my people, to the poor among you, you shall not deal with them as a creditor; you shall not exact interest from them. If you take your neighbor's cloak in pawn, you shall restore it before the sun goes down.

READING II *1 Thessalonians 1:5–10*

Revised Common Lectionary: 1 Thessalonians 2:1–8
You know what kind of persons we proved to be among you for your sake. And you became imitators of us and of the Lord, for in spite of persecution you received the word with joy inspired by the Holy Spirit, so that you became an example to all the believers in Macedonia and in Achaia.

For the word of the Lord has sounded forth from you not only in Macedonia and Achaia, but in every place your faith in God has become known, so that we have no need to speak about it. For the people of those regions report about us what kind of welcome we had among you, and how you turned to God from idols, to serve a living and true God, and to wait for God's Son from heaven, whom God raised from the dead—Jesus, who rescues us from the wrath that is coming.

GOSPEL *Matthew 22:34–46*

When the Pharisees heard that Jesus had silenced the Sadducees, they gathered together, and one of them, a lawyer, asked Jesus a question to test him. "Teacher, which commandment in the law is the greatest?" He said to him, " 'You shall love the Lord your God with all your heart, and with all your soul, and with all your mind.' This is the greatest and first commandment. And a second is like it: 'You shall love your neighbor as yourself.' On these two commandments hang all the law and the prophets."

Now while the Pharisees were gathered together, Jesus asked them this question: "What do you think of the Messiah? Whose son is he?" They said to him, "The son of David." Jesus said to them, "How is it then that David by the Spirit calls him Lord, saying, 'The Lord said to my Lord, "Sit at my right hand, until I put your enemies under your feet" '? If David thus calls him Lord, how can he be his son?" No one was able to give Jesus an answer, nor from that day did anyone dare to ask him any more questions.

Monday, November 1, and Tuesday, November 2, 2002

ALL SAINTS

Revelation 7:2–4, 9–14 *The crowd stood before the Lamb.*

1 John 3:1–3 *We shall see God.*

Matthew 5:1–12 *How blest are the poor in spirit.*

We welcome the winter with a harvest homecoming. All God's people are gathered into the new Jerusalem to begin the supper of the Lamb. The poor, the mourning, the meek and the lowly remove their masks and see themselves as they truly are: the beloved children of God, the saints of heaven.

ALL SOULS

Daniel 12:1–3 *The dead will rise to shine like stars.*

Romans 6:3–9 *Like Christ, we will live a new life.*

John 6:37–40 *I will never reject one who comes.*

In the northern hemisphere, nature shows forth the awesome beauty of the harvest. Yesterday we rejoiced in the harvest of the saints. Today we reflect on what made this harvest possible: self-sacrifice, completed labors and death.

REFLECTION

The rabbis and teachers debated constantly about which of the 613 laws in the Torah or Pentateuch of the Hebrew Scriptures was the most important, which was the greatest. Some would argue that laws regarding the common life of the community were more important, that they were necessary for obedience to the Law. Others offered that the laws concerning behavior toward God were more important, since right relationship with God meant right relationship with one's neighbors. Even the Ten Commandments are divided, with three laws pertaining to God and seven applying to the community of faith. As the reading from Exodus tells us, the people are compassionate toward their neighbors because God has first been compassionate to them.

Into this theological debate comes Jesus, who sums up all the laws into two briefly stated commandments. "You shall love the Lord your God with all your heart, and all your soul, and all your mind" is the great *shema* for Jews. In Deuteronomy, the command begins: "Shema (hear) Israel." For the faithful Jew, to hear is to obey. Action follows listening. The second command is actually found in Leviticus as part of the holiness code. To love one's neighbor as oneself is to move further on the path to holiness. And Israel was called to be holy because God is holy.

Jesus forces us to see that right relationship with God and right relationship with neighbor are inextricably entwined. If one sins against God, the community is hurt as well. If a person turns his or her back on a neighbor, God suffers the consequences, too. Jesus fights against the assumption that offering the right sacrifices and prayers relieves the responsibility for taking care of those around us. Jesus denies the possibility that we can do good works without also praising and thanking God.

■ **Sometimes loving one's neighbor as one's self is not such a good deal for the neighbor. How do we begin to love ourselves as God loves us? How do we expand that love to our neighbor?**

■ **The reading from Exodus is a blueprint for social justice. How do Christians today respond to this challenge?**

PRACTICE OF FAITH

FOR ALL THE SAINTS. The feasts of All Saints and All Souls give us the opportunity to remember the vast communion of saints who have preceded us. Some are officially proclaimed holy men and holy women by the church; others we know from our experience of the holiness of their lives.

Pray a litany of the saints and add your own personal favorites. We who are living need the prayers and intercessions of those who now share in God's eternal life.

PRACTICE OF HOPE

"HOW MANY LAWYERS DOES IT TAKE..." In the time of Jesus, people were terribly burdened by the obligations of the law and its interpretations. Jesus makes it simple: Love God, love your neighbor. Love does no harm, breaks no law. The one who loves, does what is right. Before, the poor had no hope of being able to follow every letter of the law, and therefore had no hope of being acceptable to God. But Jesus frees them from all that legalism, and gives them new hope for the Reign of God. In his great love, Jesus fulfills the Law and the Prophets, making it possible for his followers to be holy and acceptable to God, by imitating him. Jesus reveals a compassionate and loving God, rather than a harsh and stringent judge. What will you do with the hope that this new freedom promises?

PRACTICE OF CHARITY

BE CHOOSY. Are you on the list of every charity in the country? They are all sending out their end-of-the-year appeals now. How do you decide which of these worthy causes you will support? Perhaps you do as I did for many years—send a small check to each of them. Recently I learned a much more satisfactory approach. Consider which groups you most want to support and triple the amount you give them. The others will just have to be taken care of by other people who consider that cause to be a major concern of theirs. In that way I've been able to pare my donation list down from 50 worthwhile organizations to 15 groups whose work I really want to support. Also, be sure to indicate that you do not want your name sold to other organizations. Then you won't need to agonize over every request you receive or throw darts to choose which ones to answer.

WEEKDAY READINGS (Mo)Ephesians 2:19–22; (Tu)5:21–33; (We)6:1–9; (Th)6:10–20; (Fr)All Saints, see box; (Sa)All Souls, see box.

READING I *Malachi 1:14—2:2, 8–10*

Revised Common Lectionary: Micah 3:5–12

For I am a great King, says the LORD of hosts, and my name is reverenced among the nations.

And now, O priests, this command is for you. If you will not listen, if you will not lay it to heart to give glory to my name, says the LORD of hosts, then I will send the curse on you and I will curse your blessings; indeed I have already cursed them, because you do not lay it to heart.

But you have turned aside from the way; you have caused many to stumble by your instruction; you have corrupted the covenant of Levi, says the LORD of hosts, and so I make you despised and abased before all the people, inasmuch as you have not kept my ways but have shown partiality in your instruction.

Have we not all one father? Has not one God created us? Why then are we faithless to one another, profaning the covenant of our ancestors?

READING II *1 Thessalonians 2:7–13*

We were gentle among you, like a nursing mother tenderly caring for her own children. So deeply do we care for you that we are determined to share with you not only the gospel of God but also our own selves, because you have become very dear to us.

You remember our labor and toil, brothers and sisters; we worked night and day, so that we might not burden any of you while we proclaimed to you the gospel of the God. Your are witnesses, and God also, how pure, upright, and blameless our conduct was toward you believers. As you now, we dealt with each one of you like a father with his children, urging and encouraging you and p leading that you lead a life worthy of God, who calls you into God's own dominion and glory.

We also constantly give thanks to God for this, that when you received the word of God that you heard from us, you accepted it not as a human word but as what it truly is, God's word, which is also at work in you believers.

GOSPEL *Matthew 23:1–12*

Jesus said to the crowds and to his disciples, "The scribes and the Pharisees sit on Moses' seat; therefore, do whatever they teach you and follow it; but do not do as they do, for they do not practice what they teach. They tie up heavy burdens, hard to bear, and lay them on the shoulders of others; but they themselves are unwilling to lift a finger to move them. They do all their deeds to be seen by others; for they make their phylacteries broad and their fringes long. They love to have the place of honor at banquets and the best seats in the synagogues, and to be greeted with respect in the marketplaces, and to have people call them rabbi. But you are not to be called rabbi, for you have one teacher, and you are all students. And call no one your father on earth, for you have one Father—the one in heaven. Nor are you to be called instructors, for you have one instructor, the Messiah.

"The greatest among you will be your servant. All who exalt themselves will be humbled, and all who humble themselves will be exalted."

Saturday, November 9, 2002

DEDICATION OF THE LATERAN BASILICA IN ROME

Ezekiel 47:1–2,8–9, 12 *Saving water flowed from the temple.*

1 Corinthians 3:9–11, 16–17 *You are God's holy temple.*

John 2:13–22 *Zeal for God's house consumes me.*

Human flesh is God's dwelling place. In November, a season of ingathering, we assemble in the Spirit. Our own flesh and blood is becoming God's holy temple. All creation is becoming Jerusalem.

REFLECTION

"Do as I say, not as I do." Nearly every child has heard these words from parents when the parents have been caught in an inconsistency between word and action. The child hears, "Smoking is bad for you," and the parent lights up a cigarette. The child is told, "Do not cheat," and then watches as parents cheat on their taxes.

Jesus observes that the scribes and Pharisees teach rightly. They understand what the Law is saying about ethical behavior and right worship. But Jesus also points out that their example is inconsistent with their teaching.

Obedience to the Law was never imagined as a burden. Rather, it was the grateful response of the Jews to everything God had done for them. Jesus accuses the scribes and Pharisees of using the Law to make others feel unworthy or sinful. As teachers, the deference they received made them feel important and better than anyone else. They exaggerated their status at the expense of the people they were supposed to serve.

The urge to get ahead by stepping on someone else seems to be part of the contemporary condition. Status symbols include fine cars, big houses, a fat bank account, and a name that is known in the right circles and heard in the right places. Unfortunately, the economic system that supports this version of success does so by maintaining a gap between rich and poor, between those who have a name and those who are nobody.

Jesus eliminates the division between the teachers of the Law and the people they affect by reminding everyone that God is their true father and the Messiah is their teacher. The only title to which a disciple may aspire is servant of all. Servants follow the Law, respect and help those they serve, and do not exalt themselves. Above all, servants know who their master is. For disciples, God is the only master they will ever need.

■ **Paul uses a nursing mother as an image for his servanthood. A nursing mother is available on demand and shares her life with her baby in a unique way. What actions does this image suggest for the work of Christians? Is this a good image for God's relationship to us?**

■ **Malachi asks the question: "Why do we break faith with each other?" What are the ways we break faith? To begin thinking about this, look to last week's readings.**

PRACTICE OF FAITH

STRONG. Like Judaism, the early church also distinguished between talk and action. Heeding a teaching is easier if we see it demonstrated. This may be one of the reasons God became human in Jesus—to give us an example of how to live. All of us tend to imitate those we admire. Who do you admire? Why? Think about how having a model in Jesus enables us to live more fully as Christians.

PRACTICE OF HOPE

"BAD SHEPHERDS' SUNDAY"? This week the laity get to sit back and listen while those who have the care of souls get a little lecture from the Lord. Jesus was pretty hard on the Pharisees and scribes, and by extension, all who claim authority in the name of God. Much is expected of those who are called to leadership of God's people. Those who are called to lead must place themselves at the service of their people, not vice versa. The Lord gave us the best example of servant leadership.

But this is not an excuse for the laity to gloat. This is serious. Jesus encourages us and gives us hope, even when we may have to endure heavy burdens. The Lord knows that people suffer when leaders misconstrue their mission. We have one Father—God—and one Teacher—Christ. The rest of us are learners and servants. It is good for all of us to remember this.

PRACTICE OF CHARITY

OPT FOR THE POOR. This section of Matthew's gospel contrasts the religious practices of the scribes and Pharisees with the spirituality Jesus asks of us. Instead of working for those things the world values—recognition and honor—we are told to be humble and make ourselves the servant of others. We are to care for widows and orphans and all those who most need our help. At the Medellín Conference in 1962, the bishops reminded us that we should exercise a "fundamental option for the poor." Church World Service, an ecumenical organization, started in 1947 with shipments of food and other supplies through its CROP program. Today CROP raises funds through more than 2,000 hunger walks. They have also resettled 400,000 refugees. More recently CWS has focused on projects to support local development efforts. Call CWS at 800-297-1516; email cws@nccusa.org.

WEEKDAY READINGS (Mo)Philippians 2:1–4; (Tu)2:5–11; (We)2:12–18; (Th)3:3–8a; (Fr)3:17—4:1; (Sa)Dedication of the Lateran Basilica, see box.

READING I *Wisdom 6:12–16*

Wisdom is radiant and unfading,
and she is easily discerned by those who love her,
and is found by those who seek her.
She hastens to make herself known
   to those who desire her.
One who rises early to seek her
   will have no difficulty,
for she will be found sitting at the gate.
To fix one's thought on her is perfect understanding,
and one who is vigilant on her account
   will soon be free from care,
because she goes about seeking those worthy of her,
and she graciously appears to them in their paths,
and meets them in every thought.

READING II *1 Thessalonians 4:13–18*

We do not want you to be uninformed, brothers and sisters, about those who have died, so that you may not grieve as others do who have no hope. For since we believe that Jesus died and rose again, even so, through Jesus, God will bring with him those who have died. For this we declare to you by the word of the Lord, that we who are alive, who are left until the coming of the Lord, will by no means precede those who have died. For that very Lord, with a cry of command, with the archangel's call and with the sound of God's trumpet, will descend from heaven, and the dead in Christ will rise first. Then we who are alive, who are left, will be caught up in the clouds together with them to meet the Lord in the air; and so we will be with the Lord forever.

Therefore encourage one another with these words.

GOSPEL *Matthew 25:1–13*

Jesus said: "Then the dominion of heaven will be like this. Ten bridesmaids took their lamps and went to meet the bridegroom. Five of them were foolish, and five were wise. When the foolish took their lamps, they took no oil with them; but the wise took flasks of oil with their lamps. As the bridegroom was delayed, all of them became drowsy and slept.

"But at midnight there was a shout, 'Look! Here is the bridegroom! Come out to meet him.' Then all those bridesmaids got up and trimmed their lamps. The foolish said to the wise, 'Give us some of your oil, for our lamps are going out.' But the wise replied, 'No! there will not be enough for you and for us; you had better go to the dealers and buy some for yourselves.' And while they went to buy it, the bridegroom came, and those who were ready went with him into the wedding banquet; and the door was shut. Later the other bridesmaids came also, saying, 'Sir, sir, open to us.' But he replied, 'Truly I tell you, I do not know you.'

"Keep awake therefore, for you know neither the day nor the hour."

R E F L E C T I O N

At the end of *The Wizard of Oz*, Dorothy comes to the realization that there is no place like home. The scarecrow says he should have thought of that for Dorothy when she was struggling so hard to remember what she had learned. But Glinda answers that Dorothy needed to find out for herself. She never would have believed it otherwise. Matthew's gospel applies this same principle to the story of the wise and foolish bridesmaids.

At first glance, this parable seems to celebrate selfishness as a virtue, for the five bridesmaids who have oil do not share with those who do not. A closer reading, though, emphasizes the personal responsibility of everyone to be ready for the bridegroom. Every bridesmaid has a lamp. Each one is responsible for bringing what is needed to the night watch.

In one allegorical interpretation, we might consider the lamp to be the light of faith for those who are ready to celebrate Jesus' return. The oil, then, is whatever keeps faith active and alive; it is teaching of scripture, faithful witness to the work of Jesus and love of one another. These are not things one person can give to another. Rather, they must be cultivated within the individual heart to be effective.

Jesus did not come as soon as the early church expected. In the face of that, Matthew needed to help his readers continue the work of faith. The mistake of the foolish bridesmaids was not that they fell asleep; all ten did that. The mistake lay in allowing the light of faith to dwindle. The foolish bridesmaids are told to get oil from the merchants for themselves. By the time they return it is too late. Matthew's cautionary tale warns his readers that faith is not easy to keep when the cares of the world are pressing. All of us must find for ourselves the grace and strength to continue.

■ **The reading from the book of Wisdom talks about the one who keeps vigil. He or she will not be disappointed. In the light of Jesus' parable, how will you wait? How will you get ready for the coming of God?**

■ **How does the church help the community to cultivate faith? What is the oil that keeps our lamps lit?**

PRACTICE OF FAITH

SHINE. I attended a baptism in a church whose undecorated paschal candle stood tall. It was especially noticeable because of its large flame, which, without any adornment to distract the eye, seemed to burn more brightly than ordinary candles' flames. Jesus reminds us with his parable to be vigilant, ready and willing. There was some discussion in our house about unadorned paschal candles, but I cannot forget the flame. Jesus reminded us early in Matthew's gospel that we "are the light of the world." Not a compliment, but a challenge to be radiant and to shine.

PRACTICE OF HOPE

LIKE THOSE WHO HAVE NO HOPE. As the liturgical year draws to a close, here in North America the weather cooperates in setting the mood. Summer is over, the harvest is in, the leaves have fallen and the weather is growing colder every day. We have celebrated the Feasts of All Saints and All Souls, and death, like a gray winter day, is a quiet but insistent presence in the back of our consciousness.

If we have nourished our hope, we, like the wise bridesmaids, will have the oil of gladness to keep our lamps burning brightly. The Bridegroom is indeed coming, and now is the time for wakefulness, not sleep. We know that death is not the end, but the beginning of the fullness of life. Buried with the seed that "dies" in the earth, we shall rise again with the coming of the Light of the World. Keep the lamp lighted! Christ, our hope, is coming.

PRACTICE OF CHARITY

WHAT IS WISDOM? Surely it is that which Monica Cahill possesses. At age 85, Monica directs Taproots, a program on Chicago's West Side for single parents and their infants. Sister Monica knows that some of these young people need her mothering before they can care for their own babies. Then there is Sister Theresa Kane, who stood up during a papal visit to the United States in 1979 and publicly requested that women ("half of humankind") be "included in all the ministries of the church." We can recognize their wisdom and work by supporting retired sisters and their religious communities. A good way to donate to this cause is SOAR, 1400 Spring Street, Suite 320, Silver Spring MD 20910; 301-589-9811.

WEEKDAY READINGS (Mo)Titus 1:1–9; (Tu)2:1–8, 11–14; (We)3:1–7; (Th)Philemon 7–20; (Fr)2 John 4–9; (Sa)3 John 5–8

READING I | *Proverbs 31:10–13, 19–20, 30–31*

Revised Common Lectionary: Zephaniah 1:7, 12–18

A capable wife who can find?
She is far more precious than jewels.
The heart of her husband trusts in her,
and he will have no lack of gain.
She does him good, and not harm,
all the days of her life.
She seeks wool and flax,
and works with willing hands.
She puts her hands to the distaff,
and her hands hold the spindle.
She opens her hand to the poor,
and reaches out her hands to the needy.
Charm is deceitful, and beauty is vain,
but a woman who fears the LORD is to be praised.
Give her a share in the fruit of her hands,
and let her works praise her in the city gates.

READING II | *1 Thessalonians 5:1–6*

Now concerning the times and the seasons, brothers
and sisters, you do not need to have anything written to you. For you yourselves know very well that
the day of the Lord will come like a thief in the
night. When they say, "There is peace and security,"
then sudden destruction will come upon them, as
labor pains come upon a pregnant woman, and
there will be no escape!

But you, beloved, are not in darkness, for that
day to surprise you like a thief; for you are all children of light and children of the day; we are not of
the night or of darkness. So then let us not fall asleep
as others do, but let us keep awake and be sober.

GOSPEL | *Matthew 25:14–30*

Jesus said: "For it is as if a man, going on a journey,
summoned his slaves and entrusted his property to
them; to one he gave five talents, to another two, to
another one, to each according to his ability. Then he
went away.

"The one who had received the five talents went
off at once and traded with them, and made five
more talents. In the same way, the one who had the
two talents made two more talents. But the one who
had received the one talent went off and dug a hole
in the ground and hid his master's money.

"After a long time the master of those slaves
came and settled accounts with them. Then the one
who had received the five talents came forward,
bringing five more talents, saying, 'Master, you
handed over to me five talents; see, I have made five
more talents.' His master said to him, 'Well done,
good and trustworthy slave; you have been trustworthy in a few things, I will put you in charge of
many things; enter into the joy of your master.' And
the one with the two talents also came forward, saying, 'Master, you handed over to me two talents; see,
I have made two more talents.' His master said to
him, 'Well done, good and trustworthy slave; you
have been trustworthy in a few things, I will put you
in charge of many things; enter into the joy of your
master.'

"Then the one who had received the one talent
also came forward, saying, 'Master, I knew that you
were a harsh man, reaping where you did not sow,
and gathering where you did not scatter seed; so I
was afraid, and I went and hid your talent in the
ground. Here you have what is yours.' But his master replied, 'You wicked and lazy slave! You knew,
did you, that I reap where I did not sow, and gather
where I did not scatter? Then you ought to have
invested my money with the bankers, and on my
return I would have received what was my own
with interest. So take the talent from him, and give it
to the one with the ten talents.

"'For to all those who have, more will be given,
and they will have an abundance; but from those
who have nothing, even what they have will be
taken away. As for this worthless slave, throw him
into the outer darkness, where there will be weeping and gnashing of teeth.'"

R E F L E C T I O N

Jesus tells of a man going on a journey and what he leaves behind for his servants to care for. The industrious and reliable servants return double the amount they received. One servant plays it safe and simply buries his gift, knowing the man to be a hard master.

Playing it safe is something we are familiar with. Common wisdom suggests that we err on the side of caution: "Better safe than sorry." The master in this parable lives more on the edge: "No guts, no glory."

The anticipation of the imminent second coming of Christ in the years after his resurrection gave rise to many practices. Some Christians lived ascetic lives in the manner of John the Baptist; others proclaimed the message of Jesus in the towns and villages: "Repent, the dominion of God is at hand." Still others lived quiet lives of service. They all started with the same belief. They believed they had been given a gift from God in Jesus Christ. They believed the Messiah had come at last. They knew that at the end of the age, God's reign would be established and justice would prevail. Such belief could not be buried in fear or limited to a quiet meal with friends in an upper room. Those first Christians knew that baptism meant transformation. They made conscious decisions to live as Christ would have them live. They shared things in common, worshiped at a common table, and faced rejection, persecution and death for the promise of eternal life with God. In the towns or on the road, Christians felt the need to spread the good news—to bring back double what they had been given.

Christian discipleship is uncompromising in its demands. If we accept the gift of faith, we are required to double its yield in whatever way of life we choose. We know it as certainly as the cautious servant knew his master. Matthew does well to include this story in his gospel as a reminder that belief is not enough.

■ **What gift has God given you? What have you done to make a return on the investment?**

■ **The letter to the Thessalonians repeats the image of God as a thief in the night. Paul envisions a violent time when those who are complacent or asleep will be ruined. How do you see the second coming: Is it the end of the world? a battle between good and evil? something else entirely?**

PRACTICE OF

FAITH

TRUE PROFIT. Meditating on the day of the Lord, that unknown moment of Christ's glorious return, Paul emphasizes light: You are all children of the light. He admonishes us to "keep awake and be sober." The selection from the Book of Proverbs personifies Wisdom as a capable wife who devotes her energies to her household while also being mindful of and responsive to the poor and the needy outside of her home. Such loving attention requires stamina and courage. One way we stay awake is by paying attention to the needs of the community around us—in our household, in our neighborhood and beyond.

PRACTICE OF

HOPE

TIMES AND SEASONS. Paul could not have chosen a better image of inevitability than labor coming on a pregnant woman. The outcome of such pain and hard work is almost always joy and new life, but sometimes, it is disappointment and sorrow. So it is a good image for the coming of the reign of God in all its certainty and unpredictability.

We may not know the day or the hour when our longing will be fulfilled, but we do know it is inevitable, and therefore, we have hope. We mark the times and the seasons of our lives, doing the best we can with the talents we are given, while we wait in joyful hope for the coming of the Lord.

PRACTICE OF

CHARITY

INVEST YOUR TALENTS WISELY. Is Jesus really talking about investing money to get the highest return? Most likely not. We are told to use the gifts we have been given to the best of our ability. In this time of unprecedented wealth, we must not forget to recognize these riches as a gift from the Lord to be used wisely. When you look at your investments, consider their impact on the environment and the poor. Co-op America can provide you with all the information you need to make socially responsible decisions. They issue a catalogue with the names and addresses of socially responsible funds, banks and corporations. The return on such investments is comparable to others. Check out their suggestions. Co-op America, 1612 K St., NW, Suite. 600, Washington DC 20006; 202-872-5307; www.coopamerica.org

WEEKDAY READINGS (Mo)Revelation 1:1–4; 2:1–5a; (Tu)3:1–6, 14–22; (We)4:1–11; (Th)5:1–10; (Fr)10:8–11; (Sa)11:4–12

READING I *Ezekiel 34:11–12, 15–16*

Thus says the Lord GOD: I myself will search for my sheep, and will seek them out. As shepherds seek out their flocks when they are among their scattered sheep, so I will seek out my sheep. I will rescue them from all the places to which they have been scattered on a day of clouds and thick darkness. I myself will be the shepherd of my sheep. I will seek the lost, and I will bring back the strayed, and I will bind up the injured, and I will strengthen the weak, but the fat and the strong I will destroy. I will feed them with justice.

READING II *I Corinthians 15:20–26*

Revised Common Lectionary: Ephesians 1:15–23

Christ has been raised from the dead, the first fruits of those who have died. For since death came through a human being, the resurrection of the dead has also come through a human being; for as all die in Adam, so all will be made alive in Christ. But each in the proper order: Christ the first fruits, then at his coming those who belong to Christ. Then comes the end, when Christ hands over the dominion to God, the Father, after destroying every ruler and every authority. For Christ must reign until he has put all his enemies under his feet. The last enemy to be destroyed is death.

GOSPEL *Matthew 25:31–46*

Jesus said: "When the Son-of-Man comes in his glory, and all the angels with him, then he will sit on the throne of his glory. All the nations will be gathered before him, and he will separate people one from another as a shepherd separates the sheep from the goats, and he will put the sheep at his right hand and the goats at the left.

"Then the king will say to those at his right hand, 'Come, you that are blessed by my Father, inherit the dominion prepared for you from the foundation of the world; for I was hungry and you gave me food, I was thirsty and you gave me some-thing to drink, I was a stranger and you welcomed me, I was naked and you gave me clothing, I was sick and you took care of me, I was in prison and you visited me.' Then the righteous will answer him, 'Lord, when was it that we saw you hungry and gave you food, or thirsty and gave you something to drink? And when was it that we saw you a stranger and welcomed you, or naked and gave you clothing? And when was it that we saw you sick or in prison and visited you?' And the king will answer them, 'Truly I tell you, just as you did it to one of the least of these who are members of my family, you did it to me.'

"Then he will say to those at his left hand, 'You that are accursed, depart from me into the eternal fire prepared for the devil and the devil's angels; for I was hungry and you gave me no food, I was thirsty and you gave me nothing to drink, I was a stranger and you did not welcome me, naked and you did not give me clothing, sick and in prison and you did not visit me.' Then they also will answer, 'Lord, when was it that we saw you hungry or thirsty or a stranger or naked or sick or in prison, and did not take care of you?' Then he will answer them, 'Truly I tell you, just as you did not do it to one of the least of these, you did not do it to me.' And these will go away into eternal punishment, but the righteous into eternal life."

Thursday, November 28, 2002

THANKSGIVING DAY (UNITED STATES)

Sirach 50:22–24 *And now bless the God of all.*

1 Corinthians 1:3–9 *Grace to you and peace.*

Luke 17:11–19 *On the way to Jerusalem.*

God has given us the earth, a land flowing with milk and honey. We show our thankfulness by being wise and selfless stewards of the earth and by sharing our gifts with one another.

REFLECTION

The church year begins with a king. Jesus is unlike any king we know. Israel's king had one job: The king was to be the example of one who followed the law of God. In Israel's history, kings were judged on how well they did this. Sadly, not many measured up.

In Matthew's vision, Jesus teaches what the law of "love your neighbor" requires. Many scholars think the passage refers to the way people treat a disciple who preaches the good news. The least "brother" or disciple is worthy of respect as a messenger of God.

On another level, however, the real challenge of this reading comes from the one thing that the sheep and the goats shared. Neither one knew it was Jesus when they encountered the naked, the homeless or the imprisoned. The reading has nothing to do with our behavior when we see Christ in someone else; it has everything to do with our behavior when we do not see Christ in someone else. The sheep did what the king did. They had compassion on those who needed help. They served the disenfranchised, marginalized people of the world. The sheep acted on their hearts filled with gratitude for what had already been done for them. They did not need to know Jesus in those they served. They already knew him in their hearts.

The goats, on the other hand, did not know Jesus in themselves or anyone else. They acted as though they had been asleep for the whole of Matthew's gospel and its focus on readiness and transformation in Christ. This parable is a graphic example of the consequences of inattention and laziness. It is a wake-up call for all of us as we head into another year.

■ **Ezekiel's image of God as shepherd sounds like the Good Shepherd in Jesus' parable. How is it that the sheep are scattered?**

■ **How does the church work in the world to see that the corporal works of mercy are done? What more can we do?**

PRACTICE OF FAITH

FAITH DOING JUSTICE. Jesus' parables these last three weeks have painted a picture of separation between those who let their light shine, even in the face of danger, and those who fail to act. Catholic theology teaches that divine judgment and mercy make sense together. That truth surpasses our human categories, but today's readings help us understand their meaning a little better. Notice that the righteous did not do their generous acts in order to win the dominion of God: Lord, when was it that we saw you? They did not know that they had attended to Jesus. They acted in response to the needs they saw. My Jesuit community has the expression, "Faith doing justice." In what way does your faith shape your actions for justice?

PRACTICE OF HOPE

I MYSELF WILL SHEPHERD THEM. There are great words of comfort today for all the poor and the weak, the hurt and the suffering, and for those who have been scattered and lost for lack of good leadership. Christ proclaims his own dominion over all and God's promise of protection for the little ones of the earth. This king of ours does not come as a domineering slave-driver, but as a gentle shepherd, binding our wounds and healing our hurts, feeding us and giving us rest. No matter how trying and hopeless our situation has been, we can place our trust in our shepherd king, who hears our cries for help.

All of our hopes for the reign of God—justice and peace, love and forgiveness and mercy—will be realized. This is the promise, and it will come to pass, because the One who makes the promise is worthy of trust.

PRACTICE OF CHARITY

WHATEVER YOU DO FOR THE LEAST. On this last Sunday of the liturgical year, Matthew tells us one last time what is expected of us as disciples of Jesus, just in case we weren't listening before. Give food to the hungry, drink to the thirsty, welcome to the stranger and clothing to the naked. As long as we put these things at the top of our priority list, we'll be all right. We are approaching winter, the coldest, darkest part of the year. Don't forget the older people you know from church or the neighborhood. This can be a difficult time for them to get out. One of the most difficult changes for the elderly is when they can no longer drive. If you can take an older person to the store or a doctor's appointment, you will be offering much-needed help.

WEEKDAY READINGS (Mo)Revelation 14:1–3, 4b–5; (Tu)14:14–19; (We)15:1–4; (Th)18:1–2, 21–23; 19:1–3, 9a; (Fr)20:1–4, 11—21:2; (Sa)Romans 10:9–18

Information on the License to Reprint from
At Home with the Word 2002

The low bulk rate prices of *At Home with the Word 2002* are intended to make quantities of the book affordable. Single copies are $7.00 each; 5–99 copies, $5.00 each; 100–499 copies, $4.00 each; 500 or more copies, $3.00 each. We encourage parishes to buy quantities of this book.

However, Liturgy Training Publications makes a simple reprint license available to parishes that would find it more practical to reproduce some parts of this book. Reflections (and questions), Practices, Prayers of the Season, and/or the holy day boxes can be duplicated for the parish bulletin or reproduced in other formats. These can be used every week or as often as the license-holder chooses. The page size of *At Home with the Word 2002* is 8 x 10 inches.

The license granted is for the period beginning with the First Sunday of Advent— December 2, 2001—through the solemnity of Christ the King—November 24, 2002.

Note also that the license does *not* cover the scriptures, psalms, or morning, evening and night prayer texts. See the acknowledgments page at the beginning of this book for the names and addresses of these copyright owners. Directions for obtaining permission to use these texts are given there.

The materials reprinted under license from LTP may not be sold and may be used only among the members of the community obtaining the license. The license may not be purchased by a diocese for use in its parishes.

No reprinting may be done by the parish until the license is signed by both parties and the fee is paid. Copies of the license agreement will be sent on request. The fee varies with the number of copies to be reproduced on a regular basis:

Up to 100 copies: $100
101 to 500 copies: $300
501 to 1000 copies: $500
More than 1000 copies: $800

For further information, call the reprint permissions department at 773-486-8970, ext. 268, or fax your request to 773-486-7094, att: reprint permissions.

LISTENING TO GOD'S WORD

by Eileen Drilling and Judy Rothfork

Initiation into the Christian life is fundamentally a sharing of faith. Whether passed from parent to child or from teacher to student, faith involves the whole family of God. The authors have put together an exciting approach to faith-sharing. Children will enjoy the time spent talking about God with an adult, and adults will be inspired by their child's growth in faith. This is an easy way to support our children in their relationship with God and for them to interiorize the gospel. It is an easy way for families to express verbally and ritually their experience of God and to strengthen their life together by sharing experiences, prayers and blessings. Although *Listening to God's Word* is designed for 8-12 year-olds, younger children will enjoy the stories and activities, and older children may use the Adult Journal or assist younger children.

Available for Years A, B and C

Activities and Stories	**$15**
Child's Journal	**$5**
Adult's Journal	**$5**

LISTENING TO GOD'S WORD **is:**

- intergenerational faith-sharing
- based in the Sunday gospels
- composed of three resources
- activities with scripture and ritual

Use *LISTENING TO GOD'S WORD*
as a resource for:

- children's catechumenate
- sacramental preparation
- parish family programs
- faith formation in the home
- religion class
- vacation Bible school
- children's liturgy of the word

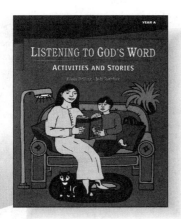

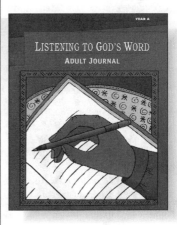

Above: pages 96 & 97 from Activities and Stories, Year A

ORDER FROM YOUR LOCAL BOOKSTORE OR CONTACT:

 LITURGY TRAINING PUBLICATIONS
1800 North Hermitage Avenue
Chicago IL 60622-1101

PHONE   1-800-933-1800

BOOKS FOR EVERYONE IN THE FAMILY

Sunday Morning
by Gail Ramshaw

Introduce youngsters to the words, images and gestures that give life to our Sunday liturgy. With vibrant and multicultural art by Judy Jarrett.

Hardcover
Order code: **SUN/AM** **$16**

Paperback
Order code: **PSUNAM** **$9**

Blessings and Prayers

Traditional and scriptural prayers that can be learned at an early age. All accompanied by Judy Jarrett's art.

Hardcover
Order code: **BLESS** **$16**

Paperback
Order code: **PBLESS** **$9**

Winter
Celebrating the Season in a Christian Home
by Peter Mazar

A wonderful, colorful family book about honoring Advent and celebrating all the days of Christmas. Includes numerous do- it-yourself ideas for St. Nicholas' Day, tree trimming, card sending, an Epiphany cake, house blessing and more. For families, singles, young and old alike, and everyone who wants to support Christian traditions in the home.

Order code: **WINTER** **$15**

Winter Saints
by Melissa Musick Nussbaum
art by Judy Jarrett

A collection of stories about saints and other winter characters, one for each day of Advent and the twelve days of Christmas. Lively illustrations and colorful narratives about people such as Nicholas, Lucy, Elizabeth, Mary, Zechariah, Rosa Parks and Dorothy Day will enchant children of all ages. Also includes seasonal prayers, maps and a timeline showing when the stories took place.

Order code: **WINST** **$15**

Patrons and Protectors
Occupations
by Michael O'Neill McGrath, OSFS

An enchanting presentation of saints as patrons of particular occupations. Twenty-four wonderfully unique images present saints in contemporary settings, performing the tasks of modern-day occupations. Each image is accompanied by information about the saint and an essay from someone in that line of work who shares how their life's work and their faith life support one another. A must-have for any family book collection!

Order code: **PPOC1** **$18.95**

I Will Lie Down This Night
by Melissa Musick Nussbaum

A mother of five tells family stories to reawaken in us the anticipation, the resolution, the vulnerability that the dark end of the day used to call to mind before we "grew up." A special reminder of what a special invitation nighttime is from God.

Order code: **NPRAY** **$10**

I Will Arise This Day
by Melissa Musick Nussbaum

Like her popular *I Will Lie Down This Night,* this delightful little book is full of anecdotes, prayers and reflections about morning prayer. These vignettes of her family engaged in the challenge to arise to the day are supported by sound theology and gutsy, earthy spirituality.

Order code: **ARISE** **$10**

Bible Stories for the Forty Days
stories adapted by Melissa Musick Nussbaum
art by Judy Jarrett

Here are the stories of our ancestors from Adam and Eve and Esther to the unnamed woman who smashes the jar to anoint Jesus for burial. Here are Abraham and Solomon entertaining guests. Here is Judith risking her life for her people and Shadrach strolling with friends in the fiery furnace. Quite a crowd! Each day of Lent introduces children to these great persons of the Bible (but don't wait 'til Lent!)

Order code: **ARKBK** **$15**

Child of God
A Book of Birthdays and Days In Between
by Gertrud Mueller Nelson
illustrations by Annika Maria Nelson

Child of God is the story of a child—your child. And it grows as your child grows. It is a place to gather what should never be forgotten: memories, photos, special letters and lost teeth. Capture important facts, record sacraments, and preserve poignant stories. When the book is bursting, put it away for 15 or 20 years. What a gift to present to your grown child!

Order code: **BDBOOK** **$15**

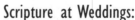

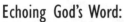

Daily Prayer 2002
by Bryan M. Cones

An exciting new annual resource for personal and small group prayer! *Daily Prayer 2002* contains a simple order of prayer for each day of the liturgical year. This book draws on the long tradition of Christian prayer, especially the liturgy of the hours. It provides the perfect way to get into a habit of daily prayer and is ideal for use by older students, teachers, catechumens, candidates, and any Christian who wants to pray each day according to the rhythm of the church. Each daily prayer page is dated and includes a psalm, a scripture reading, a reflection, intercessions, the Lord's Prayer, and a closing prayer. The introduction provides brief background on the tradition of daily prayer as well as ideas for using the book for prayer alone or with a small group. If you've ever wished that you could find an adult version of *Children's Daily Prayer*, this is it. The portable size of this "everyday" book makes it convenient to carry in a purse, briefcase or backpack.

Order code: **ADP02 $15**

Tell Me Your Name
Images of God in the Bible
by Arthur E. Zannoni

All of us who treat religion and faith as a serious part of our lives are constantly wrestling with the meaning of God. Our existence is derived from God and destined for God. And, in between, we long to know God. But how? This important book offers an opportunity to relate to God on a new level of intimacy, awe, wonder and humility. Each chapter looks at various names, images and metaphors for God—male and female, animate and inanimate—used in both testaments of the Bible, including images of Jesus and images used by Jesus.

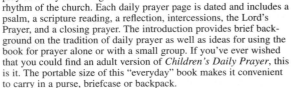

Order code: **TELL $12**

Remembering the Women
Women's Stories from Scripture for Sundays and Festivals
compiled by J. Frank Henderson
foreword by Marjorie Proctor-Smith
art by Luba Lukova

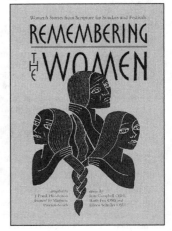

You are invited into the beautiful and inspiring, sometimes difficult and painful, women's stories of our heritage, stories that allow our community to see itself as a whole people once again.

Remembering the Women embraces what has been omitted by the two major lectionaries of western Christianity. This book contains both the stories that are told in churches and the ones that are forgotten. Discover hundreds of scriptural passages witnessing to the presence of women in the Bible. Find stories that use feminine images of God, stories about named and anonymous women, stories that use imagery based on the physical life of women, and stories that refer to the female figure of holy Wisdom. Also included are essays by Jean Campbell, OSH, Ruth Fox, OSB, and Eileen Schuller, OSU, that further explore the topic of women in the Bible and in the lectionary.

Remembering the Women is ideal for groups praying in common, for inspiring sermons and homilies, for preparing liturgies for which specific readings are not prescribed by the churches, and for personal reflection and discussion.

Order code: **WOMEN $25**

ORDER FROM YOUR LOCAL BOOKSTORE OR CONTACT:

 LITURGY TRAINING PUBLICATIONS
1800 North Hermitage Avenue
Chicago IL 60622-1101

PHONE   1-800-933-1800

Prayers for Catechists

For the catechists you know—on RCIA teams, in weekend religious education classes, in schools and in adult formation programs—this little book will offer wisdom and refreshment. Prayers and reflections focus on the vocation of catechesis: the call, preparation, self searching, and feeding of the catechist's spirit. Expressing the needs and insights of catechists in many different times and situations, this book creates a bond through time and space among all who share the ministry. A thoughtful way to express your appreciation to the dedicated volunteer catechists in your life Bulk pricing makes is possible for parishes to thank all of their catechetical staff with this beautiful book.

Order code: **PCATS $4** *each*

Come Holy Spirit

Newly confirmed disciples and others will turn to the prayers and reflections in this book to keep them growing the the gifts of the Spirit received at confirmation. Families and friends of the newly confirmed will find this a perfect confirmation gift. Catechists who prepare your people for the sacrament will want to supplement the process, either before or after the rite. For all who desire a deeper connection to the this person of the Holy Trinity, these words will awaken sensitivity to the Spirits' work. Each book includes a special dedication page in the front.

Order code: **PCONF $3** *each*

Catholic Prayers

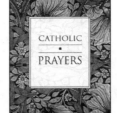

This book contains the cornerstone prayers of our faith life—texts every Catholic needs and wants to know. You'll find classic prayers such as the Lord's Prayer, the Hail Mary, the Memorare, and the Apostles' Creed as well as beloved psalms, the litany of the saints, a guide to saying the rosary, and more.

Order Code: **CATH $3** *each*

Giving Thanks at the Table

This prayer book is a portable collection of blessing prayers, graces for mealtime and inspiration quotes. It is ideal for use at any meal or for special times of the year, including Sundays and Friday7s, Advent, Christmas, Lent Triduum, Easter, summer and autumn.

Order Code: **THBL $3** *each*

Special quantity pricing available!

GIFTS OF PRAYER, INSTRUMENT OF PEACE

Use these pocket-sized prayer books to pray for and with those who are in need or to celebrate various ministries in our lives. LTP's prayer books have a distinctive design that reflects the dignity of prayer and provides a means for family ritual and group prayer. All of these prayer books make excellent gifts and fit easily into most greeting card envelopes. Give the enduring gift of prayer to yourself and to loved ones.

ORDER FROM YOUR LOCAL BOOKSTORE OR CONTACT:

LITURGY TRAINING PUBLICATIONS
1800 North Hermitage Avenue
Chicago IL 60622-1101

PHONE   1-800-933-1800